David Laing, John Wedderburn, James Wedderburn, Robert Wedderburn

A Compendious Book of Psalms and Spiritual Songs

David Laing, John Wedderburn, James Wedderburn, Robert Wedderburn

A Compendious Book of Psalms and Spiritual Songs

ISBN/EAN: 9783744767194

Printed in Europe, USA, Canada, Australia, Japan

Cover: Foto ©Lupo / pixelio.de

More available books at **www.hansebooks.com**

THE GUDE AND GODLIE BALLATES.

Edinburgh: .... W. PATERSON.
Dundee: .... FREDERICK SHAW.
London: .... J. RUSSELL SMITH.

A COMPENDIOUS BOOK OF PSALMS AND SPIRITUAL SONGS,

COMMONLY KNOWN AS

"THE GUDE AND GODLIE BALLATES."

I   R

EDINBURGH:
REPRINTED FROM THE EDITION OF 1578.
M.DCCC.LXVIII.

PREFACE.

I.—*The Gude and Godlie Ballates, and the reputed Authors.*

 Garden of Spiritual Flowers, to adopt one of the quaint English titles of an early date, might have been quite as appropriate for this collection as that of A Compendious Book, &c. The flowers it exhibits may not be remarkable either for poetical fragrance or beauty, although variegated both as to form and colour. But whatever estimate we may form of the collection, it has its own peculiar value, in connexion with the literature of the Reformation period in Scotland; and

being the only one of its kind, this little volume deserves to be better known than it is at the present day. Its history, indeed, is rather singular. Having passed through several editions, of which hundreds of copies were printed towards the close of the sixteenth century, it may seem strange to add, that the book itself had a somewhat narrow escape ever to have reached our times. During the last century no public library was known to possess a copy; and the only one discovered in any private collection was that of Andro Hart's, with the date of printing cut off. It was from this solitary copy that Lord Hailes printed selections as a "Specimen" of the work in 1765; and that further selections were included in Sibbald's "Chronicle of Scottish Poetry," in 1802; while a literal reprint of the entire book (thus affording some security for its future preservation) formed the chief portion of Dalyell's "Scotish Poems of the Sixteenth Century," in 1801.

A few years later a second copy of Hart's edition, with the title-page entire, dated 1621, and also the earlier edition by Smyth in 1600, chanced to make their appearance, and have since passed through the hands of successive collectors. Still more recently, a copy of the hitherto unknown edition of 1578 occurred in a London sale, and was purchased for a late zealous collector of early poetical literature. Having, for the purpose of collation or transcription, obtained from Mr CHRISTIE MILLER of Craigentinny the liberal use of this unique copy, preserved in the library at Britwell House, Bucks, I found that the three known editions of these " Gude and Godlie Ballates " were essentially the same; yet it occurred to me that a good service would be rendered by reprinting it verbatim, in a small convenient form, so that copies, at a moderate price, might be placed within reach of many persons who take an interest in such remains of Popular Poetry, but who know nothing of Dalyell's collection, which, besides, has now become scarce, and expensive. The present volume, accordingly, is a literal reprint, page for page, of the 1578 edition, but supplying some of its defects, correcting the punctuation and several obvious typographical errors, while adopting the common form of type, instead of the black-letter, as best suited for ordinary readers.

The Collection, it will be observed, divides itself naturally into three separate parts or divisions. The first is Doctrinal, including a Catechism, the Creed, &c., in metre, with various Spiritual Songs. The second contains versions of twenty-two Psalms, and a number of Hymns, chiefly translations from the German. The third, which gives its peculiar character to the collection, consists of secular Songs, but converted from profane into religious poetry. This mode of adapting popular rhymes and tunes to sacred subjects, but often clothed in a very incongruous form, was not unknown in other countries. But before considering this matter in relation to the present volume, although it is obviously impossible to ascribe the contents, either in whole or in part, to the respective Authors, we may inquire what is known or reported on this head.

This "Compendious Book" should properly be regarded as a POETICAL MISCELLANY by various authors, yet tradition, and the concurrent testimony of some old writers, assign the authorship to two brothers, JOHN and ROBERT WEDDERBURN, of Dundee, who flourished about the year 1540. That either of them was the collector or editor of the volume, or that any considerable portion of it was printed in Scotland prior to the Reformation, are points which seem

Preface. ix

to be highly improbable. We find no reference to the book earlier than to an impression about 1570, and "the augmentation of ballatis not contained in the first edition" may have been made when the volume was reprinted at Edinburgh, in 1578.

In adding some notices respecting the reputed Authors, I can, however, do little more than recapitulate what has previously been gleaned by Dalyell, M'Crie, and others, derived chiefly from Calderwood's MS. History. As this industrious historian obtained his information from manuscript sources, which are not now preserved, his own words, without abridgment, may be quoted. Under the year 1540 he says :—

"This yeere JAMES WEDDERBURNE, eldest sonne to James Wedderburne, merchant at Dundie, called James Wedderburne at the West Kirk Stile, was delated to the King, and letters of captioun directed to take him. He departed secreetlie to France, and remained at Rowan and Deep till he deceassed. He had beene brought up in Sanct Leonard's Colledge in his youth, in the time of the governement of Johne Duke of Albanie, and was reasonablie weill instructed in philosophie and humanitie. Thereafter he went to France, where he played the merchant. After his returne, he was instructed in religioun by James Hewat, a Blacke frier at Dundie. He confirmed the doctrine which the other had receaved in his youth, in St Leonard's Colledge, under Mr Gawin Logie. This James had a good gift of poesie, and made diverse comedeis and tragedeis in the Scotish tongue, wherein he nipped the abusses and superstitioun of the time. He composed in forme of tragedie the beheading of Johne the Baptist, which was acted at the West Port of Dundie, wherin he carped roughlie the abusses and corruptiouns of the Papists. He compiled the Historie of Dyonisius the Tyranne, in forme of a comedie, which was acted in the play-feild of the said burgh, wherin he likewise nipped the Papists. He counterfooted also the conjuring of a ghaist, which was, indeed, practised by Frier Laing, beside Kingorne, which Frier Laing had beene Confessor to the King. But after this conjuring the King was constrained, for shame, to remove him. When he was at Deepe the factors at Deepe, Johne Meldrum, Henrie Tod, Johne Mowat, Gilbert Scot, delated him to the Bishop of Rowan; but the Bishop refused to meddle with him, becaus they could prove nothing against him. They informed the Bishop and Channons of Rowan that he was declared an heretick in Scotland: the Bishop desired them to send for the processe, and that being tryed, he sould have no residence there. We heare no farther, but that he remained as factor at Deepe, and deing, said to his sonne,— 'We have beene acting our part in the theater: you are to succeed; see that you act your part faithfullie.'

"Mr JOHNE WEDDERBURNE, his brother, brought up also in the course of philosophie, under Mr Gawin Logie, being perswaded by his friends, albeit against his will, he tooke on the order of preesthood, and was a preest in Dundie. But soone after he beganne to professe the (reformed) religioun. Being summouned, he departed to Almaine [Germany], where he heard Luther and Melancton, and became verie fervent and zealous. He translated manie of Luther's dytements into Scotish meeter, and the Psalmes of David. He turned manie bawdie songs and rymes in godlie rymes. He returned after the death of the King, in December 1542, but was againe persued by the Cardinall, and fled to England.

"Mr ROBERT WEDDERBURNE, the youngest brother, brought up also under Mr Gawin, excelled his brother both in humanitie and knowledge of the Scriptures. He succeeded to Mr Robert Barrie, Vicar of Dundie. He went to Parise, where he remained cheeflie in companie of those that were instructed in religioun, as Mr Alexander Hay, N. Sandelands, sonne to the Laird of Calder, in West Lothiane, and Lord of Sanct Johne, whose father and whole familie were most zealous in advancing of religioun. After the death of the Cardinall he returned to Scotland. The Vicar, his mother's brother, being departed, he gott possessioun of the vicarage, but remained for the most part with the Laird of Calder. When he was comming home out of the east countreis, in a Danskein ship, the shippe was driven by contrarie winds upon Norway, where the passengers landed at Ripperwicke, and remained certane dayes. In the meane time, upon the Saturday before Whitsonday even, 1546, after continuall disputing and reasoning among the passengers, some Popish, and some Protestants, he, and the rest of his fellowes, tooke the boldnesse, notwithstanding they understood nothing of the Cardinall's death, to make his pourtraiture, or statue, of a great oaken blocke, and therupon write his name in paper affixed theron. They accuse him, condemne him, and burne his statue in a great fire of timber. The Cardinall was slaine that same verie day, in the morning,[1] in his owne Castell of Sanct Andrewes."[2]

In addition to these notices, it may be stated that more than one family of the Wedderburns flourished in Dundee, or its neighbourhood, at an earlier period. Sir Robert Douglas, in his Baronage of Scotland,[3] has given a detailed account of the Wedderburns of Blackness and the Wedderburns of Gosford. According to Nisbet[4] the name was local, taken from the lands and barony of Wedderburn, in Berwickshire; and Douglas says,—" That the first who settled in Angus was James Wedderburn, burgess in Dundee, in the Reign of James III. He had two sons, David, mentioned in a charter[5] 19th

[1] On the 29th of May 1546. (Knox's Works, vol. i. p. 174).

[2] Calderwood's History, MS., 1636 (Advocates Library); and Wodrow Society edition, vol. i. p. 141.

[3] Edinb. 1798, p. 278.

[4] Heraldry, vol. i. p. 371.

[5] The charter to which Douglas here refers, under a wrong date, is Lib. xii. No. 186. It contains no reference

February 1489-90, who died without issue; and James, merchant-burgess of Dundee, who married Janet, daughter of David Forrester of Nevay, by whom he had a son, John, who was town-clerk of Dundee, and had charters in 1527 and 1533, and whose son, David, also became town-clerk of Dundee," &c.

This account by Douglas is not quite correct; but the persons we have specially to notice were James Wedderburn, merchant-burgess, and his sons, three of whom seem to have received a liberal education. In extracting from the Registers of the University of St Andrews between 1500 to 1540, the names of the Wedderburns (who are usually marked as natives of Angus, or that district of the country to the north of the Tay), I will not pretend either to assign the exact relationship that may have existed between them, or to account for various apparent discrepancies in the notices we have in regard to their history.

to James Wedderburne, burgess, but simply mentions the house called a land belonging to David Wedderburn, in Dundee, in describing the boundaries of a property assigned to one of the Chaplains in the parish church of Dundee, 19th February 1489-90.

Preface.

Nomina Incorporatorum.—ACTA RECTORUM.

(1504).—Johannes Wedderburne, nac. Ang..(in Collegio).
(1505).—Ro[bertus] Wedderburne, nac. Ang. (in Pedagogio).
1507.—Johannes Wedderburne (in Collegio).
1509.—Jacobus Wedderburn (in Collegio).
1514.—Jacobus Wedderburne, nacionis Angusie.
1525.—Johannes Wedderburn (in Pedagogio).
1526.—Robertus Wedderburne, An. (in Collegio).

Nomina Determinatorum et Licentiatorum.— ACTA FACULTATIS ARTIUM.

1509.—Robertus Wedderburn, primus actus Collegii, pauper—(Determ.)
1511.—Robertus Wedderburn—(Licent.)
1526.—Johannes Wedderburn, quartus actus, dives —(Determ.)
1528.—Johannes Wedderburn—(Licent.)
1529.—Robertus Wedderburn, in Collegio Divi Leonardi—(Determ.)
1530.—Robertus Wedderburn, in Collegio Divi Leonardi—(Licent.)

I. JAMES WEDDERBURN.—In the preceding list we find a Jacobus Wedderburn incorporated in

St Salvator's College, St Andrews, in the year 1509, and another of the same name in 1514, neither of whom seems to have taken the Degree of Bachelor, or of Master of Arts. James, who became a burgess of Dundee, is said to have spent some time in France connected with his mercantile affairs. He married Janet Forrester, and had at least two sons, John and Robert, as appears from the public records:—

1527-8, January 20. A charter of confirmation granted to John Wedderburn, son of James Wedderburn junior, burgess of Dundee, procreated between him and Janet Forrester, his spouse, of the lands of Croft, with a part of the land of Tullohill, &c. in Forfarshire.[1]

1533, October 14. Another charter of confirmation, granted to James Wedderburn junior, burgess of Dundee, and Janet Forrester, his spouse, and John Wedderburn, their son, of thirteen acres of the lordship of Dudhope, in Forfarshire.[2]

The name of the other son, Robert, occurs in a less enviable manner than that of others of the family, who were accused of heresy.

[1] Regist. Magni Sigilli, Lib. xxii. fol. 77.
[2] Regist. Magni Sigilli, Lib. xxv. fol. 53.

Preface. xvii

"Ane respitt maid to Robert Wedderburn, sone to James Wedderburn, burges of Dundee, for the slaughter of umquhill (blank) Malisoun, and for all actioun and cryme that may follow therupoun, and for xix zeris to indure, &c. At Linlithgow, the sext day of Januar the zere forsaid [1537-8] *per Signaturam.*"[1]

This JAMES WEDDERBURN, as Calderwood relates, exhibited proofs of his dramatic talents, having converted the History of John the Baptist into a dramatic poem, and also the History of Dionysius the Tyrant, both of which are said to have been acted at Dundee. Such performances involved him in trouble, and obliged him, in the year 1540, to escape abroad; and Calderwood adds, that he continued to reside at Dieppe or Rouen until his death, which we may conjecture was about the year 1550. Of his dramatic pieces no trace has been discovered.

II. Mr JOHN WEDDERBURN, second son of the elder James, was educated at St Andrews, but not at St Leonard's College, under Gawin Logye, as usually reported: his name occurs among the students in the *Pædagogium* (a name at first applied

[1] Regist. Secreti Sigilli, vol. xi. fol. 43.

to the New or St Mary's College), who were incorporated in the year 1525, at the same time with George Buchanan and his brother Patrick. Wedderburn took his Bachelor's degree in 1526, and became Master of Arts in 1528. He then entered the priesthood.

Lindesay of Pitscottie, under the year 1530, calls "Mr Johne Wedderburn" Vicar of Dundee. He cannot, however, be trusted for minute accuracy, but the incident he records is worthy of notice. Lord William Howard having come to Scotland that year as Ambassador, with a large retinue of persons skilled in all kinds of games, among trials of skill which took place one was that of archery. The Queen Dowager, sister of Henry VIII., laid a wager with her son, the young King, of one hundred crowns and a tun of wine, on the superiority of the English over the Scots. Six persons were chosen on each side, and the trial took place at St Andrews. Pitscottie says, the six chosen for the Scots were three of the landed men, David Wemyss of that ilk, David Arnot of that ilk, and *Mr Johne Wedderburn, Vicar of Dundee*, with three yeomen. " They shot (he says) very near, and warred (got the better of) the Englishmen of the enterprise, and wan the hundred crowns[1] and the tun of wine; which made the King very merry, that his men wan the victory." In some copies of Pitscottie it is added, they " went thereafter to the toun, and maid ane banquett to the King, and the Queene, and the Inglisch Ambassadour, with the whole two hundred crounes, and the two tuns of wyne. Albeit that the Inglismen confessed that the Scottismen sould have been freed of the payment of that banquett, quhilk was so gorgeous that it was of no less availl than the said gold and wyne extended to."

It appears from the Treasurer's Accounts for the year 1538-1539 that 40s. was received as the composition of the escheat of the goods of Mr John Wedderburn, convicted of heresy (de certis criminibus hereseos), granted in favour of his brother Henry. Among various persons in Dundee who, at that time, were condemned upon a similar charge of heresy, was James Rollok, burgess; and in March 1539 a pursuivant was directed " to pass to Dundee and serche James Rollokkis gudis, and Maister Johnne Wedderburn[is]." In the previous

[1] The crown, in the reign of James V., was a gold coin, equivalent to one pound Scots, or 1s. 8d. sterling, no inconsiderable sum at that time.

year we also find that Gilbert Wedderburn, burgess of Dundee, had been convicted of heresy.

III. Mr ROBERT WEDDERBURN, a younger son, as a student in the University of St Andrews, was incorporated in 1526, and took his degrees of Bachelor and of Master of Arts in 1530, under Mr Gawin Logye, Principal of St Leonard's College. Logye took his degree of A.M. at St Andrews in 1512. In 1518 he is styled *Regens Collegii S. Leonardi*, and, in 1523, Principal of that College. He fled, it is supposed, in 1535, to avoid the accusation of heresy; and the name of his successor occurs two years later.[1] Calderwood says that Robert Wedderburn succeeded his uncle, Mr Robert Barrie,[2] as Vicar of Dundee. There was

---

[1] Knox's Works, vol. i. pp. 36, 528.

[2] The name of Barry or Barrie was not uncommon at this time. In the St Andrews University Registers we find the name of Robertus Barry as a Determinant in 1462, and a Licentiate or A.M. in 1465. Other names might be mentioned of a later date. I have a volume in the old wooden boards, containing :—1. Liber Alexandri Magni de Preliis. 2. Historie notabiles collecte ex Gestis Romanorum. 3. Mag. Jac. de Theramo Consolatio Peccatorum et vulgo Belial appelatur: Printed by Jo. Veldener, 1474, folio. On the fly-leaf is written, " Iste liber constat Magistro Henrico Barry, Rec-

a Mr John Barry, Vicar of Dundee, at an earlier period.[1]

In the Registrum Episcopatus Brechinensis (vol. ii. p. 184), we find the names of James Wedderburn, one of the bailies of Dundee, also Cristina Jameson, spouse of David Wedderburn senior, and Henry Wedderburn, 7th December 1532. In the appendix to the same register (ib. p. 319) is an indenture between the burgh of Dundee and Andro Barry, kirkmaster for the tyme of the paroch kirk of our Lady, 23d March 1536, to which Mr Jhone Barry, George Rollok, James Wedderburn junior, and others, were witnesses.

It is usually supposed that the three brothers shared in the persecutions to which the adherents of what was termed the Lutheran doctrines were exposed, and that, being tried, and condemned for heresy, they escaped to the Continent. All this may have happened, but we have no direct evidence of

tori de Culass, empt. 11 Aprilis anno 147[6?];" also "Liber Henrici Barry, Rectoris de Culess, qui dedit fratribus Ordinis Predicatorum de Dwnde." In a later hand is written, " Et nunc ex voluminibus G[eorgii] Ogiluy."

[1] Mr John Berri, Vicar of Dundee, 9th June 1483 (Registrum de Aberbrothok, i. p. 194)—Mr John Barry, Vicar of Dundee, 1495 (Reg. Episc. Brechin., vol. ii. p. 134).

the facts, except in the case of John, the second brother. Had Robert been convicted, he necessarily would have been deprived of his preferment in the Church; his name, however, occurs in the public records as the father of two illegitimate sons, having (what was not uncommon for priests in those days) obtained letters of legitimation, under the Great Seal, granted by the Governor, in the Queen's name, in favour of Robert and David Wedderburns, bastard sons natural of Mr ROBERT WEDDERBURN, Vicar of Dundee, dated at Linlithgow on the 13th January 1552-3. As the term *olim* or *quondam* is not applied either to the Vicar's office or person, we may conclude, without absolutely asserting the fact, that he was then alive, and still retained his office as Vicar.[1] This is a question intimately connected with a disputed point in our literary history, to which I shall, in a subsequent page, take occasion to advert.

David Wedderburn above mentioned is not to be confounded with his namesake the town-clerk of

---

[1] "Legitimatio Roberti et Davidis Wedderburn bastardorum filiorum naturalium MAGISTRI ROBERTI WEDDERBURN, Vicarii de Dundee—Apud Linlithquo, 13. Januarij 1552, et Regni nostri vndecimo." (Reg. Mag. Sig., Lib. xxxi. No. 114).

Dundee, who, according to Douglas's Baronage, was son of John, styled son of James Wedderburn junior, in 1527, and having married Helen Lawson, he " lived to a great age, and died about the year 1590." David Wedderburn, burgess of Dundee, and Helen Lawson, his spouse, had conjoint charters, under the Great Seal, of lands in Forfarshire, &c., dated 10th February 1538-9, confirming a grant in their favour by John, Abbot of Lindores, 9th October 1535; also two others on 8th October 1542 and 8th August 1552.

The preceding notices may not be very satisfactory; and unfortunately, so far as the subsequent history of the Wedderburns is concerned, no precise information has been recorded. That some of the following ballads belong to a later period than that of the Wedderburns, is evident from internal evidence. For instance, at p. 49, the words,

—— thy word at lenth
Is preichit cleir befoir our ene,

with the satirical allusions in *Hay trix, hay trim*, at p. 178-181, and the mention made of the Protestants, at p. 178, as *The Congregation*, may certainly be referred to the year 1559.[1] In like manner, the

[1] I find that in this view I am not singular. The author

words alluding to the destruction of some of the Abbey Churches and Religious Houses, at p. 185—

>Had not your self begun the weiris,
>Your stepillis had bene standand yet

In George Bannatyne's MS. collection of Scottish poetry, 1568, the four following poems are attributed to WEDDERBURN, but no Christian name is given. They evidently are of the time of James the Fifth :—

Ballatis in prayis of Wemen.
"I marvell of thir vane fantastik men,"
    34 stanzas of 7 lines, . . . fol. 239 b.
"My lufe was fals and full of flattery,"
    9 stanzas of 7 lines, . . . fol. 260.
"I think thir men ar verry fals and vane,"
    14 stanzas of 7 lines, . . . fol. 279.
"O man, transformit and unnaturall!"
    18 stanzas of 7 lines, . . . fol. 287 b.

John Jonston, Professor at St Andrews (1593-1611), in his unpublished work, entitled "ΠΕΡΙΣΤΕΦΑΝΩΝ Sive de Coronis Martyrum in Scotia, of a Memoir of Sir John G. Dalyell, referring to his republication of the Gude and Godlie Ballates in 1801, says:—
"From the frequent allusion in them to the Queen Regent, the Pope, and the priesthood, it is evident that many of them were written in the heat of the Reformation." Lond. 1858, 4to, p. xxii.

necnon Peculium Ecclesiæ Scoticanæ" (from which Dr M'Crie, in his Life of Knox, selected the most interesting portions), thus commemorates the three brothers:—

JOHANNES WEDDERBURNUS.
Pulsus in exilium, an. 1546. Exul in Anglia moritur 1556.

I.

Non meriti est nostri, meritas tibi dicere grates,
    Aut paria, aut aliqua parte referre vicem.
Quæ meruisse alii vellent, nec posse mereri est:
    Hæc velle, hæc posse, hæc te meruisse tuum est.
Sic facis atque canis sacra: sic agis omnia, nil ut
    Sanctius, et nusquam purior ulla fides.
Hinc nullum magis invisum caput hostibus: hinc et
    Nemo umquam meruit charior esse bonis.
Grandius hoc meritum, nil te meruisse fateris,
    Humanis meritis nec superesse locum.

II.

DE JOHANNE, JACOBO, ET ROBERTO WEDDERBURNO, FRATRIBUS.

Divisvm imperium, per tres, tria Numina, Fratres,
    Infera quæque vides, quæque superna, canunt.
Vos miror potius tres vero nomine fratres,
    Vosque supra veneror, Numina vana, Deos;
Concordes animas, clarissima lumina gentis,
    Tres paribus studiis, tres pietate pares.
Felices qui vos tales genuere parentes,
    Quæque orbi tellus pignora rara dedit.
Progenitos Cælo Alectum dedit inclyta terris:
    Inde Dei-Donum nomen habere putem.

II.—*The Psalms and Hymns of the Reformed Churches.*

The practice of singing psalms and hymns in Christian worship has prevailed in all ages. Of the early Latin hymns some still retain their place in the Service Book of the Romish Church, and have also been translated, for that purpose, into different languages, and continue to be sung or chaunted in the English and other Reformed Churches. The Hussites, or Bohemian Brethren, in the fifteenth century, had their devotional songs. But it remained for the great German Reformer to give a permanent form and character to the hymnology of his fatherland, by the publication of his " Gesangbuch " in 1524. This was a collection of hymns enlarged from time to time by himself and others, suited as well for private edification as for public worship, being written in the vernacular tongue, and set in many instances to popular airs or melodies. It is easy to conceive that no method could have been better adapted to excite the enthusiasm of the German people, and, by setting an example to other countries, materially to promote the spread of the Protestant faith.

The chief source of modern hymnology may, therefore, be clearly traced to a German origin. The collections published by Dr Wackernagel and the Chevalier Bunsen exhibit the great variety and extent of such compositions. Miss C. Winkworth's " Lyra Germanica," first and second series, and other works of a recent date,[1] have served to introduce such hymns to the notice of English readers. In the preface to the first series, or " Hymns for the Sundays and Chief Festivals of the Christian Year, translated from the German," Miss Wink-

[1] Among these may be noticed a little volume by the Rev. George Walker, minister of Kinnell, Presbytery of Arbroath, entitled, " Hymns translated or imitated from the German: To which is prefixed a Preface, giving an account of the origin of the Lutheran Hymns: By a Clergyman." Lond., 1860, 12mo., pp. xxiv., 116. Mr Walker refers to the earlier *Gesangbuchs* as the source of both Wedderburn and Coverdale's translations. See also Professor Lorimer's interesting volume, " The Scottish Reformation; a Historical Sketch." Lond. 1860, small 4to. Two excellent articles, " Hymnology, German and English," occur in " The Christian Observer," 1859, pp. 704, 834. But the subject has recently been illustrated in a more detailed manner by Professor Mitchell of St Andrews. See page liv.

worth says,—" Ever since the Reformation, the German Church has been remarkable for the number and excellence of its hymns and hymn-tunes. Before that time it was not so. There was no place for congregational singing in public worship, and therefore the spiritual songs of the latter part of the middle ages assumed for the most part an artificial and unpopular form. Yet there were not wanting germs of a National Church poetry in the verses rather than hymns which were sung in German on pilgrimages and at some of the high festivals, many of which verses were again derived from more ancient Latin hymns. Several of Luther's hymns are amplifications of verses of this class, such as the Pentecostal hymn here given, 'Come, Holy Spirit, God and Lord,' which is founded on a German version of the '*Veni Sancte Spiritus, Reple.*' By adopting these verses, and retaining their well-known melodies, Luther enabled his hymns to spread rapidly among the common people. He also composed metrical versions of several of the Psalms, the *Te Deum*, the Ten Commandments, the Lord's Prayer, the *Nunc Dimittis*, the *Da nobis Pacem*, &c., thus enriching the people, to whom he had already given the Holy Scriptures in their own language, with a treasure of that sacred poetry which is the precious inheritance of every Christian Church."[1]

Similar attempts, but not with the same success, were made in other countries, to provide metrical versions of the psalms and hymns, suited for public worship. In such countries, however, as France, Italy, and Flanders, the progress of the Reformation was not only rudely checked, but the people generally were not actuated by the same innate love of popular and sacred music as in Germany. Moreover, in these countries the practice of singing in the Reformed churches, during public worship, was in a great measure limited to metrical versions of the Psalter. In France, the thirty psalms translated by Clement Marot, and increased to fifty in 1541, being set to popular airs, found favour for a time among the French courtiers. This version was finally completed by Theodore Beza in 1562, accompanied by musical notes, and it has since continued in use by the Protestant Churches both in France and Switzerland.

In Switzerland the practice of singing psalms in the vernacular tongue by the congregation at

---

[1] New edition, p. viii. Lond., 1859, 12mo.

large, in place of chaunting Latin Canticles or hymns by the clergy alone, had been introduced at Basel by Œcolompadius, so early as 1527. Various circumstances seem to have prevented this mode prevailing to any extent.

In England there is a singular coincidence in the history of metrical psalmody with that in France. The version which came into general use was commenced by Thomas Sternhold, Groom of the King's Chamber. A selection of nineteen psalms in metre was first printed at London, without date, but apparently in the year 1549, with a dedication to the young King Edward the Sixth. Two years afterwards the number of psalms by Sternhold was increased to thirty-seven; and others, after his death, were added by John Hopkins. This version received further additions by the English exiles of Geneva; and being finally completed and printed, with the tunes, in 1562, it was "allowed," but not enjoined, to be used in churches, by authority of Queen Elizabeth.

Had the use of metrical psalmody been generally adopted in the Church of England during the reign of Queen Elizabeth, its effects might have more nearly resembled that of Germany. We find, at least, a notice confirming this in a letter of

Preface. xxxi

Bishop Jewell to Petrus Martyr, 5th March 1560, which may stand alongside of the often quoted description of the Edinburgh congregation of about 2000 people welcoming the return of their minister, John Dury, on 3d September 1582, by singing in the streets the cxxiv. psalm, " till haevin and erthe resoundit." In Scotland, it is well known that song schools were maintained in all the larger towns; and the old Psalm books having in most editions the tunes, this implies some knowledge of musical notation. Bishop Jewell thus writes :—

"Religio nunc aliquanto confirmatior est, quam fuit. Populus ubique ad meliorem partem valde proclivis. Magnum ad eam rem momentum attulit ecclesiastica et popularis musica. Postquam enim semel Londini cœptum est in una tantum ecclesiola cani publice, statim non tantum ecclesiæ aliæ finitimæ, sed etiam longe disjunctæ civitates, cœperunt idem institutum certatim expetere. Nunc ad Crucem Pauli videas interdum sex hominum millia, finita concione, senes, pueros, mulierculas, una canere, et laudare Deum. Id sacrificos et diabolum ægre habet. Vident enim sacras conciones hoc pacto profundius descendere in hominum animos, et ad singulos pene numeros convelli et concuti regnum suum. Nihil tamen habent, quod jure ac merito quere possint." [1]

"Religion is now somewhat more established than it was. The people are every where exceedingly inclined to the better part. The practice of joining in church music has very much conduced to this, for as soon as they had once commenced singing in public, in only one little church in London, immediately not only the churches in the neighbourhood, but even the towns far distant, began to vie with each other in the same practice. You may now sometimes see at St Paul's Cross, after the service, six thousand persons, old and young, of both sexes, all singing and praising God. This sadly annoys the mass-priests and the devil, for they perceive that by these means the sacred discourses sink more deeply into the minds of men, and that their kingdom is weakened and shaken at almost every note. There is nothing, however, of which they have any right to complain." [2]

At the close of the following century the version of Sternhold and Hopkins was superseded by

---

[1] Zurich Letters, 1558-1579. Epist. Tigurinæ, p. 40. Cambridge, 1842, 8vo.

[2] Zurich Letters, p. 71. Parker Society, 1842, 8vo.

the new, but not superior version, of Brady and Tate. In Scotland, the old version of the Psalms by Sternhold and others was adopted in 1564-5, with certain alterations, in having different translations of forty-one Psalms in place of those peculiar to the English copies.[1] In this amended form it continued in use for nearly a century, until our present version was completed, and received, by authority both of Church and State, in May 1650.

III.—Psalms by Coverdale and Wedderburn.

There are two English metrical versions of select Psalms prior to those of Sternhold, which require to be specially noticed. The authors were Myles Coverdale, and, it is presumed, John Wedderburn. The first of these versions belongs to the reign of Henry VIII., and the only edition that seems to have been printed, could never have obtained much circulation in England;

[1] See Knox's Works, vol. vi., pp. 334-340; Baillie's Letters and Journals, Appendix, vol. iii.

and it became of such rarity as to be wholly unknown till a comparatively recent date, when the copy preserved in the Library of Queen's College, Oxford, was described by the Rev. Archdeacon Cotton, D.C.L., in his valuable work, a List of "Editions of the Bible and parts thereof in English," Oxford, 1821, enlarged in 1852, 8vo. This Psalter has since been reprinted in Coverdale's Remains, Lond. 1846, for the Parker Society, omitting the musical notes. The original title is as follows:—

"Goostly Psalmes and Spirituall Songes drawen out of the holy Scripture, for the comforte and consolacyon of such as love to reioyse in God and his worde." (Colophon.) "Imprynted by me Johan Gough. Cum privilegio Regali." 4to.

On the title page, after short quotations from Psalm cxlvi., Collos. iii., and Jaco. v., are the following lines by the Author:—

To the Boke.

Go, lytle Boke, get the acquaintaunce
   Amonge the lovers of God's worde,
Geue them occasyon the same to auaunce,
   And to make theyr songes of the Lorde,
   That they may thrust under the borde
All other Ballettes of fylthynes,
   And that we all with one accorde
May geue ensample of godlynes.

> Go, lytle Boke, amonge men's chyldren,
>   And get thé to theyr companye;
> Teach them to synge the Commaundementes ten,
>   And other Ballettes of God's glorye:
>   Be not ashamed, I warrande thé,
> Though thou be rude in songe and ryme,
>   Thou shalt to youth some occasion be,
> In godly sportes to passe theyr tyme.

This volume, which has no date of printing, is usually assigned to the year 1539, from the circumstance that it appears in the List of prohibited books which Foxe, in the first edition of "The Booke of Martyrs" (p. 573), annexed to "Certane Injunctions" issued by Henry VIII., 6th of November 1539. He introduces the list with this note: "Hereafter folow the names of certen Bokes which either after this Injunction, or some other in the said Kinges daies, were prohibyted: the names of which bokes heare folowe in order expressed." The books first named are works by Myles Coverdale; and include,—" Item, Psalmes and Songes, drawen, as is pretended, out of Holy Scripture." This list was unquestionably misplaced: it should have accompanied what Foxe, at p. 676 of that edition, calls "A streight and cruell Proclamation, set forth and devised for the abolishing of English Bookes, about the same time of the death of Anne Askew, the viii. of July, and the xxxviii. yere of the reigne of King Henry."—[A.D. 1546]; as upon examining the list, we find books named in it (some of John Bale's, for instance), which were not printed earlier than 1545 and 1546. Foxe, when revising his great work for a second edition in 1570, at p. 1295, withdrew this list; nor was it restored in any of the later impressions until the republication, edited by the Rev. R. S. Cattley (Lond. 1838, 8 vols., 8vo.), when it was inserted, under its proper year 1546 (vol. v. p. 565); omitting, however, what is of importance, the names of authors which the original edition has on the margin.

Notwithstanding the date of Foxe's list, I consider that Coverdale's Psalms must have been printed between 1536 and 1540, during his residence in England. The books printed by or for John Gough extend from 1536 to 1543, and one, a Sermon by Osiander, "translated out of hye Almayn (or German) into Englyshe by Myles Coverdale," has the date 1537. Now, it is well known that after the fall of his great patron, Thomas Cromwell, Earl of Essex (beheaded on the 28th July 1540), Coverdale made his escape to the Continent, where he remained till the accession of Edward VI. in

January 1547, when he was recalled to England, and was, in 1552, promoted to the see of Exeter. His volume contains translations of thirteen Psalms, the 2, 11, 14, 25, 46, 51 (two versions), 67, 124, 128 (two versions), 130, 133, 137, and 147.

In Coverdale's volume four of these Psalms are nearly *verbatim* with those in the present collection. These are—

    Page 57.—I call on thee.   Parker vol. p. 560.
    „ 119.—O God be mercyfull to us. „   580.
    „ 125.—My saull dois magnifie the Lord. „   565.
    „ 127.—Christ is the onlie Son of God. „   553.

A question might arise in regard to their authorship. As fellow-exiles, Wedderburn and Coverdale may have been personally acquainted during their residence abroad, and the former might have contributed some portions to that volume. I do not imagine, however, that such was the case. Coverdale himself makes no allusion either to the fact that most of the pieces were translations from the German, or to assistance received; but his volume having been printed in England not later than the year 1539, selections from it must have found their way into the later collection of "Gude and Godlie Ballates," which has neither the name of author nor editor. So far as we know, it was not printed till nearly thirty years after the English Reformer had given to the world the earliest attempt that had been made in the English language to replace profane and licentious songs and ballads with sacred hymns and psalms, adapted for singing to suitable melodies, according to the practice in the Protestant churches in Germany.

The editor of Coverdale's Remains, 1846, in republishing his psalms and hymns, was seemingly not aware of their German origin, or that they formed one of the many works which he employed himself, during his *first* exile, in translating from one of the numerous volumes of German Hymns printed between 1524 and 1537, as, "PSALMEN UND GEYSTLICHE LIEDER" (Psalms and Spiritual Songs). In the list of Coverdale's works, given by his fellow-exile, Bishop Bale, one has the title of "Cantiones Wittenbergensium, Lib. i."

Mr John Wedderburn, living as an exile in Germany, must have been familiar with the collections of hymns by Luther and other contemporaries; and if we give him the credit of writing and translating most of the pieces which form the second portion of the present volume, he, like Coverdale, availed himself of the hymn-books then in circulation. Indeed, at page 74, it is expressly stated that the Psalms and other new pleasand Ballads were "Translated out of Euchiridion Psalmorum, to be sung." In the "Aufzählung und Beschreibung der alten Deutschen Gesangbücher und Gesangblätter," (an Enumeration and Description of the older German Song-books and Song-leaves), given by Dr Wackernagel, we find several volumes under the titles of *Enchiridion* and of *Kirchenlieder*, in 1524 and subsequent years, printed at Nuremburg, Strasburg, Wittenburg, and other places.

That both Wedderburn and Coverdale were in a great measure indebted to such collections, retaining, for the sake of the music, their peculiar form and structure, is too evident to be doubted. Several of these hymns having been derived from the common source of the Latin hymns sung by the primitive Christians, as handed down from one age to another, although translated at different times and into different languages, would necessarily retain a kind of family likeness.

It is quite impossible, with the scanty information we possess, to assign the various Spiritual Songs and Psalms contained in the present collection to the respective authors or translators.

Each of the three Wedderburns may have contributed to this Miscellany,

> Tres paribus studiis, tres pietate pares.[1]

If their names are to be associated with the present collection, I would conjecture that the Second portion was chiefly the work of Mr John Wedderburn, while residing in Germany; and that the Third portion, consisting of parodies or alterations of Popular Songs or Ballads, might more properly be assigned to his younger brother, the Vicar of Dundee. Judging from the language, we might have attributed the composition of most of these "Godlie Ballates" to the middle of the sixteenth century; but, looking at the history of the reputed authors, the year 1540 would require to be given as the more precise date.

Knox, in his History of the Reformation, records that the night before George Wishart's apprehension at Ormiston,—that is, the night preceding the 16th of January 1545-6,—" After suppar he [Wishart] held confortable purpose of the death of Goddis chosen childrin, and mearely [merrily] said, 'Methink that I desyre earnestlye to sleap;' and thairwith he said, 'Will we sing a

[1] See *supra*, p. xxv.

Psalme?' and so he appointed the 51st Psalme, which was put in Scotishe meter, and begane thus:—

> Have mercy on me now, good Lord,
> After thy great mercy, &c."

It will be seen that these lines occur in the second verse of that psalme, in the present collection, p. 104. Nearly similar words, however, may be found in other translations; but there is no good reason to call in question that this version was the one which Wishart used on the occasion referred to, without admitting that the entire collection then existed in a printed form. Knox, under the year 1555, also says that Elizabeth Adamson, a little before her death, " desyred hir sisteris, and some otheris that was besyd hir, to sing a psalme, and amonges otheris she appointed the 103 Psalme, begynnyng—*My saule, praise thou the Lord alwyes.*"[1] In the note to this passage, I said " This was apparently a metrical version of Psalm 103, but the line does not correspond with any of the known versions of the Psalms in metre. The

[1] Knox's Works, vol. i. p. 139. In the note to this passage, and also at p. 531 of the Appendix, I inadvertently called the Vicar of Dundee John Wedderburn. He is so called by Pitscottie, see *supra*, p. xviii. It was his brother Robert who appears to have held this office.

Wedderburns, however, may have versified a greater number of psalms than those contained in the volume best known as 'The Gude and Godlie Ballates.'[1] At the time, I overlooked the fact that these words form the commencement of Psalm 146, being one of the seven which were contributed by John Hopkins as his first addition to Sternhold's, and as such printed in the year 1551.[2] Knox, in 1561, quotes Sternhold's version of Psalm 103, v. 19—*The hevins hie ar maid the seat.*[3]

At the close of the sixteenth century the present collection of psalms and spiritual songs would seem to have passed under the name of THE DUNDEE PSALMS, thus contributing to fix the place of its origin. In the inventories of some of the Edinburgh booksellers and printers, copies of various editions of the Psalms occur.[4] In particular, in Bassandyne's inventory, who died 18th October 1577, there were 323 "Douglas Psalmes, price the pece vi. d. Summa, £8, 1s. 6d.;" Item, "150 Douglas Psalmes, with Quene Ka-

[1] Knox's Works, vol. i. p. 246.
[2] See the Rev. Mr Livingston's very elaborate introduction to his handsome edition of "The Scottish Metrical Psalter, of A.D. 1635." Glasgow, 1864, folio.
[3] Knox's Works, vol. ii. p. 154.
[4] Bannatyne Miscellany, vol. ii. pp. 191-233.

Preface. xliii

tharine Prayer, the pece x. d. Summa, £6, 5s."
What collection this was, unless the name was
written by mistake, I cannot conjecture. But in
the stock of Robert Smyth, bookseller, who died
1st May 1602, we find,—"*Item*, ane thowsand
xxxiiij. [1034] Dundie Psalmes." Of Smyth's
edition of the present volume, in 1600, only one
copy has reached our days.

But popular as this collection may have been at
that time, it neither was authorised by the General Assembly, nor was it known to have ever been
employed in the public services of the Church. But
the same cause which rendered Luther's hymns
so popular in Germany may have produced a
similar effect in this country subsequent to the
Reformation,—by the adaptation of devotional
poetry to popular tunes.

Another circumstance that falls to be noticed in
connexion with the name of WEDDERBURN is the
authorship of that curious little prose work, The
Complaynt of Scotland, printed, it is supposed, at
St Andrews in 1549. Two "slight and contradictory notices constitute (says Dr Leyden) all the
information which has as yet been discovered concerning the author." In the catalogues of the Har-

leian Library, 1742 and 1745, a copy of the book is twice entered as "Vedderburn's Complainte of Scotland," 1549. It was conjectured that Wedderburn's name might have occurred on the title-page, which is not preserved in any existing copy. On the other hand, Dr George Mackenzie, who is extremely innaccurate in his statements, describes the work as having been written by a Sir James Inglis, knight, who, he says, died at Culross in 1554. It is quite clear that he confounded some imaginary person with the Sir James Inglis, Abbot of Culross, whom Sir D. Lyndsay commemorates among the Scottish Poets, but who was murdered in 1531. Regarding Inglis's claim, I may refer to a long note in Dunbar's Poems, vol. ii. p. 398. Dr Leyden, in republishing the Complaynt itself (Edinburgh, 1801), attempted, but not successfully, to establish a claim for Sir David Lyndsay to have been the author.

As this question of authorship is one in the literary history of Scotland which some persons may consider to be of greater interest than even that of "The Godlie Ballates," I may add a few words on the subject. I do not apprehend that the name either of author or printer occurred in the book itself. The Harleian copy was probably obtained by Harley, Earl of Oxford, with other similar books relating to Scotland, from James Anderson, author of the *Diplomata Scotiæ*, and it may have had the name of Vedderburn written on the title-page or fly-leaf. In the note to Dunbar's Poems, to which I have just referred, I was not foolish enough to indorse Dr George Mackenzie's account of Sir James Inglis, knight, when pointing out that another priest of that name, also one of the Pope's Knights, was alive after "The Complaynt of Scotland" had appeared in 1549. But an old obscure chaplain, whose name is in no way connected with history or literature, may now be summarily set aside for that of Wedderburn.

The ordinary statements that the three brothers Wedderburn became exiles on account of religion, and the supposed time of their decease, seemed to place their claims out of the question. According to Johnston's verses, printed at p. xxv., John Wedderburn, indeed, is said to have been driven into exile in 1546, and to have died in England in 1556. But these dates cannot be relied upon—as we know that he was in exile in 1539—and, after Cardinal Beaton's death in 1546, there was something like toleration in Scotland, which cannot be said to have existed in England during the fires of persecution in Queen Mary's reign (1553 to 1558). Mr Robert Wedderburn, Vicar of Dundee, having, however, survived till after the date of printing, leads me now to add, that, notwithstanding some apparent discrepancies, by far the most probable conjecture is, that he was the author of The Complaynt. Indeed, from what has been stated above, as the Vicar, in 1553, was still alive, and officially connected with the Romish Church, I have little hesitation in assigning to MR ROBERT WEDDERBURN, VICAR OF DUNDEE, the credit of being the author of that remarkable production, THE COMPLAYNT OF SCOTLAND, printed (at St Andrews) in 1549. In coming to this conclusion we have his residence in the vicinity of St Andrews, the general tone and character of the book, as conveying the sentiments of one who was perhaps inclined in his heart to be a Reformer, although retaining his connexion with the Romish Church, and who imitated Sir David Lyndsay in exposing (with a deal of pedantic learning) the prevailing abuses of the time; and more especially his familiarity with the popular literature of the time, while enumerating the names of songs, dances, &c., of which Dr Leyden mentions seven among those which Wedderburn himself is supposed to have "metamorphosed" in the present collection of "GUDE AND GODLIE BALLATES."

It is generally admitted that this collection of Godly Ballads was not only popular, but had considerable influence on the minds of the common people, who could easily appreciate words sung to popular airs. The number of such satirical invectives against the corruptions and abuses which prevailed in the Romish Church, could not fail to enlighten the ignorant portion of the laity, and tend to facilitate the progress of the Reformed doctrines.

It is to be observed that no mention of the Wedderburns, by Knox or others, is met with until the days of James Melville, when he refers to an unknown edition of the present volume about 1570. In giving an account of his education at the school of Montrose, he relates, in his autobiography, that in the year 1571 John Erskine, the Laird of Dun, "dwelt oft in the town, and of his charitie interteined a blind man, wha had a singular guid voice. Him he caused the Doctor (teacher) of our school teach the whole Psalms in metre, with the toones thereof, and sing them in the kirk; be hearing of whom I was so delyted, that I learned many of the psalms and toones thereof in metre, quhilk I have thought ever sensyne a great blessing and comfort. . . . . "There was also there a post (a carrier or messenger) that frequented Edinburgh, and brought hame Psalme-books and Ballates, namely, of Robert Semple's making, wherein I took pleasure, and learned some thing baith of the estate of the Countrie, and of the measours and cullors of Scottes ryme. He shew me first WEDDERBURN'S SONGS, wherof I learned diverse *par cœur* (by heart), with great diversitie of toones."[1]

In like manner, Mr John Row, minister of Carnock (1592-1646), and son of John Row, the Reformer, minister of Perth (1560-1580), in his History of the Kirk of Scotland, under the year 1558, mentions certain books which were sett out, "whereby many in Scotland got some knowledge of God's trueth," and, along with Sir David Lyndsay's writings, he enumerates "WEDDERBURN'S PSALMES and GODLY BALLADS, changeing many of the old Popish Songs unto godlie purposes."[2]

---

[1] Autobiography and Diary of James Melville, Bann. Club edition, 1829, 4to, p. 18. Edinb. Wodrow Society edition, pp. 22, 23, 1842, 8vo.

[2] Wodrow Society edition, 1846, p. 6.

IV.—*Profane Songs Spiritualized.*

It is not likely that I am singular in expressing a wish that the original songs and ballads which the Wedderburns "changed to godly purposes" had also been preserved. Several of these, no doubt, were of an indecent character, but others, like such satirical effusions containing references to local and personal as well as public events, would have furnished curious and interesting illustrations of popular literature, and of the history and manners of the time. It has so happened that of these "ballatis, sangis, and rhymes," in a printed form, not one is known to exist, although they were extensively circulated in the face of prohibitions by Acts of Parliament, Acts of Town-Councils, and Canons issued by the Clergy.

In referring to "the Gude and Godlie Ballates," Dr M'Crie gives the following information:—

"The title (he says) sufficiently indicates their nature and design. The air, the measure, the initial line, or the chorus of the ballads most commonly sung by the people at that time, were transferred to hymns of devotion. Unnatural, indelicate, and gross as this association appears to us, these spiritual songs edified multitudes in that age. We must not think that this originated in any peculiar depravation of taste in our reforming countrymen. Spiritual songs, constructed upon the same principle, were common in Italy—(Roscoe's Lorenzo de Medici, vol. i. p. 309, 4to). At the beginning of the Reformation, the very same practice was adopted in Holland as in Scotland.

"The Protestants first sung in their families and private assemblies the Psalms of the noble Lord of Nievelte, which he published in 1540, ut homines ab amatoriis, haud raro obscœnis, aliisque vanis canticis, quibus omnia in urbibus et vicis personabant, avocaret. Sed quia modulationes vanarum cantionum (alias enim homines non tenebant) adhibuerat," &c.—"Gisberti Voetii Politica Ecclesiastica, tom. i. p. 534—Amstælod. 1663, 4to. Florimond de Remond objected to the Psalms of Marot, that the airs of some of them were borrowed from vulgar ballads. A Roman Catholic version of the Psalms in Flemish verse, printed at Antwerp by Simon Cock, in 1540, has the first line of a ballad printed at the head of every psalm."[1]

The passage from Roscoe's Life of Lorenzo de Medici mentioned by Dr M'Crie may be quoted as follows :—

"In an ancient collection of Laude, or Hymns, printed at Venice in 1512, I find that several of these devout pieces are directed to be sung to the air of *Ben venga Maggio*. From this collection it appears that it was then a general custom in Italy, as it now is, or lately was, the practice of a certain sect in this country, to sing pious hymns to the most profane and popular melodies, for the purpose of stimulating the languid piety of the performers, by an association with the vivacity of sensual enjoyments. Thus the hymn *Jesu sommo diletto*, is sung to the music of *Leggiadra damigella*; *Jesu fammi morire*, to that of *Vaga bella e gentile*; *Genetrice di Dio*, to that of *Dolce anima mia*; and *Crucifisso a capo chino*, to that of *Una Donna d'amor fino*, one of the most indecent pieces in the *Canzoni a ballo*"[2]

In order to appropriate the original airs in the

[1] Bayle, Dict. art. Marot, note N; M'Crie's Life of Knox, vol. i. p. 379, 2 vols. Edinb. 1831, 8vo.

[2] Roscoe's Lorenzo de Medici, vol. i. p. 309, edit. 1796.

German *Gesangbuchs*, it has already been remarked, the same structure of verse was adopted by Wedderburn as well as by Coverdale, which to some extent rendered their translations less flowing and easy. But the great object which both of them had in view, and of which Coverdale may claim the merit of being the first in the English language to have made the attempt, was to replace profane and licentious songs and ballads with sacred hymns and metrical psalms. In England, Sternhold's Psalms were harmonized by various persons. There is a rare edition in four parts or separate volumes, imprinted at London, by John Daye, in 1563, professing to be "The whole Psalmes in foure partes, whiche may be song to al Musical Instrumentes, set forth for the encrease of Vertue, and abolyshyng of uther vayne and triflyng Ballates." Another has this title, "The Psalmes of David in English Meter, with Notes of foure partes set unto them by Gulielmo Damon, for John Bull, to the use of the godly Christians for recreating themselves instede of fond and unseemely Ballades. Anno 1579," oblong quarto. This was republished, in 1585, by Iohn Cosyn, and in 1591, by W. Swayne. But these were superseded by Thomas Este's Psalter of

1592,[1] and by Thomas Ravenscroft's Psalms and Hymns, in 1621 and 1633. In Scotland, the Psalms in four parts, were not published until 1635. The Scottish Psalter of 1566, by Thomas Wood, has, it may be said, been only lately discovered. According to his statement, the Parts of the Psalm Tunes " conform to the Tenor" were set in harmony by David Peblis, one of the Canons of St Andrews, at the special request of the Prior, afterwards Earl of Murray, and Regent of Scotland.[2] Alexander Hume, in his Hymnes and Spirituall Songs, printed in 1599, in his address "To the Scottish Youth," makes use of similar arguments with Coverdale in recommending poetry of a religious nature instead of " that naughty subject of fleshly and unlawfull love. In such sort (he adds), that in Princes Courts, in the houses of greate men, and at the assemblies of yong gentilmen and yong damesels, the chiefe pastime is, to sing profane

---

[1] Republished by Dr E. F. Rimbault for the Musical Antiquarian Society, 1844, with a learned introduction.

[2] Three of the original volumes are now in my possession; the *Contra tenor*, required for completing the set, has not been recovered. Two volumes of a duplicate set (the Treble and Bassus) are in the University Library, Edinburgh. See notices of the MSS. in a forthcoming volume of Proceedings of the Society of Antiquaries of Scotland.

sonnets, and vaine ballats of love, or to rehearse some fabulos faits of Palmerine, Amadis, or other such like raveries."[1]

Myles Coverdale, in the preface to his "Goostly Psalmes and Spirituall Songes," thus urges the propriety of his attempt to supply the place of the profane and licentious ballads which were in ordinary circulation. The greater part of this address is equally suitable to Wedderburn's volume, as the following extracts will evince:—

"MYLES COVERDALE UNTO THE CHRISTIAN READER."

(After some general remarks on the unthankfulness manifested to the Father of Mercy for spiritual benefits, he exclaims:—)

"O that men would praise the goodness of the Lord, and the wonders that he doth for the children of men! O that we would remember what great things the Father of Mercy hath done, doth daily, and is ever ready to do, for our souls! O that men's lips were so opened, that their mouths might shew the praise of God! Yea, would God that our Minstrels had none other thing to play

[1] Reprinted for the Bannatyne Club, 1832, 4to.

upon, neither our carters and ploughmen other things to whistle upon, save psalms, hymns, and such godly songs as David is occupied withal! And if women, sitting at their rocks, or spinning at the wheels, had none other songs to pass their time withal, than such as Moses' sister, Glehana's wife, Debora, and Mary the mother of Christ, have sung before them, they should be better occupied than with *Hey nony nony*, *Hey troly loly*, and such like phantasies.

"If young men also that have the gift of singing, took their pleasure in such wholesome ballads as the three Children sing in the fire, and as Jesus the Son of Sirac doth in his last chapter, it were a token, both that they felt some spark of God's love in their hearts, and that they also had some love unto him; for truly, as we love, so sing we; and where our affection is, thencĕ cometh our mirth and joy.   .   .   .   .   .   .
.   .   .   .

"Seeing, then, that, as the prophet David saith, it is so good and pleasant a thing to praise the Lord, and so expedient for us to be thankful; therefore, to give our youth of England some occasion to change their foul and corrupt ballads into sweet songs and spiritual hymns of God's honour, and for their own consolation in him, I have here, good reader, set out certain comfortable songs grounded on God's word, and taken some out of the holy scripture, specially out of the Psalms of David, all whom would God that our musicians would learn to make their songs! And if they which are disposed to be merry, would in their mirth follow the counsel of St Paul and St James, and not to pass their time in naughty songs of fleshly love and wantonness, but with singing of psalms, and such songs as edify, and corrupt not men's conversation.

"As for the common sort of Ballads which now are used in the world, I report me to every good man's conscience, what wicked fruits they bring. Corrupt they not the manners of young persons?

. . . .

" By this thou mayst perceave what spiritual edifying cometh of Godly Psalms and Songs of God's word; and what inconvenience followeth the corrupt Ballads of this vain world. Now, beloved Reader, thou seest the occasion of this my small labour: wherefore, if thou perceavest that the very word of God is the matter thereof, I pray thee accept it, use it, and provoke youth unto the same. And if thou feelest in thine heart, that all the Lord's dealing is very mercy and kindness, cease not then to be thankful unto him therefore: but in thy mirth be always singing of him, that his blessed name may be praised now and ever. Amen."[1]

The last poem in Coverdale's volume of "Goostly Psalmes and Spirituall Songes," is more of a satirical cast than the others. It is too long to quote entire, but the first four of twelve verses may be given; and it may suggest whether other pieces in the present collection, besides the four which are pointed out in the Notes, might not also claim him as the writer:—

LET GO THE WHORE OF BABILON.

Let go the Whore of Babilon,
 Her kyngdome falleth sore;
Her merchauntes begyne to make theyr mone,
 The Lorde be praysed therefore.
Theyr ware is naught, it wyll not be bought,
 Great falsheed is founde therin:
Let go the Whore of Babilon,
 The mother of al synne.
No man wyll drynke her wyne any more,
 The poyson is come to lyghte;
That maketh her marchauntes to wepe so sore,
 The blynde have gotten theyr syghte.

[1] Works of Myles Coverdale—Remains, p. 537. Parker Society, 1846. 8vo.

For now we se God's grace frelye
   In Christ offred us so fayre:
Let go the Whore of Babilon,
   And bye no more her ware.

Of Christen bloude so much she shed
   That she was dronken withall;
But nowe God's worde hath broken her head,
   And she hath gotten a fall.
God hath raysed some men in dede,
   To utter her great wickednesse:
Let go the Whore of Babilon
   And her ungodlynesse.

Ye ypocrites, what can ye saye?
   Wo be unto you all!
Ye have begyled us many a daye;
   Heretikes ye did us call,
For lovynge the worde of Christ the Lorde,
   Whom ye do alwaye resiste.
Let go the Whore of Babilon,
   That rydeth upon the Beast.

In the volume known as the Aberdeen Cantus (editions, 1666-1682), there is a later but by no means a happy adaptation of a popular song. The song itself, *Come Love let's walk*, seems to have first appeared in the "Canzonets to three voyces, newly composed by Henry Youll, practicioner in the Art of Musicke," Lond. 1608, which has also a second part, *In yonder dale*, and a third part, *See where this nymphe.*[1] Not having Youll's collection to compare, it is sufficient, for the present object, to copy the first verse from the Aberdeen Cantus, and also the first of three verses of the imitation :—

The XIV. Song.
Come, Love, let's walk in yonder spring,
Where we shall hear the Blackbird sing,
The Robin red-breast, and the Thrush,
The Nightingale in thorny bush,
The Mavis sweetly caroling :
   This to my Love, this to my Love,
     Content will bring.

Another of the same.
Come, Lord, let's walk on Sion Hill,
There to remain for ever still;
Where Prophets, 'Postles, and just folk,
With Martyrs on a row do walk,—
The Angels sweetly caroling :
   This to my soul, this to my soul,
     Content shall bring.

In concluding these notices, I have to acknowledge that my attention to various points connected with the origin of portions of this volume, as having been translated from the German, was specially called by my Reverend friend PROFESSOR MITCHELL of St Andrews. He himself has fully and

[1] Rimbault's Musical Bibliography, p. 27.

ably illustrated the subject in a Lecture, recently published, including in the Appendix several of the German hymns, and of Coverdale's in parallel columns with the corresponding "Godlie Ballates." It is entitled—

"The Wedderburns, and their Work on the Sacred Poetry of the Scottish Reformation, in its Historical Relation to that of Germany: A Lecture by Alex. F. Mitchell, D.D., Professor of Hebrew, St Andrews. Wm. Blackwood and Sons, Edinburgh and London, 1867." 4to, pp. 88.

I have gladly availed myself, in the Notes, of the author's learned researches.

I have also much pleasure in expressing my best thanks to S. CHRISTIE MILLER, Esq., of Craigentinny, for the liberal use of the original edition of 1578; and to Mr JAMES WALKER, for carefully revising and enlarging so fully that portion of the Glossary subjoined to Sir John Graham Dalyell's "Scotish Poems of the Sixteenth Century," which is applicable to "the Godlie Ballates."

DAVID LAING.

1867.

ANE
Cōpendious buik

of godlie Psalmes and spirituall Sangis
collectit furthe of sindrie partis of the
Scripture, with diueris vtheris Ballattis changeit out of prophane Sangis
in godlie sangis, for auoyding of
sin and harlatrie. With augmentation of sindrie gude
and godlie Ballatis
not contenit in the
first editioun.

✠

ℂ Imprentit at

Edinburgh be IOHNE ROS
for Henrie Charteris.
M. D. LXXVIII.
Cum priuilegio Regali.

ANE ALMANACK

for ix. zeiris.

The zeir of our Lord.	Pasche day.	The Goldin number.	The Sondayis Letter.	The Leip zeir.
M.D.lxxviii.	30 Marche	2	E	
M.D.lxxix.	19 Aprill	3	D	
M.D.lxxx.	3 Aprill	4	C B	
M.D.lxxxi.	26 Marche	5	A	
M.D.lxxxii.	15 Aprill	6	G	
M.D.lxxxiii.	21 Marche	7	F	
M.D.lxxxiiii.	19 Aprill	8	E D	
M.D.lxxxv.	11 Aprill	9	C	
M.D.lxxxvi.	3 Aprill	10	B	

January xxxi. dayis.

iii	A	Circumcision.	i
	b		ii
xi	c	At viij. and iiij.	iii
	d		iv
xix	e		v
viii	f	Epiphanie.	vi
	g	The 6. day the three wyse men	vii
xvi	A	acknawledged Christ, and offerit	viii
v	b	giftis vnto him.	ix
	c		x
xiii	d	Sunne in Aquarius.	xi
ii	e		xii
	f	S. Mungo in Glasgow, a Fair.	xiii
x	g		xiv
	A		xv
xviii	b		xvi
vii	c		xvii
	d		xviii
xv	e	The 19. day the middis of Wyn-	xix
iv	f	ter efter Ptolomie.	xx
	g		xxi
xii	A		xxii
i	b	At vij. and ane half, ànd iiij. and	xxiii
	c	ane half.	xxiv
ix	d	Conversioun of Paull.	xxv
	e		xxvi
xvii	f		xxvii
vi	g		xxviii
	A		xxix
xiv	b		xxx
iii	c		xxxi

February xxviii. dayis.

	d		i
xi	e	Purificatioun of Marie.	ii
xix	f		iii
viii	g		iiii
	A		v
xvi	b		vi
v	c	The 8. day, the beginning of the	vii
	d	Spring time, among the Romanes,	viii
xiii	e	efter Plinius.	ix
ii	f	At vij. and v.	x
	g	Sunne in Pisces.	xi
x	A		xii
	b		xiii
xviii	c		xiiii
vii	d		xv
	e		xvi
xv	f		xvii
iv	g		xviii
	A		xix
xii	b		xx
i	c		xxi
	d		xxii
ix	e	The place of the Leip zeir.	xxiii
	f	Mathew Apostle.	xxiiii
xvii	g		xxv
vi	A		xxvi
	b	At vij. and ane half, and v. and	xxvii
xiv	c	ane half.	xxviii

Marche xxxi. dayis.

xj	d	In S. Monence ane Fair.	i
	e		ii
iij	f	The iij. day the Temple of Je-	iii
	g	ruſalem was buyldit againe,	iiii
xix	A	and confecratit with greit fo-	v
viii	b	lempnitie. Efdra 6. befoir the	vi
	c	birth of Chriſt 515. zeiris.	vii
xvj	d		viii
v	e		ix
	f	at vi. and vi.	x
xiii	g	Sone in Aries.	xi
iii	A		xii
	b		xiii
x	c		xiiii
	d		xv
xviii	e	Aprilis.	xvi
vii	f	S. Patrik in Dunbartane ane	xvii
	g	Fair.	xviii
xv	A		xix
iiii	b	S. Cudbert in Langtoun in the	xx
	c	Mers ane Fair.	xxi
xii	d		xxii
	e		xxiii
	f		xxiiii
ix	g	Lady day in the weſt Wemis	xxv
	A	ane Fair.	xxvi
xvii	b	The 25. day Veneis was be-	xxvii
vi	c	gun to be buyldit, anno 423.	xxviii
	d		xxix
xiiii	e		xxx
ii	f		xxxi

April xxx. dayis.

xj	g		i
	A	The first day Rome was de-	ii
xix	b	stroyit be Alarik king of Go-	iii
viij	c	this, efter ij. zeiris seige. anno	iiii
	d	412. Blondus. The Temple	v
xvj	e	of Jerusalem is purgit from	vi
v	f	Adolatrie be king Ezechias.	vii
	g	2. Paral. 29.	viii
xiij	A		ix
ij	b		x
	c	at v. and vi.	xi
x	d		xii
	e		xiii
xviij	f	Maij.	xiiii
vii	g		xv
	A	The 11. day Josue circumciseth	xvi
xv	b	the pepill in Gilgall. Jos. 5.	xvii
iiii	c		xviii
	d	The 18. day the pepill passit	xix
xii	e	saif throw the reid sey, and	xx
j	f	Pharao with his Oist drownit.	xxi
	g	Exod. 14. 15.	xxii
ix	A	-	xxiii
	b		xxiiii
xvii	c	Mark Euangell.	xxv
vj	d		xxvi
	e		xxvii
xiiii	f		xxviii
iij	g	at iiij. and ane half,	xxix
	A	and vij. and ane half.	xxx

Maii xxxi. dayis.

xi	b	Philip and Jacob.	i
	c		ii
xix	d	Haly Croce day in Kinnocher	iii
viii	e	and in Peblis ane Fair.	iiii
	f		v
xvi	g	The 6. day Rome was takin	vi
v	A	be the Duke of Burbone. an.	vii
	b	1527.	viii
xiii	c		ix
ii	d		x
	e	Sone in Gemini.	xi
x	f		xii
	g		xiii
xviii	A		xiv
vii	b	The 15. day God did raine	xv
	c	Manna to the pepill. Exo. 15.	xvi
xv	d		xvii
iiii	e	The 17. day Noe enterit in	xviii
	f	the Arke. Gene. 7.	xix
xii	g		xx
i	A	at iiij. and viij.	xxi
	b		xxii
ix	c		xxiii
	d		xxiiii
xvii	e		xxv
vi	f		xxvi
	g	The 27. day Noe came furth	xxvii
xiiii	A	of the arke. Genes. 8. 9.	xxviii
iii	b	The 29. day Constantinople was	xxix
	c	takin be Mahomete.	xxx
xi	d		xxxi

June xxx. dayis.

	e	The firſt day the pepill of Iſra-	i
xix	f	ell come in the hill of Sinai : v-	ii
viii	g	therwiſe callit Caſius, & thair	iii
xv	A	abaid almaiſt ane zeir. Exo. 19.	iiii
v	b		v
	c	The vi. day Alexander the greit	vi
xiij	d	is borne.	vii
ij	e		viii
	f		ix
x	g		x
	A	S. Barnabie, Lawder fair	xi
xviii	b		xii
vii	c	Sone in Cancer.	xiii
	d	Junij langeſt day.	xiiii
xv	e		xv
iiii	f	Quarter before iij.	xvi
	g		xvii
xii	A		xviii
j	b	The 19. day James the Sext	xix
	c	king of Scotland was borne	xx
ix	d	Anno. 1566.	xxi
	e		xxii
xviii	f		xxiii
vi	g	S. Jhone in S. Johnſtoun	xxiiii
	A	ane Fair.	xxv
xiiij	b		xxvi
iij	c		xxvii
	d		xxviii
xi	e	Peter [A]poſtle.	xxix
	f		xxx

July xxxi. dayis.

xix	g		i
viii	A		ii
	b		iii
xvi	c		iiii
v	d		v
	e	Canicular dayis begin.	vi
xiii	f	at iiij. and vij.	vii
ii	g	The 8. day John Hus was brunt	viii
	A	in the Counfall of Conftance,	ix
x	b	for the treuth, 1415.	x
	c		xi
xviii	d	Sun in Leo.	xii
vii	e		xiii
	f		xiiii
xv	g		xv
iv	A	The 16. Rome wes overthro-	xvi
	b	wen be the Galles, befoir Chriftis	xvii
xii	c	birth 376 zeiris.	xviii
i	d		xix
	e		xx
ix	f		xxi
	g	Marie Magdalene. In Linlith-	xxii
xvii	A	gow, and Pettenweme, ane Fair.	xxiii
vi	b		xxiiii
	c	S. James. In Cowper of Fyfe,	xxv
xiv	d	in Lanerk, and in auld Rox-	xxvi
iii	e	burgh, ane Fair.	xxvii
	f		xxviii
xi	g	This 29. James the Sext King of	xxix
xix	A	Scotland wes crowned in Striuiling	xxx
	b	the fecond zeir of his age, Anno 1567.	xxxi

August xxxi. dayis.

viii	c	Lambes day, in Inuerkething,	i
xvi	d	in Sanctandrois, and in Dunbar-	ii
v	e	tane, ane Fair.	iii
	f		iiii
xiii	g		v
ii	A		vi
	b		vii
x	c		viii
	d		ix
xviii	e	S. Laurence, in Selkirk, in Dun-	x
vii	f	blane, and in the Raine, ane	xi
	g	Fair.	xii
xv	A	at v. and vij.	xiii
iv	b		xiiii
	c	Lady day. In Dundee, ane Fair.	xv
xii	d	Sun in Virgo.	xvi
i	e		xvii
	f		xviii
ix	g	The 19. day Octavius Auguftus	xix
	A	the Emperour died, the 79. zeir	xx
xvii	b	of his age, efter Chriftis birth	xxi
vi	c	16. zeiris.	xxii
	d		xxiii
xiv	e	Bartholomew Apoftle, in Lin-	xxiiii
iii	f	lithgow, and in Kincarne of	xxv
	g	Neill, ane Fair.	xxvi
xi	A		xxvii
xix	b		xxviii
	c	S. Johnis day, in S. Johnftoun.	xxix
viii	d	at v. and ane half,	xxx
	e	and v. and ane half.	xxxi

September xxx. dayis.

xvj	f		i
v	g		ii
	A		iii
xiii	b		iiii
ij	c	Heir endis the Canicular dayis.	v
	d		vi
x	e		vii
	f	Lady day in Striuiling and Dun-	viii
xviii	g	die ane fair.	ix
vii	A		x
	b		xi
xv	c	at vi. and vi.	xii
iiii	d		xiii
	e	Rude day in Craill and Jed-	xiiii
xii	f	burgh ane fair.	xv
j	g	Sone in Libra.	xvi
	A	Nicht and day of ane lenth.	xvii
ix	b		xviii
	c		xix
xvii	d	Mathew Apostle in Linlithgow	xx
vj	e	ane fair.	xxi
	f		xxii
xiiii	g		xxiii
iii	A		xxiiii
	b		xxv
xi	c		xxvi
xix	d	at vi. and ane half, and v. and	xxvii
	e	ane half.	xxviii
viii	f	S. Michael in Hadingtoun, in	xxix
	g	Leslie, and in Air ane fair.	xxx

October xxxi. dayis.

xvi	A		i
v	b	The first day the feist of the	ii
xiii	c	Trumpettis in remembrance that	iii
ij	d	Isaac was delyverit from the	iiii
	e	Sacrifying. Leuit. 23.	v
x	f		vi
	g		vii
xviii	A		viii
vii	b	S. Dinneis in Atoun in the Mers	ix
	c	& in Peblis ane fair.	x
xv	d		xi
iiii	e		xii
	f	at vii. and v.	xiii
xii	g	Sone in Scorpio.	xiiii
	A		xv
	b	Nouembris.	xvi
ix	c		xvii
	d	S. Luke in Lawder, in Kin-	xviii
xviii	e	rofcheir, and in Ruglane ane	xix
vi	f	Fair.	xx
	g	The 15. day the feist of the Ta-	xxi
xiiii	A	bernackles continewit vii. dayis.	xxii
iij	b	Leuit. 23. John 7.	xxiii
	c		xxiiii
xi	d		xxv
xix	e		xxvi
	f		xxvii
viii	g	Simon and Jude.	xxviii
	A		xxix
xvi	b	at vij. and ane half,	xxx
v	c	and iiij. and ane half.	xxxi

Nouember xxx. dayis.

	d	Hallow day ane fair in Edin-	i
xiij	e	burgh viij. dayis, and in Falk-	ii
ij	f	land ane day.	iii
	g		iiii
x	A		v
	b	The 10. day Martine Luther	vi
xviij	c	was borne in Iſlebia, the zeir of	vii
vij	d	Chriſt. 1483.	viii
	e		ix
xv	f		x
iiij	g	S. Martine in Dunbar, in Cow-	xi
	A	per of Fyfe, and in Hammiltoun	xii
xij	b	ane Fair.	xiii
j	c	Decembris.	xiiii
	d	The 15. day Jeroboam efter	xv
ix	e	the defectioun of the ten Try-	xvi
	f	bes from Roboam, erectit ij.	xvii
xvij	g	Goldin Calues in Dan, and Be-	xviii
vj	A	thell, and cauſit the pepill to	xix
	b	ga worſchip thame, that thay	xx
xiiij	c	ſuld not go vp to Jeruſalem.	xxi
iij	d	1. Kings 12.	xxii
	e		xxiii
xi	f		xxiiii
xix	g	S. Katherene in Dunfermling	xxv
	A	ane Fair.	xxvi
xviii	b		xxvii
	c		xxviii
xvi	d		xxix
v	e	S. Andro in S. Johnſtoun, in Peblis, in Sanctandrois, and in Chirneſyde, in the Mers ane Fair.	xxx

December xxxi. dayis.

xiii	f		i
ii	g		ii
	A		iii
x	b		iiii
	c		v
xiiii	d	S. Nicolas in Abirdene a fair.	vi
vii	e		vii
	f	Lady day in the west wemis	viii
xv	g	ane fair.	ix
iiii	A		x
	b	Sone in Capricorne.	xi
xii	c		xii
j	d	Luce, schortest day.	xiii
	e	January.	xiiii
ix	f	at viii. and ane quarter, and	xv
	g	ane quarter before iiij.	xvi
xvii	A		xvii
vi	b		xviii
	c		xix
xiiii	d		xx
iii	e	Thomas Apostle.	xxi
	f		xxii
xi	g		xxiii
	A		xxiiii
	b	Zule day.	xxv
viii	c	S. Steuin.	xxvi
	d	S. Johne Euangell.	xxvii
xvi	e	• Innocentis day.	xxviii
v	f		xxix
	g		xxx
xiiii	A		xxxi

The Lamentatioun of a Sinner.

O LORD in thee is all my truſt,
   giue eare vnto my wofull cry:
Refuſe me not that am unjuſt,
   bot bowing doun thy heavenly eye,
Behald how I do ſtill lament
   my ſinnes quhairin I do offend;
O Lord, for thame ſall I be ſchent?
   ſen thee to pleaſe I do intend.

No, no, not ſo thy will is bent,
   to deale with ſinners in thyne ire;
Bot quhen in hart thay ſall repent,
   thow grantſt with ſpeid thair juſt deſyre:
To thé thairfoir ſtill ſall I cry
   to waſh away my ſinful cryme:
Thy blude (O Lord) is not zit dry
   bot that thow may help me in tyme.

For quhy? whill I on eirth remaine
   oppreſt, allace, with wo and greif!
My febill hart plunged in paine,
   doth ſigh and ſew for thy releif.
Sweit Chriſt, will thow not then appeir,
   to comfort thame that comfort laik?
Will thow not bow thyne eir to heir?
   Lord Jeſus, cum and be not ſlake!

For then ſall thyne reſſave thair reſt;
   thair joy, thair blys, thair perfite peice,
                            And

The Lamentatioun.

And fé thy face of treafure beft,
   O Lord, that dois our joyes incres.
Then fall thow give thofe Nobill crownes,
   quhilk thine awin blud hes deirly bocht.
Then fall thofe Pfalmes and hie Renownes
   be gevin in grace moft richely wrocht.

Then fall thy Saintes redemed deir,
   from baill to blys remoued be:
And fweiteft Chrift, thy fweit voyce heir
   cum vnto me Babes, cum to me.
Cum Reigne in joye Eternalie,
   cum reigne in blys that hes na end,
Cum thairfoir Lord, cum Chrift we pray,
   our preffed greif with fpeid amend.

Hafte thee (O Lord) hafte thee I fay,
   to powre on me the giftes of grace;
That quhen this lyfe muft flit away,
   in heuin with thé I may haue place.
Quhair thow doft reigne Eternally,
   with God, quhilk once did doun thee fend,
Quhair Angels fings continually,
   to thee be praife, warld without end.

So be it.

¶ THE PROLOGVE.

PAVLE writand to the Coloss. in his thrid Chap. sayis, "Let the word of God dwel in zow plenteouslie in all wisdome; teiching and exhorting zour awin selfis with Psalmes, & Hymnis, and Spirituall sangis, quhilkis haue luse to God, & fauouris his word." We haue heir ane plane Text, that the word of God incressis plenteouslie in vs, be singing of the Psalmes, and Spiritual sangis, and that speciallie amang zoung persons, and sic as ar not exercisit in the Scriptures: for thay wil soner consaue the trew word, nor quhen thay heir it sung in Latine, the quhilks thay wait not what it is. Bot quhen thay heir it sung in thair vulgar toung, or singis it thame selfis, with sweit melodie, then sal thay luse thair Lord God, with hart and minde, and cause them to put away baudrie & vnclene sangis. Pray God. Amen.

THE text of the Catechifme, or Inftructioun of Chriftiane men, quhilk is neceffarie till euerie man that wald be fauit, to knaw and exercife thame felfis daylie thairin, contening the Ten Commandementis of God, the Twelve Articklis of our Faith, the Lordis Prayer, of our Baptifme, and of the Lordis Supper.

And firft, the Ten Commandementis of God, as thay ar writtin in Exodus the twentie Chapter.

I Am the Lord thy God quhilk haue brocht thé out of the land of Egypt, and furth of the hous of bondage. Thow fail haue nane vther godis befoir my face.

Thow fall not mak to thy felf ony grauin Image, nor the fimilitude of ony thing that is in heuin aboue, nor in the eirth beneth, nor in the watter vnder the eirth: thow fall not bow downe to them nor worfchip them. For I the Lord thy God am a jelous God, and vifitis the finnes of the Fatheris vpon the Children vnto the thrid and fourt generatioun of them that hait me, and fchew mercie vnto thoufandis of them that lufe me, and keipis my commandementis.

Thow fall not tak the Name of the Lord thy God in vane : [For the Lord wil not hald him giltles that taketh his name in vaine. *Edit.* 1621.]

Remember that thow keip haly the Sabboth day.

Honour thy Father and thy Mother.
Thow fall do na Murther.
Thow fall not commit Adulterie.
Thow fall not Steill.
Thow fall not beir fals witnes aganis thy Nicht-
bour.
Thow fall not couet thy Nichtbouris hous: thow
fall not couet thy Nichtbouris wyfe, nor his
feruand, nor his mayd, nor his oxe, nor his
affe, nor ony thing that is thy Nichtbouris.

¶ *The threitning of God, maid to them that brekis
his Commandementis, and His promeis maid
to them that keipis them. Deut. xvij.*

Curfit ar thay that continewis not in all the wordis of this Law to do them: and all the pepil fall fay Amen. Exod. xx. Chap.

¶ *The twelf Articklis of our Faith, as thay war writtin be the Apoftillis to the Thre Perfones in Trinitie.*

1 I Beleue in God the Father Almichtie, maker of heuin and eird.
2 And in Jefus Chrift his only Sone our Lord.
3 Quhilk was confauit be the Haly Gaift, borne of the Virgine Mary.
4 Sufferit vnder Ponce Pylate, was crucifyit, deid, and buryit, and difcendit into hell.
5 The thrid day he rais againe from the deid.
6 He afcendit into heuin, and fittis at the richt

The Articklis of the Faith.

    hand of God the Father Almichtie.
7 And efter sall cum to judge the quicke and the deid.
8 I Beleue in the Haly Gaist.
9 The haly Kirk vniuersall, the communioun of Saintes.
10 The Remissioun of Sinnis.
11 The Resurrectioun of the body.
12 And life Euerlasting.   So be it.

¶ *The Lordis Prayer, as it is writtin in the 6. Chap. of Mathew, quhilk Christ leirnit vs to pray, contening sex petitiounis, and all thingis necessarie for vs. &c.*

1 OVR Father that art in heuin, hallowit be thy Name.
2 Thy Kingdome cum.
3 Thy will be done in eirth, as it is in heuin.
4 Giue vs this day our daylie breid.
5 Forgiue vs our trespassis, as we forgiue them that trespas aganis vs.
6 And leid vs not into temptatioun. Bot deliuer vs from euill. For thine is the Kingdome, the power and the glorie, for euer. Amen.

¶ *Of our Baptisme.*

GO zour way, and teiche all Natiounis, and Baptise them in the name of the Father & of the Sone, and of the Haly Gaist. Math. xvj. Chap. Go zour way into all the warld, and preiche the Euangell till all creatures : and quha that beleuis and is Baptifit, fall be faif; bot quha beleuis not, fal be condempnit. ad Titum. Cap. 3. Not for the workis of righteoufnes that we haif wrocht, bot efter his greit mercie, God hes fauit vs be the fontane of the new birth, and renewing of the Haly Gaift; quhilk he fched on vs aboundantly throw Jefus Chrift our Sauiour, that we being maid richteous be his grace, fuld be airis of Eternal Life, according to hope, this is trew, Rom. vj. Thairfoir we are buryit with Chrift be Baptifme into deid: like as Chrift was raifit fra deid be the glorie of his Father, euin fa we alfo fuld walk in a new life.

¶ *The Lordis Supper, as it is writtin in the firft Epiftil to the Cor. xj. Chap.*

THAT quhilk I haue deliuerit vnto zow, I reffauit of the Lord: for the Lord Jefus, the fame nicht in the quhilk he was betrayit, tuke the breid, brak it, gaue thankis, and faid, Tak ze, eit ze, this is my body quhilk is brokin for zow, do ze this in remembrance of me. Efter the fame maner alfo, he tuke the coupe, quhen the Supper was done, and faid, This coupe is the new Teftament in my blude, do this als oft as ze drink it in the remembrance of me, for als oft as ze fall eit of this breid, and drink of this coupe, ze fall declair the Lordis deith vntill his cumming. Quhairfoir, quhafaeuer fall eit of this breid, and drinke of this coupe of the Lord vnworthely, falbe gyltie of the body and blude of the Lord. Bot let euerie

man examine him felf, & let him eit of this breid,
and drink of this coupe. For he that eitis and
drinkis vnworthely, eitis and drinkis his
awin dampnatioun, becaus he makis
na difference of the Lordis
body and blude.

¶ *The power of binding and lowfing grantit to the
trew preicheris of Goddis word.
Mathew xvj. Chapter.*

THE keyis of heuin will I giue vnto thé, quhat
faeuer thow fal bind vpon the eird, falbe bound
alfo in heuin : and quhatfaeuer thow fall loufe v-
pon the eird, falbe lowfit alfo in heuin. Quhais
finnis ze forgiue, ar forgeuin vnto them, & quhais
finnis ze retene, ar retenit vnto them.

¶ *Heir followis the Catechifme put in Meter, to
be fung with the tune, and firft the Ten
Commandementis.*

MOYSES vpon the Mont Sinay,
with the greit God fpak face for face,
Faftand and prayand but delay,
The tyme of fourtie dayis fpace.
  O God be mercyfull to vs.

  And God gaue him thir ten Commandis,
To teiche to mankinde euerie one,

And wrait them with his awin handis
Twyſe on twa Tabillis maid of ſtone.
  O God be mercyfull to vs.

j. I am thy God allanerlie,
Serue me in feir and faith thairfoir,
Worſchip na kinde of Imagerie,
And giue na creature my gloir.
  O God be mercyfull to vs.

ij. Tak not the Name of God in vaine,
Bot let zour talk be nay and ze,
Except ane Judge do zow conſtraine
To teſtifie the veritie.
  O God be mercyfull to vs.

iij. Wirk na euill wark on Haly day,
Fle from all ſinfull luſt and ſleuth,
Walk and be ſober, faſt and pray,
Heir him that preiche the word of treuth.
  O God be mercyfull to vs.

iiij. Honour thy Elders, and them ſupplie,
Gif that thair neid of thee requyre,
Obey all Judges in their degre,
Ordand ouir thé to haue impyre.
  O God be mercyfull to vs.

v. Thow ſall not ſlay in na kin wyſe,
In counſell, thocht, nor outward deid.
Be thow ane Judge, or on ane Syſe,
In judgement ordourly proceid.
  O God be mercyfull to vs.

A. iiij

vj.   Commit na kinde of licherie,
Bot leif ane chaist and sober lyfe :
Want thow the gift of Chaistitie
Burne not in lust, bot wed ane wyfe.
   O God be mercyfull to vs.

vij.   Commit na thift, na man thow reif,
Leif on thy wage, thy rent or wark :
Hald na manis geir, let nane thé craif,
Beg not and thow be haill and stark.
   O God be mercyfull to vs.

viij.   Beir na witnes with fals report,
In contrair just and richteous men :
Defame na man in ony sort,
Suppois his fault or vice thow ken.
   O God be mercyfull to vs.

ix.   Thy Nichtbouris wyfe, hous, heritage,
Thow couet not, to thé, or wis
His hors, his oxe, his mayd, nor page,
Nor ony gudis that is his.
   O God be mercyfull to vs.

x.   Our poysound nature (allace thairfoir)
Can neuer mair this Law fulfill,
Bot greuand God ay moir and moir,
And can not wirk his godly will.
   O God be mercyfull to vs.

Then quhy to vs gaue God this Law ;
The quhilk be na way we can keip ?
That we be it our Sin suld knaw,

Repent and mend, and for it weip.
  O God be mercyfull to vs.

Trew Faith in Chrift wirkand be lufe,
Sall faue vs from the fyre of hell:
Thocht Goddis Angell wald vs reprufe,
As fals and curft ze him expell:
  O God be mercyfull to vs.

¶ *Of our Beleif.*

WE trow in God allanerlie,
  Full of all micht and Maieftie,
Maker of heuin and eird fa braid,
Quhilk hes him felf our Father maid:
And we his Sonnis ar in deid,
He will vs keip in all our neid,
Baith faull and body to defend,
That na mifchance fall vs offend;
He takis cure baith day and nicht,
To faue vs throw his godly micht
Fra Sathanis fubteltie and flicht.

We trow in Jefus Chrift his Sone,
God lyke in gloir, our Lord alone:
Quhilk, for his mercy and his grace,
Wald man be borne to mak our peace,
Of Mary mother Virgin chaift
Confauit be the Haly Gaift.
And for our faik on croce did die,
Fra fin and hell to mak vs fre:
And rais from deith, throw his Godheid,
Our Mediatour and our remeid,

Sall cum to Judge baith quick and deid.

  We trow in God the Haly Spreit,
In all diftres our comfort fweit.
We trow the Kirk Catholick be,
And faithfull Chriftin companie,
Throw all the warld with ane accord.
Remiffioun of our Sin we trow;
And this fame flefche that leuis now
Sall ftand vp at the latter day,
And bruik Eternall lyfe for ay.
FINIS.

OVR Father God Omnipotent,
  Quhen Chrift thy Sone was heir prefent,
  He bad vs euer pray to thé;
(Becaus we knew not for to pray)
He leirnit vs quhat we fuld fay,
  Syne hecht to heir vs mercyfullie.

Sen thé to call, is thy command,
Thyne awin wordis then vnderftand,
  Quhilk thow hes promeift for till heir:
Behald not my vnrichteoufnes,
Bot luke till Chriftis richteoufnes
  And with thy faith my Spreit vp fteir.

Lord, thow will haue allanerlie,
Worfchip in Spreit and veritie,
  And to nane vther giue thy gloir:
Thy Name then let vs lufe and dreid,
And call on it in all our neid,
  And thank and loue thé euermoir.

The Lordis Prayer.

Deſtroy the Deuill, his Realme and Reigne
Quhilk of this warld is Prince and King,
    And let thy Goſpell be our gyde:
Conforme our lyfe efter thy word,
That we may reigne for euer (O Lord)
    In thy Kinrik with thé to byde.

God grant that we may wirk thy will,
In eird thy pleſure to fulfill,
    Siclyke as in the Heuin impyre:
And quhat that euer we tak on hand,
May be conforme to thy command,
    And na thing efter our deſyre.

Giue vs this day our daylie breid,
And all thing that thow hes maid,
    For mennis ſuſtentatioun;
And all thing quhairof we haue neid,
Our ſaull and body for to feid,
    But ſleuth or ſoliſtatioun.

Forgiue our ſinnis, and our treſpas,
For Chriſtis ſaik quhilk geuin was,
    To deid for our Redemptioun;
As we forgiue all Creature,
Offendand vs, baith riche and pure,
    Hartfully without exemptioun.

Defend vs from temptatioun,
The feind and his vexacioun,
    The warld ſa fals, the fragill fleſche;
Saif vs from ſchame, and from diſpair,
    From vnbeleue and Lollaris lair,

And Deuillis doctrine mair or les.

Deliuer vs from euillis all,
Baith spirituall and corporall,
   And grant vs grace quhen we sall die,
And fra this present lyfe we wend,
That we may mak ane blyssit end,
   Syne reigne with thé eternallie.

Power nor gloir, impyre nor tryne,
Is nane in heuin nor eirth bot thyne,
   And euer mair sall sa remaine:
Thairfoir thow may and wil releue
All them that can in Christ beleue,
   From Deid, the Deuill, and Hellis paine.

FINIS.

¶ *The effect of the Sacrament of Baptisme, and first institution thairof; declaring alswa quhat singular comfort we obtene be the samin.*

CHRIST baptist was be Johne in Jordan flude,
   For to fulfil for vs all richteousnes,
And our Baptisme dotit with sanctitude,
   And greit vertew, to wesche our sinfulnes,
   To drowne the deid, and hell for to oppres,
Quhen Goddis word with water joynit be,
Throw Faith to gif vs life Eternallie.

For our waiknes God of his mercy sweit,
   To strenth our Faith ordand this Sacrament,
In Name of Father, Sone and Haly Spreit,
   To wesche our body, and in our minde to prent

That worde and water outward reprefent,
Throw wirking of the Spirit into our hart,
That Chriftis blude wefchis away the fin inwart.

Our Baptifme is ane takin, and ane figne,
   That auld Adame fuld drownit be and die,
And grauit in the deid of Chrift our King,
   To rife with him to life Eternallie :
That is, we fuld our fin ay mortifie,
Refiftand vice, leif haly, juft and trew,
And throw the Spirit daylie our life renew.

Be figure and be word, Chrift did vs teiche,
   The Fatheris voyce was hard fayand full cleir,
Jefus, quhome I haue fend my word to preiche,
   He is my weilbelouit Sone fa deir,
In word, in wark, allone ze fall him heir :
In him is all my plefure and delyte,
To him I zow commit baith fmall and greit.

The Haly Gaift come downe to teftifie,
   His doctrine and his Baptifme to declair,
In forme of Dow fat on him foberlie :
   In Baptifme to dout not nor difpair,
   Baith Father, Sone, and Haly Gaift ar thair
To be our gyde, the Trinitie him fell,
Hes geuin in eird with vs to dwell.

Chrift bad his Apoftillis preiche to all creature
   That thay with fin and hell war all forlorne;
Ouha will beleue, and traift my wordis fure
   And bapteift is, and new againe is borne,
   And Sathan and his warkis hes forfworne,

Thay fall be faif, and neuer mair fall die,
Bot ring in gloir perpetuall with me.

Quha will not this greit grace beleif, to hell
   Salbe condempnit, with eternall deid
Quhair Purgatorie and Pardounis will not fell,
   And gude intent, thair Pylate plicht and leid:
   Dum ceremonies, the quhilk themfelf hes maid
And vowis vaine, quhilk thay did neuer keip,
Sall gar thame gnafhe thair teith, & eyis weip.

Our eine feis outward bot the watter cauld,
   Bot our pure faith the power fpirituall
Of Chriftis blude, inwart it dois behauld,
   Quhilk is ane leuand well celeftiall
   Zit for to purge the penitent with all
Our natiue fin, in Adame to expell,
And all trefpas committit be our fell.

Our Baptifme is not done all on ane day,
   Bot all our lyfe it leftis identlie:
Remiffioun of our fin, induris for ay:
   For thocht we fall, throw grit fragylitie,
   The cunnand anis contract faithfullie
Be our grit God, at Font, fall euer remaine,
Als oft as we repent, and fin refraine,

We can not giue to God louing conding
   For fa greit grace, and mercy infinite,
Quhilk inftitute this Sacrament and Signe,
   Quhais greit vertew in veirs I can not dyte;
   Bot mony cunning Clerk of it dois wryte
Full Chriftianely, als the Catechifme buke

Declaris at length, quha lift to luke.

¶ *The Supper of the Lord, and richt vſe of it, to be ſung.*

OVR Sauiour Chriſt, King of grace,
With God the Father maid our peace;
And with his bludie woundis fell,
Hes vs redemit from the Hell.

And he, that we ſuld not forzet,
Gaue vs his body for to eit
In forme of breid, and gaue vs ſyne
His blude to drink in forme of wyne.

Quha will reſſaue this Sacrament,
Suld haue trew faith, and ſin repent;
Quha vſis it vnworthelie,
Reſſauis deid eternallie.

We ſuld to God giue praiſe and gloir,
That ſched his blude vs to reſtoir;
Eit this is his remembrance,
In ſigne of thy delyuerance.

Thow ſuld not dout, bot faſt beleue,
That Chriſtis body ſall releue
All them that ar in heuines
Repentand fair thair ſinfulnes.

Sic grace and mercy nane can craif
Bot thay that troublit hartis haif:
Feill thow then ſin, abſtene thy ſell,

Or thy rewaird fall be in hell.

 Chrift fayis, Sinners, cum vnto me,
Quhilk myfter hes of my mercie:
Neidis thow nocht my medicine,
I lois my paine and trauel tyne.

 Giue thow thy felf thy Saull culd win,
In vaine I deit for thy fin:
My Supper is nocht graithit for thé,
Gif thow can mak thy felf fupplie.

 Will thow thy finfull life confes,
And with this wark thy faith expres,
Sa ar ze worthie, fmall and greit,
And it fall ftrenth zour faith perfite.

 And thow fall thankfull be thairfoir,
And loue thy God for euirmoir;
Thy Nichtbour lufe, and als fupplie
His neid, as Chrift hes done for thee.

¶ *Certaine Graces to be fung, or faid, befoir or efter meit.*

ALL meit and drink was creat be the Lord,
 Reffauit for to be with thankfulnes,
Til all faithful knawers of the trew word,
To fatisfie thair neid with fobernes.
All fude is gude, the quhilk God creat hes,
And not to be refufit ony day,
Only to God geuing the louing ay,
Be prayer, and be Goddis word all meit

The Graces.

Unto the clene, all thingis is clene to eit;
Thairfoir, we pray his godly Maieſtie
To blys our meit, and all our companie,
And ſaif vs fra exces and drunkinnes;
Efter our meit to thank his gentilnes.

CHRIST leirnit vs on God how we ſuld call,
And bad vs pray, ſyne hecht to heir vs all.
OUR Father God quhilk is in heuin ſa hie,
Thy glorious Name with vs mot hallowit be.
Let cum to vs thy kingdome and thy gloir.
Thy will mot be fulfillit euermoir
In eird, as it is in heuin, but variance.
Giue vs this day our daylie ſuſtenance.
Forgiue our dettis, for Chriſtis paine and ſmart,
As we forgiue our detteris with our hart.
And leid vs not into temptatioun,
Bot, for Chriſt Jeſus bitter paſſioun,
Delyuer vs from euillis ſpirituall
And corporall, now and perpetuall.
Saif vs, gude Lord, for thy promeis deuyne:
For Kingdome, power, gloir and all is thyne.

WE thank our God baith kynde and liberall,
His grace and mercy dois euer indure :
He geuis ſuſtentatioun to vs all,
  To man and beiſt, and euerie creature;
  And he allone, dois feid baith riche and pure.
Thairfoir to God be gloir allanerlie,
Throw Jeſus Chriſt we thank him hartfullie.

ALL Creature on the Lord dependis,
Thair ſuſtenance for to reſſaue of thé;

B. j

Thair meit & drink in tyme to them thow fendis,
  Thow oppinnis furth thy hand full gracioufly
  And fatiffyis all flefche aboundantly:
Blys vs gude Lord into thir giftis gude,
Quhilk thow hes geuin to be our daylie fude.

TO our gude God, of warldis Lord and King,
  Full of mercy, only trew and wyfe,
Be louing, honour, gloir, without ending,
  Kingdome, impyre, hieft renoun and pryfe:
With mynde and mouth, giue we ane thoufand [fyfe
All gloir to him, quhilk alone worthie is,
Afking for Chrift to bring vs to his blis.

WE thank thé God, of thy gudnes,
  Throw Jefus Chrift our gracious Lord,
For thy greit mercy and gentilnes,
  Quhilk feidis vs with thy fweit word:
Sen all that euer tuke lyfe of thé,
Thow fatiffyis aboundantlie,
  We praife thé all with ane accord.

As thow hes fed this finfull flefche,
  Quhilk fone fall die, and turne in affe:
Siclyke the fillie faull refrefche,
  The quhilk immortall creat was.
God, for thy grace and mercy greit,
Grant vs ane fteidfaft faith perfite,
  And in thy gloir with thé to pas.

To God on heich be louing maift,
  Quhilk lowfis fin allanerlie,
Till all that will repent, and traift

On

On Jesus Christ his Sone onlie:
Thow makis them thy sone and air,
Throw him thow will them saif from cair,
To quhome be gloir eternallie.

¶ *Certaine Spirituall Sangis, togidder with ane Confessioun of Sin, and ane Prayer.*

SORE I complaine of Sin,
 And with King Dauid weip:
I feill my hart within
 The wraith of God full deip.
I wyte my greit trespas
 Is caus of all my wo,
Quhairwith God greuit was
 Full sore, and oft also.

O God! I me confes
 Ane sinfull creature,
Full of all wretchitnes
 Fragill, vaine, vyle and pure.
Thair is na gude in me
 Bot pryde, lust, and desyre,
And warldis vanitie,
 The way to hellis fyre.

Except God do me saue
 From hell and endles paine,
My sin will me dissaue,
 Quhilk I can not refraine.
My only hope and traist,
 Help my fragillitie
My sinnes to detest,
   B. ij

Resistand constantlie.

O cast me not away
    For my grit sinne, O Lord,
I grant my vices all
    Blasphemit hes thy word.
God, for thy grit mercie,
    And Christis woundis wyde,
Ane steidfast faith grant me
    Allone to be my gyde.

Christ Goddis Sone allone,
    Victour of deid and hell,
Thow tuke my nature one
    My sinnes to expell,
And gaif thyself to plaige,
    Me catiue to conuoy,
To my richt heritage,
    From paine to heuinlie ioy.

Thy seruand Lord defend,
    Quhome thow hes bocht sa deir;
Trew preichours to me send
    Thy word to schaw me cleir:
Lat me my lyfe amend,
    And thairin perseueir,
Grant me ane blyssit end
    Quhen I sall part from heir.

O Lord God, Haly Spreit,
    Full of benignitie,
Trew Chrits promeis sweit,
    Teiche me the veritie.

Expell

Expell my ignorance,
My finnis mortifie,
Grant me perfeuerance
Unto the end trewlie.
FINIS.

¶ *Ane Sang of our corrupt nature, and the only remeid thairof.*

WE wretchit finners pure,
Our fin hes vs forlorne,
Thairin all creature confauit is and borne:
Sin hes wrocht vs fic paine,
That we, without remeid,
Condempnit ar and flane to hell, the deuil, & deid.
Lord haue mercy on vs. Chrift haue mercy, &c.

Our warkis can nocht be
As dois the Law requyre,
Nor zit can fatiffie our Fatheris wraith and ire:
Na deid can mak vs fre
From our greit finfulnes,
Bot Goddis Sone muft die, for our vnrichteoufnes.
Lord haue mercy on vs. Chrift haue, &c.

Or had not Chrift bene fend,
Cled in our vyle nature,
Fra hell vs to defend, our deidly wound to cure,
And willingly to die,
Fra Sin to mak vs clene,
We had eternallie in hell condampnit bene.
Lord haue mercy on vs. Chrift haue, &c.

Man now hes thy peace,

B. iij

Sic lufe God fchawis thé;
He takis thé in his grace, his mortall ennemie.
Throw Faith in Chrift fa kynde,
Quhilk frely gaif him fell
On Croce for to be pynde, to faif vs fra the hell.
Lord haif mercy. Chrift haif mercy. Lord, &c.

 This we fuld euer beleue,
And nocht difpair for fin :
For hell cannot vs greue, the deid nor deuil thairin:
We ar maid juft and rycht,
And fred from panis fore,   [more
Throw Chrift that Lord of micht, bliffit for euer-
Lord haif mercy. Chrift haif mercy. Lord, &c.

 Thairfoir lat vs loue and pryfe,
God the Father feruentlie.
We thank ane thoufand fyfe, his Sones Maieftie:
We pray the Haly Gaift
Our fin to mortifie,   [fullie.
And not difpair, bot traift Goddis word moft faith-
Lord haif mercy. Chrift haif mercy, &c.

¶ *Ane Sang of the Flefche and the Spreit.*

ALL Chriftin men tak tent and leir,
How faull and body is at weir:
Upon this eird baith lait and air,
With cruell battell identlie,
And nane may not ane vther fle.

¶ The Flefche.

 The Flefche faid, Sen I haue haill,
I will in zouth with luftis daill,
Or age with forrow me affaill :

With joy I will my tyme ouirdriue,
And will not with my luſtis ſtryue.
¶ The Spreit.
The Spreit ſaid, Thocht I charge thé nocht,
Dreid God, and haue his Law in thocht:
Thow hecht quhen thow to Font was brocht,
Efter his Law luſt to refraine
And not to wirk his word againe.
¶ The Fleſche.
The Fleſche ſaid, I am ſtark and wicht,
To wacht gude wyne, freſche, cauld and bricht,
And tak my pleſure day and nicht,
With ſinging, playing, and to dance
And ſet on ſex and ſeuin the chance.
¶ The Spreit.
The Spreit ſaid, Think on the riche man,
Quhilk all time in his luſtis ran,
Body and ſaull he loiſſit than,
And ſone was buryit into hell
As Chriſt Jeſus hes ſaid him ſell.
¶ The Fleſche.
The Fleſche ſaid, Quhat hald I of this?
Laſer aneuch, and time thair is
In age for till amend my mis;
And from my vitious lyfe conuert
Quhen ſadnes hes ouirſet my hart.
¶ The Spreit.
The Spreit ſaid, Power thow hes none
In zouth, nor zit in eild bygone,
With twinkling of ane eye anone
God ſall thé tak at euin and morne,
Na certaine tyme ſet thé beforne.

B. iiij

The Flesche and the Spreit.

¶ The Flesche.
The Flesche said, All time air and lait,
I se all warldlie wise estait
Hald lust vertew in thair consait,
With thame I will persew my weird
Als lang as I leue on this eird.
¶ The Spreit.
The Spreit said, Zit sall cum the day
The saull sall part the body fray;
Then quhat sall help thy game or play,
Quhen thow mon turnit be in as,
As first in eird quhen thow maid was.
¶ The Flesche.
The Flesche said, Thow hes vincust me,
I traist eternall gloir to se:
Christ grant that I may cum thairby,
Now will I to my God returne,
Repent my sin, richt sore I murne.
¶ The Spreit.
The Spreit said, Nane to schame I driue,
Ane contrite hart help God aliue,
The flesche mon die, with paine and striue,
For it was borne to that intent,
In eird with wormes to be rent.
¶ The Flesche.
The Flesche said, O Lord God of peace,
Help me to turne, throw Christis grace;
O Haly Gaist my faith incres,
That I may thoill this eirdly noy,
My hope is in eternall joy.
¶ The Spreit.
The Spreit said, Now I haue my micht,
Thocht

Thocht I be ane vnworthie Knicht:
Thow God the quhilk is only richt,
Thow faue me from the Deuillis net:
Thairfoir thow on the Croce was plet.
¶ The Dyter.
Now hes this Ballat heir ane end,
God grant ilk man his hart fa kend,
To fin na mair, fyne to Chrift wend:
Than fall he turne againe to vs,
And giue vs his eternall blys.
FINIS.

¶ *Ane Sang of the Croce, and the frute thairof.*

CVM heir, fayis Goddis Sone to me,
  Sinneris, that heuie ladin be,
  I will zour fillie Saull refrefche:
Cum zoung and auld, baith man and wyfe,
I will zow giue eternall lyfe,
  Thocht troublit heir fair be zour flefche.

My zok is fweit, my burding fmall,
Quha drawis efter me, thay fall
  Efchaip eternall deid and fyre:
For I fall help them in thair draucht,
That thay fall cum, as I haue taucht,
  To gloir and joy, and heuin impyre.

Quhat I haue teichit lait and air,
Quhat I haue tholit les and mair,
  That preis zow euer to fulfill;
And thocht zour flefche be heir oppreft,
Zit all thing wirk fall for the beft;
  For fa is richt, and Goddis will.

26 *Cum heir, sayis Goddis Sone to me.*

The warld wald fauit be, and faine,
And cum to gloir but croce or paine;
   Quhilk Chriſtis flock muſt ſuffer heir.
Bot paine, thair is nane vther way
To cum to gloir, and put away
   Eternall hellis paine, but peir.

That the faithfull muſt the Croce indure,
Witnes beiris all creature,
   Subdewit vnto vanitie:
Quha will not thoill in Chriſtis name,
The Deuill ſall wirk him ſic ane ſchame,
   With peirles paine perpetuallie.

To day ane man is freſche and fair,
The morne he lyis ſeik and ſair,
   Syne dulefully domeit to deid:
Euin lyke as in the feild ane flour,
The day is ſweit, the morne is ſour:
   Sa all this wretchit warld ſall faid.

The godles dreidis ſair to die,
Bot quhen he can na further flee,
   And fain his ſinfull lyfe wald mend:
Thay grip ſa faſt his geir to get,
The ſillie ſaull is quyte forzet,
   Quhill haiſtely gais out his aind.

Quhen he perſauis na remeid,
Then greuouſly he gais to deid,
   And gruncheand geuis up the gaiſt:
Sair I ſuſpect God do accuſe
His Sectouris, and him ſelf refuſe,

                               That

That fa vnfaithfully deceift.

The riche man, helpis not his gude,
The nobill not his royall blude;
   For thay fall baith thair quarrell tyne:
Thocht ane had all this warld fa wyde,
Zit he fall die with dule and pyne,
   With golde and precious ftanis of pryde.

Knawledge concernis not the clerk,
Nor hypocrite his haly wark;
   Bot thay but dout with deid mon dwell.
Quha will not haill to Chrift him giue,
Quhill in this prefent lyfe he liue,
   For euer mair fall die in hell.

Mark weill thairfoir, my Sonnis fweit,
How Chriftis croce is for zow meit:
   O moue zow not in mynde thairfoir,
Bot at his word ftand fteidfaftlie,
And with him fuffer pacientlie,
   Gif ze wald enter in his gloir.

Do gude for euill, and leid zour lyfe,
Without reprufe, but pryde or ftryfe,
   And thoill the warldis wraith to rage.
O enter be that narrow rod;
Giue gloir and vengeance vnto God,
   And he thair cruell ire fall fwage.

Quhen that zour flefche hes all the will,
And may zour luftis all fulfill,
   Ze ar but dout the Feindis pray:

God fendis zow the croce thairfoir,
To mortifie zour flefche fo foir,
   To faif zour fillie faull for ay.

And quhen this fchort paine to zow greif,
Than think on hell the lang mifcheif,
   Quhair mony ane for ay fall murne;
And faull and body fall remaine,
For euermoir with cruell paine,
   Endles for ay, without returne.

Bot he fall, efter warldly pyne,
Reioyce with Chrift, withouttin fyne,
   Quhair na myndis memoriall
Can think, nor toung can tell the tryne,
Nor haue the gloir quhilk fall propyne
   That michtie Lord vnto vs all.

For quhat eternall God of peace
Hes promeift, throw his Spreit of grace,
   And fyne fworne be his haly Name,
That he fall hald baith trew and fune.
God grant that we may fe his Throne,
   Throw faith in Jefus Chrift. Amen.

¶ *Ane Confolatioun in aduerfitie of the Scripture.*

BLISSIT is he quhome God dois correct;
  Thairfoir his fcurge fe thow not neglect:
For he it is quhilk geuis wan and wound,
And fuddanly he will mak haill and found.
He will thé ftryke with his maift fatherly wand,
Syne thé releue with his maift mercyfull hand.
                                   God

Blyssit is he.

God will thé slay, and giue thé lyfe anone,
And thé returne, thocht thow to graue wer gone.
And will thé sone bring into pouertie,
Syne giue thé greit riches aboundantlie.
He will thé set into a law degre,
Syne thé exalt, that euerie man may se.
Quhome God ressauis to his sone and air,
Him will he scurge with plagues said and sair;
Thairfoir vnder the croce thow perseuir:
Then as a Father sall God to thé appeir.
Quha is ane sone, and will not pacientlie
His father thoill, with all humilitie?
He schawis him as he wer bastard borne,
And heritage fra him wer all forlorne.
And sen that we our fleschely father dreid,
For eirdly thing our body for to feid,
How mekill mair our Father spirituall
Suld we obey to lyfe perpetuall.
All croce appeiris presently distres,
Voyde of all joy, bot full of painefulnes;
Bot efterwart it sall giue peace and rest,
Thocht for a tyme with paine we be oppreft,
The paine that is now present, schort and licht,
And leftis bot a moment in our sicht,
Aboue measure sall wirk eternall gloir
In till our saull, behalding not thairfoir
The present paine, quhilk is befoir our ene,
Bot luke on that quhilk now may not be sene.
All joy esteme, my brether, ane and all,
Quhen into diueris troublis ze do fall,
And knawis that of zour faith it is a preif,
To wirk in zow pacience for zour releif;

As of the croce ze ar companzeoun,
Sa fall ze be of confolatioun.
Faithfull is God, and on zow hes pitie,
And will not thoill zow temptit for to be
Aboue zour ftrenth, bot will quhen ze leift wene,
Giue zow fic grace, that ze fall weill fuftene.
Juft mennis lyfe is in the Lordis hand,
Torment of deid may not them hald in band.
Thocht befoir men thay thoill aduerfitie,
Thair hope is full of immortalitie.
God knawis innocentis temptatioun,
To faif them fra thair greit vexatioun;
And fall reffaue againe the latter day,
The wickit for to burne in hell for ay.

FINIS.

¶ *The Forlorne Sone, as it is writtin in the*
xv. Chapter of Luk.

SINNERS, vnto my fang aduert,
  Quhilk Chrift into his Vangell kend,
And from zour finfull lyfe conuert,
  Quhairwith ze do zour God offend.
For Chrift in his fweit Parabill,
To faif vs is full plyabill,
  Gif we repent, and to him wend.

Ane certaine man of riche fubftance,
  Had Sonnes twa to him full deir,
And fone with fchort delyuerance,
  The zoungeft fpak on this maneir:
Father, giue me my part of geir,
Quhilk me belangis les and mair,
  I will na mair be thirlit heir.

The

The Father did his gude deuyde,
  Betuix them, bot the zoungeſt Sone
Wald na mair with his Father byde,
  Bot tuke his part, and furth is gone:
In till ane ſtrange and far countrie,
And leuand thair richt ryatouſlie
  He waiſtit all his geir anone.

Quhen all was gone, thair rais fra hand
  Ane derth quhilk maid the vittell ſkant,
Baith far and neir throw all the land,
  And he throw neid begouth to want:
Then to ane Citizenar he zeid,
Quhilk ſend him furth his ſwyne to feid,
  For falt of fude he was full fant.

He wald haue eitin with the ſwyne,
  His houngrie ſtomak to fulfill:
Bot thocht he ſuld for hounger tyne,
  Zit nane wald giue him leif thairtill:
Quhen he come till him ſelf againe,
This him alone he culd complaine,
  In till his mynde with mourning ſtill.

How mony ſeruandis for thair wage,
  Hes fude into my fatheris hous,
And I for hounger die and rage?
  Bot my father is gracious,
Thairfoir till him I will me dres:
And ſchaw my ſin and my diſtres,
  And ſay with voyce full pitious,

O Father, I haue bene to bauld,

Sinnand contrair the heuin and thé,
And not worthie that men me hauld,
   Na mair thy Sone in ony degre:
As ane of thy feruandis me mak.
With that he did his jornay tak
   Hame till his Father haiftilie.

And quhen he come bot zit afar,
   His father had compaffioun,
And ran him till or he was war,
   And gaue him confolatioun,
And in his armes he did him fang
And euer he kiffit him amang,
   With friendly falutatioun.

The Sone faid, Father of greit micht,
   I knaw that I haue finnit foir
Contrair the heuin, and [in] thy ficht,
   And I am worthie now no more
That ony me thy fone fuld call.
Bot his Father, full liberall,
   Callit his feruandis him befoir:

And kyndely to them can he fay,
   Ze bring me furth the beft cleithing,
And cleithe my Sone courtly and gay,
   And on his finger ze put ane ring,
Ze fet on fchone vpon his feit,
The quhilk ar trym and wounder meit,
   That he be honeft in all thing.

And flay that calf quhilk now is maid
   Sa fat, and let vs mak gude cheir,

For this my Sone the quhilk now was deid,
    Againe on lyfe is haill and feir:
My Sone was loift, and now is found.
And they within ane lytill ftound
    Began to myrrie be but weir.

The Eldeft to the feild was gone,
    And quhen that he hame cummand wes,
And hard the menftraly anone,
    The danfing and the great blyithnes,
Ane of his feruandis he did call,
And faid to him, Quhat menis all
    This glaidnes, and this merynes?

Then anfwerit he, and faid him till,
    Thy Brother is cum hame againe,
Thairfoir his father hes gart kill
    His weill fed calf, and is full faine
That faif reffauit him hes he.
The Eldeft wraith was and angrie,
    And zeid not in throw greit difdaine:

And then come furth his Father kynde,
    And prayit him richt feruently:
Bot he anfwerit, richt proude in mynde,
    O Father myne, how lang haue I
Thy trew and faithfull feruand bene;
And neuer zit brak thy biddene,
    Bot thé obeyit faithfully.

Zit gaue thow nocht of thy riches,
    Sa mekle as ane fmall kyd to me,
That I micht mak fum mirrynes,

  And with my lufaris blyith to be.
Bot now, becaus is cum againe
Thy Sone quhilk waiſtit hes, in vaine,
  Thy gudis into harlatrie;

That calf quhilk foſterit was ſa fair,
  Thow hes gart kill at his pleſour.
His Father ſaid, My Sone and air,
  Of all my riches and treaſour,
Quhat ever I haue, all that is thyne,
And thow art euer with me and myne,
  And all is haill into thy cure.

Thairfoir to vs it was full meit
  For to reioyce, and blyith to be,
With all our hart and all our ſpreit,
  Thy Brother ſaif and found to ſe:
For he was loiſt, and now is win,
And he was deid from all his kin,
  And now aliue againe is he.

Our God and Father is full kynde,
  To ſinneris that ar penitent,
With all thair hart, and all thair mynde,
  Schawand warkis that thay repent:
And gif in Chriſtis blude thay traiſt,
Then ſall he neuer them deteſt,
  But ſaif them that thay be not ſchent.

FINIS.

¶ *Ane Sang of the riche Gluttoun and pure Lazarus, as it is writtin in the xv. Chapter of Sanct Luk.*

FAITHFVLL in Chrift, vfe zour riches richt,
　　Not to zour luſt and ſenſualitie:
Bot all tyme help that pure with all zour micht,
　　For in the frute fall knawin be the tre;
　　And gude and euil fall baith rewardit be,
With heuinly gloir, and hell fa terrabill,
To that effect ſpak Chriſt this parabill:—

Ane certaine man was riche, and coiſtly cled
　　With purpour, ſylk, heich and preſumpteous,
And euerie day delicioufly him fed:
　　Thair was alſwa a pure hecht Lazarus,
　　Lay ſeik at the zet of this gluttounis hous;
Throw fairis ſmart he had ane peirles pyne,
And wantit fude, quhen he wald faineſt dyne.

To ſatiſfie his ſeikly appetyte,
　　He wald haue eitin of the crummis ſmall,
Quhilk fell downe fra his buird of greit delyte;
　　But nane to gif him was fa liberall:
　　The doggis did thair office naturall,
And oft thay did this catyue man refreſche,
Lickand the fylth furth of his laithly fleſche.

It chancit ſa this begger did deceis,
　　Syne caryit was be angels gracious
In Abrahams boſome, in heuinly reſt and peace.
　　And this riche man that was fa ryatous,
　　Deceiſſit als, syne buryit glorious;
In hellis paine he lyftit vp his ene,
And ſyne afar of Abraham hes he ſene.

Quhen Lazarus he ſaw with him alſo

C. ij

In his bofome, he faid with drerie fpreit:
Father Abraham haue mercy on my wo,
 Send Lazarus his finger for to weit,
 And cuill my toung with cauld water and fweit;
For I am torment fair into this flame.
Then anfwerit him our father Abraham,

Remember, Sone, that thow reffauit hes
 Into thy lyfe thy plefure in all thing.
And, contrariwife, Lazarus had diftres,
 Bot now he is in joy and comforting,
 And thow art in wo and tormenting;
And als betuix vs thair is fa greit ane fpace,
That nane may cum till vther be na cace.

And then he faid, O Father, I thé pray,
 Unto my fatheris hous thow wald him fend
That he my fyue Brether aduerteis may,
 Leift they into this cairfull place difcend.
 Bot Abraham faid, Let them repent and mend,
And als thay haue the Prophetis & Moyfes law,
Let them heir them, gif thai the way wald knaw.

Bot he faid, Nay, my father Abraham kynde,
 Gif ony to the quick zeid from the deid,
Trewly thay fuld repent with hart and mynde.
 Bot not the les, Abraham this anfwer maid,
 Gif thay heir not the Law quhilk fuld them leid
Then fall they nocht in ony wayis beleif,
Thocht ane fuld ryfe from deid them to releif.

Unto the pure thairfoir be pietifull,
 Quhill ze ar heir, fchaw them zour cheritie,

Help, God.

Till freind and fa be all tyme mercyfull,
  As ze forgiue ze fall forgeuin be;
  Mortifie luft and fenfualitie,
Conforme zow not to wardly pomp and pryde,
Dreid God, lufe man, refraine luft at all tyde.
FINIS.

¶ *The principall pointis of the Paſſioun, ſhortlie correctit.*

HELP, God, the formar of all thing,
  That to thy gloir may be my dyte;
Be baith at end and beginning,
  That I may mak ane fang perfyte
Of Jefus Chriftis paffioun,
Sinneris only Saluatioun
  As witneffis thy word in write.

Thy word for euer fall remaine,
  As in his buke wrytis Ifay,
Baith heuin and eird fall turne againe,
  Or thy trew word cum to decay.
Thow can not lyke ane man repent,
To change thy purpois or intent:
  Bot fteidfaft is thy word for ay.

Jefus, the Fatheris Word alone,
  Difcendit in ane Virgine pure,
With meruellis greit and mony one;
  And be Judas that fals tratour,
That Lambe for fober fumme was fauld,
And gaue his lyfe, for caus he wald
  Redeme all finfull creature.

C. iij

Quhen eittin was the Paſcall Lamb,
　　Chriſt tuke the breid his hand within.
Blyſſing it, brak it, gaue the ſame
　　Till his Apoſtillis mair and min,
Eit that, for my body is this,
Quhilk for zour ſaikis geuin is,
　　In till remiſſioun of zour ſin.

Siclyke he gaue them for to drink
　　In wyne his blude, the quhilk was ſched,
Upon his precious deid to think,
　　On him remembrance to be maid.
Quha eitis this blyſſit Sacrament,
Worthely with trew intent
　　Sall neuer ſe Eternall deid.

For caus thay knew him till depart.
　　Thay ſtraif quha ſuld be ouereſt:
Bot Jeſus ſaid, with humbill hart,
　　Princes ar repute nobileſt,
The quhilk rewlis maiſt awfullie;
Sa amang zow it ſall not be,
　　Bot quha is maiſt ſall ſerue the leiſt.

Jeſus wuſhe his Apoſtillis feit,
　　Schawand exempill of lawlynes.
And chargit them with wordis ſweit,
　　That lufe amang them ſuld incres;
For thairby it ſuld cum to licht,
That ze ar my Diſcipulis richt,
　　Giue ze amang zow lufe poſſes.

Efter this prayer paſſit he,

　　　　　　　　　　　　　　　And

And met the Jewes quhilk him focht,
Quhen thay had bound him cruellie,
　　Befoir the Judges they him brocht.
Firft they him him fcurgit, and for fcorne,
Him crownit with ane crowne of thorne,
　　Syne dampnit him to deid for nocht.

That Prince on Croce thay liftit on hicht,
　　For our Redemptioun that thocht fa lang;
He faid I thrift, with all my micht,
　　To faue mankynde fra panis ftrang:
He that all warldis was beforne,
Come downe of Mary to be borne,
　　For our trefpas on croce he hang.

Then he his heid culd inclyne,
　　As wrytis Johne, and gaue the gaift,
And off the croce tane was fyne,
　　And laid in graue; bot fone in haift,
Leuand, he rais on the thrid day,
And to his Apoftillis did fay,
　　To them appeirit maift and leift.

And fyne he did his Apoftillis teache,
　　Throw all the warld for to pas;
And till all creature for to preiche,
　　As they of him inftructit was.
Quha bapteift is, and will beleue,
Eternall deid fall not them greue,
　　Bot falbe fauit mair and les.

Sanct Luk wryting his Affentioun,
　　Thocht prefent ay with vs he be,
C. iiij

As Scripture makis mentioun,
   That is to say, with vs is he
Be his sweit word, steidfast but faill,
Contrair the quhilk can not preuaill
   Sathan nor hellis tyrannie.

Ane Conforter to vs he did send,
   Quhilk from the Father did proceid,
To gyde vs trewly to the end,
   In inwart thocht and outward deid,
Call on the Lord, our gyde and licht,
To leid vs in his law full richt,
   And be our help in all our neid.

Pray for all men in generall,
   Suppois thay wirk vs richt or wrang.
Pray for zour Prince in speciall;
   Thocht thay be just, or tyrannis strang.
Obey, for sa it aucht to be.
In prison, for the veritie,
   Ane faithfull Brother maid this sang.

FINIS.

¶ *Ane Sang of the Euangell, contenand the effect of the samin.*

BE blyith, all Christin men, and sing,
   Dance and mak mirth with all zour micht,
Christ hes vs kyithit greit comforting,
   Quhairfoir we may reioyce of richt;
Ane wark to wounder that is wrocht
Christ with his blude full deir vs bocht,
   And for our saik to deid was dicht.

                       For

Be blyith.

For with the Deuill and dulefull deid,
   With hell and sin I was forlorne;
The sone of ire, at Goddis feid,
   Consauit sa I was and borne;
I grew ay mair and mair thairin,
And daylie eikit sin to sin,
   Dispair was euer me beforne.

Quhair I culd not the Law fulfill,
   My warkis maid me na supplie;
Sa blind and waik was my fre will,
   That haitit the veritie;
My conscience kest me euer in cair,
The Deuill he draif me to dispair,
   And hell was euer befoir myne eye.

God had greit pitie on my wo,
   And aboue mesure schew me grace;
Quhen I was zit his cruell fo,
   Zit he wald cure my cairfull case:
His lufe to me he did conuert
From the maist deipest of his hart,
   Quhilk coist him deir to mak my peace.

To his belouit Sone he said,
   The tyme of mercy drawis neir,
To saif man and the feind inuaid;
   Thairfoir, my hartly Sone sa deir,
Ga freith them from the feindis feid;
Thow mon ouirthraw sin, hell, and deid,
   Syne man restoir baith haill and feir.

The Sone his Father did obey,

And come downe on the eird to me,
Borne of ane Mayd, as wrytis Eſay,
   My kynde ſweit brother for to be;
He tuke on him my nature vyle,
And did his power for to exyle,
   Sathan and all his ſubteltie.

He ſaid, Thow ſall haue victorie,
   Gif thow alone on me depend:
For I will giue my ſelf for thé,
   Thy cairfull quarrell to defend;
For I am thyne, and myne thow art,
And of my gloir thow ſall haue part,
   Syne ring with me withouttin end.

They man ſched out my blyſſit blude,
   And reif alſwa my lyfe from me;
I thoill this only for thy gude,
   Beleue that firme and ſteidfaſtlie:
For my deid ſall thy deid deuoir,
That ſin ſall thé condampne no moir,
   For be that way ſaif thow mon die.

Syne fra this preſent lyfe I fair,
   To my Father Celeſtiall;
Thy Mediator trew ſall be thair
   And ſend to thé my Spreit I ſall,
To giue thé conſolatioun,
In all thy tribulatioun;
   The treuth he ſall inſtruct zow all.

My doing leirning mair and les,
   That leir and do vnfenzeitlie;

                            For

For that dois Goddis Kirk incres,
   And his greit gloir dois magnifie.
Be war of men and thair command,
Quhilk me and my word do ganeſtand,
   My Laſt Will heir I leif to thé.

FINIS.

¶ *Ane Sang of the Birth of Chriſt, to be ſung with the tune of Balulalow.*

I COME from heuin to tell,
   The beſt nowellis that euer befell:
To zow thir tythingis trew I bring
And I will of them ſay and ſing.

   This day to zow is borne ane Chylde
Of Mary meik, and Virgin mylde;
That blyſſit bairne, bening and kynde
Sall zow reioyce baith hart and mynde.

   It is the Lord Chriſt, God and man,
He will do for zow quhat he can;
Himſelf zour Sauiour will be,
Fra ſin and hell to mak zow fre.

   He is zour richt ſaluatioun,
From euerlaſting dampnatioun,
That ze may ring in gloir and blis,
For euer mair in heuin with his.

   Zé fall him find but mark or wying
Full ſempill in ane cribe lying;
Sa lyis he quhilk zow hes wrocht,

And all this warld maid of nocht.

 Let us reioyce and be blyith,
And with the Hyrdis go full fwyith,
And fe quhat God of his grace hes done,
Throw Chrift to bring vs to his throne.

 My faull and lyfe ftand vp and fe
Quha lyis in ane cribe of tre:
Quhat Babe is that, fa gude and fair?
It is Chrift, Goddis Sone and air.

 Welcome now, gracious God of micht,
To finneris vyle, pure, and vnricht,
Thow come to faif vs from diftres,
How can we thank thy gentilnes?

 O God that maid all creature,
How art thow now becummin fa pure,
That on the hay and ftray will ly,
Amang the affis, oxin and ky.

 And war the warld ten tymes fa wyde,
Cled ouir with golde and ftanis of pryde,
Unworthie it war zit to thé,
Under thy feit ane ftule to be.

 The filk and fandell thé to eis,
Ar hay, and fempill fweilling clais,
Quhairin thow gloris greiteft King,
As thow in heuin war in thy ring.

 Thow tuik fic panis temporall,

To mak me riche perpetuall;
For all this warldis welth and gude,
Can nathing riche thy Celcitude.

  O my deir hart, zoung Jesus sweit,
Prepair thy creddill in my spreit,
And I sall rocke thé in my hart,
And neuer mair fra thé depart.

  Bot I sall praise thé euer moir,
With sangis sweit vnto thy gloir;
The kneis of my hart sall bow
And sing that richt Balulalow.

  Gloir be to God eternallie,
Quhilk gaue his only Sone for me:
The Angellis joyis for to heir,
The gracious gift of this New Zeir.

            FINIS.

TO vs is borne a barne of blis,
   Our King and Empreour,
Ane gratious Virgin mother is,
   To God hir Sauiour.
Had not that blyssit Barne bene borne,
We had bene euerie ane forlorne
   With Sin and feindis fell.
Chrift Jesus, louing be to thé
That thow ane man wald borne be,
   To saif vs from the hell.

For neuer was, nor sall be man,
   Nor woman in this lyfe:

Sen Adam firſt our ſin began,
   And Eue his weddit wyfe,
That can be ſaif throw thair gude deid;
For poyſound all ar Adamis ſeid,
   And can not ſin refraine;
Quhill God him ſelf fand the remeid,
And gaue his only Sone to the deid,
   To freith vs from all paine.

We ſuld lufe God and myrrie be,
   And dryue away diſpair:
For Chriſt is cummin from heuin ſa hie,
   Our fall for to repair.
Na toung ſic kyndnes can expres:
The forme of ſeruand takin hes,
   And *Verbum caro factum eſt;*
Except Sin, lyke vnto vs all,
To freith vs from the Feindis thrall,
   And mend quhair we did mis.

Full weill is them for euer moir,
   That trowis faithfullie,
Be grace to ring with Chriſt in gloir,
   Throw faith allanerlie:
And weill is them that vnderſtude,
The gracious gift of Chriſtis blude,
   Sched ſinners for to win:
Was neuer hard fa kynde ane thing;
Chriſt for his fais on Croce did hing,
   To purge vs from our ſin.

Thus thank we him full hartfully,
   For his greit gentilnes:

In dulci jubilo.

We pray him, for his greit mercy,
   Trew Preichouris till incres;
Fals Pharisians, and fenzeit lair,
Quhome we haue followit lait and air,
   Baith them and vs forgiue,
God, Father, Sone, and Haly Spreit,
Instruct vs in thy word sa sweit,
   And efter it to liue.—FINIS.

IN *dulci jubilo*, now let vs sing with mirth & jo,
   Our hartis consolatioun lyis *in præsepio*;
And schynis as the Sone, *Matris in gremio*.
Alpha es & O, Alpha es & O.

O *Jesu parvule*, I thrist soir efter thé:
Confort my hart and mynde, *O Puer optime!*
God of all grace sa kynde, *et Princeps gloriæ*,
Trahe me post te; Trahe me post te,

Vbi sunt gaudia, in ony place, bot thair
Quhair that the angellis sing, *Noua Cantica*,
Bot and the bellis ring, *in Regis curia*.
God gif I war thair: God gif I war thair!

ONLIE to God on heich be gloir,
   And louing be vnto his grace;
Quha can condampne vs ony moir,
   Sen we ar now at Goddis peace?
In till his fauour we ar taine,
Throw faith in Jesus Christ allane,
   Be quhome his wraith sall end and ceis.

We worschip, and we loue and pryse,

Thy Maieſtie and magnitude;
That thow, God, Father only wiſe,
　　Ringis ouer all with fortitude:
Na toung can tell thy ſtrenth nor micht,
Thy wordis and thochtis all ar richt,
　　And all thy warkis juſt and gude.

Lord Jeſus Chriſt, Sone only borne,
　　Of thy Father Celeſtiall:
Thow ſauit vs that was forlorne,
　　Fra ſin and hell, and Sathans thrall,
Lord Goddis Lamb, thow tuke on thé,
For all our ſin to ſatisfie.
　　Lord be mercyfull vnto vs [all].

O Haly Gaiſt, our comfort gude,
　　From feindis feid thy flocke defend,
[Quhome Chriſt had ranſomit on the Rude:]
　　To thy keiping we them commend:
From errour and hypocriſie
Strenth vs in the veritie,
　　To perſeueir vnto the end.

FINIS.

¶ *Of the greit louing and blyithnes of Goddis word.*

LORD God, thy face and word of grace,
　　Hes lang bene hid be craft of men:
Quhill at the laſt, the nicht is paſt,
　　And we full weill thair falſet ken:
We knaw perfyte the Haly wryte,
　　Thairfoir be gloir and praiſe to Thé,
Quhilk did vs giue, this tyme to liue,
　　Thy word trew preichit for to ſe.

Our

Our barnis now weill knawis how,
  To worschip God with seruice trew;
Quhilk mony zeir, our fatheris deir,
  Allace thairfoir, full fair misknew!
Zit God did feid his chosin in deid,
  As Noe, and Lot, and mony mo:
And had respect to his elect,
  How euer the blind warld did go.

Sen throw thy strenth, thy word at lenth
  Is preichit cleir befoir our ene:
Be zit, gude Lord, misericord
  To them quhilk zit dissauit bene,
And nocht dois knaw bot mennis law,
  To thair greit dampnatioun;
Teiche them fra hand to vnderstand
  Thy word to thair saluatioun.

Quha wald be saif, first this mon haue,
  To knaw thair sin, syne trow in Christ:
Big on this ground, let lufe abound,
  With patience, prayer, hope and traist.
On God thow call, thank him of all,
  To serue thy nichtbour giue thy cure:
Thy conscience fré mon euer be,
  This can giue thé na creature.

Thow, Lord abone, mon giue alone,
  Thir giftis for thy Haly name:
Quha will thair hart to Christ conuert,
  Na man can do them skaith nor schame:
Thocht Paip or King wald sa maling,
  To mak the word of God forlorne:
D. j

Thair ſtrenth ſall faill, and not preuaill,
   Thocht thay the contrair all had ſworne.

Lord let thy hand help in all land,
   That thy Elect conuertit be,
Thy word to leir, quhilk now dar ſweir
   That thy Word is bot heriſie.
Thay giue thy word a fals record,
   Quhilk neuer hard the veritie;
Nor neuer it red bot blindlingis led,
   With Doctouris of Idolatrie.

The tyme is now, but dout I trow,
   Quhilk Paule did prophecie in writ,
Thocht heuin and eird ſuld ga areird,
   Thy word ſall ſtand faſt and perfite.
Thocht that maiſt part indure thair hart
   Setting thair ſtrenth thy word againe;
Repent thay nocht, thay ſalbe brocht
   Eternally to hellis paine.

Our Sauiour and Gouernour
   Is Chriſt, quhais bludie woundis wyde,
Redemit hes from all diſtres,
   Sinneris that will on him confide.
To him be gloir for euer moir,
   To vs quhilk hes ane promeis maid:
Us to conuoy from paine to joy,
   Baith in our lyfe and in our deid.

We hope and traiſt, the Haly Gaiſt
   Sall not forzet vs in our neid:
Sa we thy Word with one accord

                                Hald

Hald in our hart our faull to feid.
Let vs not mis thy gloir and blis,
   Quhen fra this wretchit lyfe we wend:
Grant vs thy grace to die in peace,
   And perſeueir vnto the end.

FINIS.

¶ Nunc dimittis, *the Prayer of Symeon.*
Luk ij. Chapter.

LORD, let thy ſeruand now depart
   In glaidneſs, reſt, and peace:
I am reioycit at my hart,
   To ſe his godly face,
Quhome faithfully thow promeiſt me,
   Chriſt Jeſus, King of grace.

This preſent deid ſall be full ſweit,
   And into ſleip ſall changit be:
To.reſt, ſyne ryſe, bot euer my Spreit
   Sall liue, and be alwayis with thé,
Throw faith in Chriſt my only traiſt,
   Quhome preſently I ſe.

Our Sauiour thow hes him maid,
   His deid ſall ſaue vs all
From ſin and hell, the Deuill and deid:
   His Reſurrectioun ſall
Frelie vs giue, euer for to liue,
   In gloir perpetuall.

Of Hethin folk, blindit ſo ſoir,
   He is the verray licht,
Quhilk neuer hard of him befoir,

52 *Christ Jesus gaue him self to die.*

Nor saw him with thair ficht:
He is the gloir, praife and decoir,
And ftrenth of Ifrael richt.
FINIS.

¶ *Ane fang of the Refurrectioun.*

CHRIST gaue him felf to deid,
And for our fault he mendis maid:
For vs he fched his precious blude,
With greit tryumphe vpon the Rude,
And fin and Sathan thair hes flaine,
And fauit vs from hellis paine.

For he againe fra deid vp rais,
Victour of deid, and all our fais;
He raif the obligatioun,
Contrair to our faluatioun;
Syne fpoylzeit Sathan, Hell and Sin,
And Heuinlie gloir to vs hes win.

And we ar now at Goddis peace,
Throw Chrift reffauit to his grace,
Our Father mercyfull he is,
And we fall ring with him in blis.
Allalua, allalua, *Benedicamus Domino.*
FINIS.

¶ *Certaine Ballatis of the Scripture.*

TILL Chrift, quhome I am haldin for to lufe,
I gif my thirlit hart in gouernance.
How fuld I lufe, and fra his treuth remufe,
Full

Till Chriſt, quhome, &c.

Full wo wer me, that drerie diſſeuerance,
   Is na remeid, ſaif only eſperance:
For weill, for wo, for boiſt, or zit for ſchoir,
Quhair I am ſet, I ſall lufe euer moir.

And ſen I muſt depart on neid, I ſall
   Be till him trew, with hart, and that I hecht,
And ſen that I becummin am his thrall,
   With body him ſerue, with mynde & all my micht:
   He is the rute of my remembrance richt;
The verray crop, quhome of I comfort tak:
Quhy ſuld I not do ſeruice for his ſaik?

Quhome ſuld I ſerue, bot him that did me ſaue?
   Quhome ſuld I dout, bot him that dantis deid?
Quhome ſuld I lufe, bot him attour the laif?
   Of all my wo he is the haill remeid:
   How ſuld I fle, and can not find na feid?
Quhome ſuld I lufe, bot him that hes my hart?
How ſuld we twin, that na man can depart?

Thus vmbeſet I am on euerie ſyde,
   And quhat to do I can not weill deuiſe:
My fleſche biddis fle, my ſpreit biddis me byde:
   Quhen cair cummis, then Comfort on me cryis;
   Hope ſayis get vp, then langour on me lyis,
My panis biddis my wofull hart repent,
Bot neuer mair thairto will I conſent.

Depart him fra, my hart will neuer conſent;
   It biddis me byde, and I ſall neuer fle;
For be I takin, ſlaine, or zit ſchent,
   For ſic ane King it is na ſchame to die.

Gif thair be grace into this eird for me,
It is committit from the heuin abufe,
Till Chriſt quhome I am haldin for to lufe.
FINIS.

RICHT ſoirly muſing in my mynde,
For pitie ſoir my hart is pynde,
Quhen I remember on Chriſt ſa kynde,
    that ſauit me:
Nane culd me ſaif from thyne till Ynde,
    bot only He.

He is the way, trothe, lyfe, and licht,
The verray port till heuin full richt,
Quha enteris not be his greit micht
    ane theif is he:
That wald preſume be his awin micht
    ſauit to be.

I grant that I haue faultie ſoir,
To ſtok and ſtane geuand his gloir,
And heipand warkis into ſtoir,
    for my remeid:
War not his mercy is the moir,
    I had bene deid.

Thow lytill bill thy wayis thow wend,
And ſchaw my mynde from end to end,
Till them that will repent and mend,
    thow ſchaw them till:
Beleue in Chriſt, quhome God hes ſend,
    and wirk his will.
FINIS.

Richt foir oppreſt.

RICHT foir oppreſt I am with panis ſmart
Baith nicht and day, makand my wofull mone,
To God for my miſdeid, quhilk hes my hart
   Put in ſa greit diſtres with wo begone:
   Bot gif he ſend me ſum remeid anone,
I liſt not lang my lyfe for till indure,
Bot to the deid bowne cairfull creature.

I can not do my detfull obſeruance,
   Till Him that heuin & all the world ſuld dreid:
Auld Adame is the caus of this miſchance,
   And turnis oft my faith in wickit deid.
   War not the deid of Chriſt war my remeid,
I liſt not on my lyfe for till tak cure,
Bot to the deid bowne cairfull creature.

O God of gloir! quhais micht is infinite,
   Grant me thy grace quhome ſin haldis in thrall,
To fecht aganis my fleſhe, quhilk hes the wyte
   Of all my wo, and my appeirand fall:
   Thow gaue command, in neid on thé to call,
And for thy Sonnis ſaik I ſuld be ſure,
That thow ſuld ſaue all ſinfull creature.

Remember, Lord, my greit fragilitie,
   Remember, Lord, thy Sonnis paſſioun,
For I am borne with all iniquitie
   And can not help my awin ſaluatioun:
   Thairfoir is my juſtificatioun
Be Chriſt, quhilk cled him with my nature,
To ſaue from ſchame all ſinfull creature.

O Lord! ſen thow thy word to me hes ſend,
   Thow let it neuer returne to thé in vaine,

Bot let me perseueir vnto the end;
  To my auld sin let me not turne againe:
  For then bene far better into plaine,
Not till haue hard thy precept in Scripture,
Then, knawand it, die carefull creature.

FINIS.

ALLACE, that same sweit face,
  That deit vpon ane tre,
To purches mankynde peace,
From sin to mak vs fre,
  Allone to be our remedie.
To graith our place full meit
He is ascendit hie,
And left with vs his Spreit:
To worship Spirituallie,
  Onlie to be our remedie.
He bad, quhen he was gone,
Apply vs haillelie,
To serue our God alone,
In Spreit and veritie,
  Alone to be our remedie.
Na kynde of outward deid,
How haly that euer it be,
May saif vs at our neid,
Nor zit vs justifie,
  Nor zit can mak vs remedie.
Bot Christ we neid nathing
Quhair throw sauit we suld be:
He is ane potent King,
And will alanerlie,
  Onlie be our remedie.

His Teſtament maiſt perfyte,
Plainely dois teſtifie,
Quhilk his Apoſtillis did wryte,
That nane may ſaif bot he,
      Nor zit can mak vs remedie.
Bot now, ſen he is gone
To ring eternallie,
We worſchip ſtock and ſtone,
Can nouther heir nor ſe,
      Nor zit can mak vs remedie.
We haue dwelt all to lang
In fals hypocriſie,
Trew faith, Lord, mak vs fang,
Wirkand be cheritie,
      Only to be our remedie.
        F I N I S.

I CALL on thé, Lord Jeſus Chriſt,
  I haue nane vther help bot thé,
My hart is neuer ſet at reſt,
  Till thy ſweit word comfort me.
Ane ſteidfaſt faith grant me thairfoir,
  To hald be thy word euer moir,
Abuſe all thing, neuer reſiſting
  Bot to incres in faith moir and moir.

Zit anis againe I call on thé,
  Heir my requeſt, O mercyfull Lord!
I wald faine hope in thy mercie,
  And can not be thairto reſtoird:
Except thow illuminate with thy grace
  My blind and naturall waiknes,
Caus me thairfoir haue hope in ſtoir,
  In thy mercie and ſweit promeis.

I call on thé, Lord.

Lord, prent into my hart and mynde,
   Thy Haly Spreit with feruentnes:
That I to thé be not vnkynde
   Bot lufe thé without fenzeitnes.
Lat nathing draw my mynde from thé,
   Bot euer to lufe thé erneſtlie;
Let not my hart unkyndly depart
   From the richt lufe of thy mercie.

Giue me thy grace, Lord, I thé pray,
   To lufe my enemeis hartfullie,
Howbeit thay troubill me alway,
   And for thy caus do ſclander me.
Zit Jeſus Chriſt for thy gudnes,
   Fulfill my hart with forgiuenes;
That quhill I liue, I them forgiue,
   That do offend me mair and les.

I am compaſſit rounde about,
   With foir and ſtrang temptatioun:
Thairfoir, gude Lord, delyuer me out
   From all this wickit natioun:
The Deuill, the warld, the fleſhe alſo,
   Dois follow me quhair euer I go,
Thairfoir wald I delyuerit be,
   Thy help I feik, Lord, and no mo.

Now feis thow, Lord, quhat neid I haif,
   Thair is none vther to plenze to:
Thairfoir thy Haly Gaiſt I craif
   To be my gyde quhair euer I go,
That in all my aduerſitie,
   I forzet not the lufe of thé;

Bot as thow, Lord, hes geuin thy word,
  Let me thairin baith liue and die.
FINIS.

O F mercy zit he paſſis all,
  In quhome I traiſt and euer fall;
For to nane vther will I call,
  To die thairfoir, to die thairfoir.

For thair is nane vther ſaluatioun
Bot be that Lord that ſufferit Paſſioun;
Upon our Saulis he hes compaſſioun,
  And deit thairfoir, and deit thairfoir.

That Lord ſa far had vs in mynde,
He come from heuin and tuke mankynde;
He haillit the ſeik, ſair, lamit and blinde,
  And deit thairfoir, and deit thairfoir.

To pray to Peter, James, or Johne,
Our Saullis to ſaif, power haue thay none,
For that belangis to Chriſt allone,
  He deit thairfoir, he deit thairfoir.

I traiſt to God of ſuretie,
Be Chriſtis blude ſauit to be,
In quhilk I hope ſa faithfullie,
  To die thairfoir, to die thairfoir.

Thair is na deidis, that can ſaue me,
Thocht they be neuer ſa grit plentie;
Bot throw Chriſt, and his greit mercy,
  Quhilk deit thairfoir, quhilk deit thairfoir.

Of mercies ʒit he paſſis all.

Gif deidis micht faue our Saulis from paine,
Then Chriſtis blude was fched in vaine,
As ze may reid in Scripture plaine,
 To die thairfoir, to die thairfoir.

Zit fum hes hope fauit to be
For doing deidis of cheritie;
Faith can not faue quhair na deidis be,
 Thay lie thairfoir, thay lie thairfoir.

The theif was faift be faith trewlie,
And not for deidis of cheritie,
As wrytis Luk, twentie and thre,
 To die thairfoir, to die thairfoir.

Fyre without heit can not be,
Faith will haue warkis of furetie,
Als faſt as may conuenientlie
 Be done, but moir.

Now Lord, that deit vpon ane tre,
And fched thy blude fa plenteouſlie
Reſſaue our Saullis to thy gloir
 We afk no moir, we afk no moir.
  FINIS.

WE fuld into remembrance
  Of Jefus Chriſt our King,
Without ony diſſimulance
  Be blyith, and myrrie fing.

We war condampnit to the deid,
 In hell, for Adamis mis:

Bot

We suld into remembrance.

Bot Jesus Christ the peice hes maid
   Betuix God and vs.

Christ is our God and Sauiour,
   Our help and our refuge:
Our Brother and our Mediatour
   Our Aduocate and Judge.

Sen on our syde is God him sell,
   Quha dar againe him pleid?
For he hes vincust sin and hell,
   The Deuill, and also deid.

This greit gudnes that Christ hes done,
   God let vs neuer forzet:
Bot thank and loue that Lord abone,
   With sangis sweitly set.
        FINIS.

HAY, let vs sing, and mak greit mirth,
   Sen Christ this day to vs is borne:
For had not bene that blyssit birth,
   Mankynde alwayis had bene forlorne.

All men wer borne in sinfulnes,
   Condampnit to eternall deid:
Except Christ that in richteousnes,
   Was only borne for our remeid.

And he, gif we beleue, hes coist
   His innocens for our trespas;
Had not bene Christ we had bene loist;
   O blyssit birth that euer was.
        FINIS.

In Burgh and Land.

IN Burgh and Land, eift, weft, north, south
We glorie for to fpeik of Chrift;
And his Euangell in our mouth,
    Bot far fra him our hartis, we wreift.

To Goddis Law quha will aduert,
    Sall fteidfaft in his promeis traift,
And lufe our brethren with our hart,
    And fle from fin, and vice deteft.

Lufe is fulfilling of the Law,
    As Paule reheirfis in his wryt;
Of Chrift nathing forfuith we knaw,
    That hes na faith, and lufe perfyte.

The Scripture plainely dois accord,
    Quha will not wirk his Fatheris will,
Bot fayis euerie day, Lord! Lord!
    Sall neuer cum in heuin him till.

Brether and fifteris that will refort
    Till Chrift, and with his Gofpell mell,
Do as ze fay, I zow exhort,
    And now na mair diffaue zour fell:

Or God fall tak his word againe
    Fra vs, fyne will it fend
To them that will not wirk in vaine,
    Bot perfeueir vnto the end.

FINIS.

¶ *Ane Sang contrair Idolatrie.*

WE fuld beleue in God abufe,
 And in nane vther thing;
Quha traiſtis in him, he will them lufe,
 And grant them thair aſking.

Contrair it is to Goddis command,
 To trow that help may cum,
Of Idoles maid with mennis hand,
 Quhilk ar baith deif and dum.

Quha dois adorne Idolatrie,
 Is contrair the haly writ:
For ſtock and ſtaine is Mammontrie,
 Quhilk men may carue or quhite.

The Apoſtillis that wrait the veritie,
 Expreſly do conclude,
That Idoles fuld deteſtit be,
 As contrair to Chriſtis blude.

Ze ſempill pepill vnperfite,
 Greit ignorance may ze tell,
Of ſtock and ſtaine hes mair delite,
 Then into God him fell.

FINIS.

¶ *Ane Ballat of the Epiſtill on Chriſtin-*
mes Euin.

THE Grace of God appeiris now,
 Our helth and our ſaluatioun,
To teiche and inſtruct vs how,
 In all countrie and natioun.

64 *The Grace of God appeiris now.*

That we fuld leue our wickitnes,
   And flé vaine wardly appetyte,
Juft, haly, be with fobernes,
   Leif in the warld a lyfe perfyte.

That blyffit hope for to abyde,
   The cumming of greit God of gloir,
And Jefus Chriftis woundis wyde,
   The Sauiour of les and moir.

Quhilk for our faik he gaue him fell,
   To faif from fin, and purge vs cleir,
Ane chofin pepill in fpeciall,
   In gude warkis to perfeueir.

To ftudie in them nicht and day,
   Thus we fuld ane exhort ane vther,
Of Goddis word to fing and fay,
   And euery man to lufe his brother.
            FINIS.

OF thingis twa I pray thé, Lord,
   Deny me not befoir I die,
All vanitie and leand word,
   Full far away thow put fra me.

Extreme pureteth, nor greit riches,
   Thow giue me not in na kin wife;
Bot only of thy greit gudnes,
   Giue me that may my neid fuffice.

For be I riche, I may perchance,
   Say, Quha is God, and him mifknaw;
                              And

And na thing bot my ſelf aduance,
  And him forzet and all his Law.

Or be I pure, and haue na geir,
  Than man I outher reif or ſteill.
Or than my Goddis name maneſweir,
  And ſet him at full lytill vaill.
                FINIS.

LORD, Father, God that gaif me lyfe,
  Thow leif me not to do my will:
Bot grant thy grace to me catiue,
  Thy godlie Law for to fulfill.

The prydefull luking of myne eine,
  Lat nocht be rutit in my hart:
All euill deſyre that in me bene,
  Full far from me thow wald aduart.

Ane gredie ſtomokis appetyte,
  And all ſurfet thow tak from me:
And als I pray thé mak me quyte,
  Of fleſchelie luſt and licherie.

Remouc from me all thrawardnes,
  Als weill in mynde as outward deid:
And tak from me vnſchamefaſtnes,
  And God and man to lufe and dreid.
                FINIS.

BLIS, bliſſit God, thir giftis gude,
  Quhilk thow hes geuin to be our fude;
Us blis, and mak thankfull in deid,
                E. j

Grace befoir Denner.

Be Jesus Christ, that blissit seid.
In quhome all blissing we ressaif,
Be quhome all blissing we ask and craif.
Grant blissing, Lord of michtis maist,
God, Father, Sone, and Haly Gaist.

FINIS.

Blissing, gloir, wisdome, & hartly thankfulnes,
And godly honouris all micht and fortitude,
We offer thé, Lord, with lawly humbilnes,
Committing our selfis haill to thy celsitude,
Asking, for Christ, quhilk for vs gaue his blude,
Grace for to be in hart and mynde thankfull,
For all thy gude and fre giftis plentifull.

FINIS.

Now let vs sing, with joy and mirth,
In honour of our Lordis birth,
For his lufe and humanitie,
Quha gaue him self for vs to die.

Be Adame we wer all forlorne,
Bot now Christ Jesus till vs is borne,
Hes fred vs fra captiuitie,
And vincust hes our enemie.

Quhen he was borne, nane did him snib,
To ly richt law intill ane crib:
Ane oxe, ane asse, richt tenderlie,
Refreschit his humanitie.

His Godheid mysteris na support

For

For it was full of all comfort;
Quhilk equall is in all degre,
Unto his Fatheris maieſtie.

The Angellis ſang with mirrynes,
Unto the Hyrdis mair and les,
And bad them of gude comfort be,
For Chriſtis new Natiuitie.

For we [ye] war all at Goddis horne;
This Babe to zow that now is borne,
Sall mak zow ſaif, and for zow die,
And zow reſtoir to libertie.

This Babe for zow did ſched his blude,
And tholit deid vpon the Rude:
And for his greit humanitie,
Exaltit is his Maieſtie.

And now he is our Aduocate,
Prayand for vs baith air and lait:
This can the Scripture verifie,
In ſa far as ane man is he.

Thairfoir all tyde, tyme, and hour,
Pas vnto him as Mediatour
Betuix the Fatheris wraith and thé,
Of ſin gif thow wald clengeit be.

For he hes promeiſt with his hart
To all ſinneris that will reuart,
And fra thair ſinfull lyfe will fle,
Sall ring with him eternallie.

E. ij

Quha can discriue.

To God the Father mot be gloir,
And als to Chriſt for euer moir,
The Haly Gaiſt mot bliſſit be,
Wirkar of this Natiuitie.

FINIS.

QVHA can diſcriue or put in write,
The grace and mercy of our Lord?
Quhais godly giftis infinite,
Men ſuld remember and record,
Conforme vnto his haly word.

Our Father, God, fontaine of grace,
His Sone did ſend to ranſoun vs
From Sin, and all our cairfull caſe,
And from the Deuill maiſt dangerous.
And ſlew that Serpent vennemous.

Chriſt come rycht ſweit, as ane ſeruand,
Of ſeruitude to mak vs fre:
And broken hes the Deuillis band,
Quhilk led vs in captiuitie:
Quhairfoir we thank his grit mercie.

Chriſt beand ryche in heuinlie gloir,
And we rycht pure and in diſtres,
Did mak vs riche for euer moir:
Quhairfoir we thank his gentilnes,
Be reſſoun of his greit gudnes.

Chriſt come full humbill and full law,
Us to exalt in majeſtie:
And tholit panis, as ze knaw,

Of

Of hounger, cauld, and miserie;
And we gat lyfe quhen he did die.

Chrift als difcendit to the hell,
   And vs redemit from that paine:
And from the deith did rais him fell,
   Na mair to thoill the deid againe,
   As we may reid in Scripture plaine.

Chrift maid vs juft quhen he vp rais,
   Be reffoun of his victorie:
Quhairthrow he vincuft all our fais,
   Sin, Deid, and Deuill our enemie,
   And from thair bandis maid vs fre.

Chrift paffit to the heuinnis hie,
   To graith ane place for vs in gloir,
Our Aduocate thairfoir to be:
   Heirfoir his grace let vs imploir,
   That we with him ring euer moir.

FINIS.

GIF ze haue riffin from deid againe,
   With Chrift our cheif and foueraine,
Quhilk did the inward man renew,
Gloir not in eirdly thingis vaine,
   Bot in the Croce of Chrift Jefew.

Seik thingis abufe that ar not feine,
Nor neuer fall with carnall eine:
   Do diligence for till fubdew
The flefche, the outward man I meine,
   And gloir in the Croce of Chrift Jefew.

E. iij

Honour it with feruent defyre,
And I fall fwa zour Spreit infpyre,
   Ay quhen temptatioun dois zow perfew,
Of lychorie fall flokkin the fyre,
   And gloir in the Croce of Chrift Jefew.

Quhen auarice, pryde, or ony fin,
Into zour memberis dois begin,
   Than pray with feruent hart and trew,
That ze may be of Ifackis kin,
   And gloir in the Croce of Chrift Jefew.

And delf with deip into zour land
As Ifack did, quhill that he fand·
   The water of lyfe, of heuinly hew,
Quhilk is now fillit with eird and fand,
   And gloir in the Croce of Chrift Jefew.

Honour the image of the Croce,
Not cryand out with curious voyce,
   Bot in the Spreit, as it is dew;
His gudnes that reftorit the lofe,
   And gloir in the Croce of Chrift Jefew.

His image is his word compleit,
Performit be the Haly Spreit,
   Quhilk from the Father fprang and grew,
Thair is na image half fa fweit,
   As gloir in the Croce of Chrift Jefew.

Gif ze lufe Chrift, hait not his word;
His leuing image, it is na bourd,
   Quha lichtleis it, fall not efchew

                               Of

Gif ʒe haue riſſin from deid.

Of vengeance the abbominabill ſword,
   And gloir in the Croce of Chriſt Jeſew

Siclyke of Juda the Lyoun ſtrang,
Upon the Croce he grat and hang,
   Quhen he was raiſit he ouerthrew
The Serpent, and his vennemous ſtang,
   And gloird in the Croce of Chriſt Jeſew.

The decreit and ſchairp hand write,
That ſtoppit vs fra the Father quyte,
   Furth of the myndes he withdrew,
And fixt it to the Croce perfite,
   And gloird in the Croce of Chriſt Jeſew.

Syne the Jewes that wer legall,
And Gentiles, that from Adames fall,
   Sa mony zeiris thair God miſknew
Maid baith ane body myſticall,
   And gloiris in the Croce of Chriſt Jeſew.

Let vs, thairfoir, with Paull now ſing,
Away from vs all viſibill thing,
   Sing to the Lord ane ſang of new,
Of laude, prais, and comforting,
   And gloir in the Croce of Chriſt Jeſew.

With ſpirituall lufe let vs proceid,
Nocht lyke the Jewes with feir and dreid;
   Sing to the Lord ane ſang richt trew,
That was borne of King Dauids ſeid,
   And gloir in the Croce of Chriſt Jeſew.

FINIS.
E. iiij

QVHA fuld my melodie amend,
Or folace fwiftly to me fend,
    Quha fuld me fuccour or fupplie,
Quha fuld me from the deid defend,
    Bot God, my lufe, in heuin fa hie?

Imploir his grace quhair we offend,
And do our former lyfe amend:
    Giue honour only to that King
In quhome our hope allone depend,
    And lufe him alfo ouer all thing.

Nixt lufe zour nichtbour as zour fell,
Euill thochtis from zour mynde expell:
    Quhair Spreit is waik afk comforting
At Him quhilk creat heuin and hell:
    Lufe God in heuin attour all thing.

Do gude for euill, and leif zour will,
Not gude for gude, nor euill for euill,
    Than ze prefent ane peirles fing,
Of lyfe ferene, the warld vntill:
    Lufe God in heuin attour all thing.

Thocht thow perfwaid this threid flyding
Quhilk ay increffis moir and moir,
    Think weill on heuinlie gouerning
This warld is nocht bot tranfitoir,
    And lufe thy God attour all thing.

Quha feruis the warld gais amis,
And fall be far from heuinnis blis:
    For quhy? in Scripture is founding

Na wicht can serue twa Lordis I wis:
Lufe God in heuin attour all thing.
FINIS.

The Conceptioun of Chrift.

LET vs reioce and sing,
And praise that michtie King,
  Quhilk send his Sone of a Virgine bricht.
    La.   Lay.   La.
And on him tuke our vyle nature,
Our deidlie woundis to cure,
  Mankynde to hald in richt.
    La.   Lay.   La.
Sanct Luk wrytis in his Gospell,
God send his Angell Gabriell,
  Unto that Virgine but defame.
    La.   Lay.   La.
For to fulfill the Prophesie,
Was spousit with Josaph fre,
  Mary scho had to name:
    La.   Lay.   La.
Thir wordis to hir he did reheirs.
Haill Mary! full of grace,
  The Lord God is with thé.
    La.   Lay.   La.
Thow blyssit Virgine mylde,
Thow sall consaue ane Chylde
  The pepill redeme sall he:
    La.   Lay.   La.
Quhais power and greit micht,
Sall be in Goddis sicht,
  Quhilk from the Father of micht is send,

The Conceptioun of Chriſt.

   La. Lay. La.
Jeſus his name ze call,
Quhilk ſalbe Prince ouir all
 His Kingdome ſall haue nane end.
   La. Lay. La.
Than ſpak that Virgin fre,
Behald, how ſall this be,
 Seeing I knaw na man?
   La. Lay. La.
Than ſaid the Angell chaiſt,
Be the power of the Haly Gaiſt,
 Quhilk all thing wirk he can.
   La. Lay. La.
Elizabeth thy couſing alſo,
Sex monethis with chylde can go,
 At quhais birth greit joy ſall be:
   La. Lay. La.
Call him Johne, ſayis the Angell bricht,
Quhilk is ſend be Goddis micht,
 The Lordis way prepair ſall he.
   La. Lay. La.

FINIS

Heir endis the Spirituall Sangis, and beginnis the Pſalmes of Dauid, with vther new pleaſand Ballattis. Tranſlatit out of Enchiridion Pſalmorum *to be ſung.*

  Quare fremuerunt gentes. Pſal. ij.

QVHAT is the caus, O God omnipotent,
 That all natiounis commouit ar ſa ſoir?
           The

Qubat is the caus.

The Kingis and the pepill with ane confent,
  Refiftis thé, thy power and thy gloir.
  That ftryue againe thy law ay moir and moir,
And contrair Chrift thy Sone quhome thow hes
To faif all man that will on him depend.   [fend,

Thay will not be reformit from thair fin,
  Bot will remaine blindit in ignorance,
And will not thoill to luke thy law within,
  Bot caftis it away with greit greuance:
  Thy counfell they refufe and gouernance,
And following thair awin hartis confait,
Euerie man drawis a findrie gait.

Bot thow, O God, in heuin into thy ring,
  Thow makis all thair counfels euerie one,
Quhat thay intend, that fall thay neuer bring
  To finall end; for thy wifdome allone
  Thair pregnant wittis fall fcorne, and anone,
In thy greit ire, thow fall them fair reprufe,
And from thy face thow fall them fwyith remufe.

For God hes fet a captaine ftark and wicht,
  Chrift [h]is awin Sone, God and man naturall,
On Mont Sion to reule it juft and richt,
  That is to fay, his Kirk Uniuerfall,
  To teiche his Fatheris word celeftiall:
His godly will and plefure for to fchaw,
Inftructing all the warld into his Law.

God faid to him, Thow art my Sone and air,
  I thé begat, for euer and this day,
Thy deid purcheft victorie preclair,

Syne from the deid thow rais, to ring for ay,
  My chofin in thé fall not cum to decay,
  Quha trewlie traiftis in thy godlie name,
Sall neuer die eternallie I plane.

My Sone, I will thé geue all natiounis
  In heritage, and put thame in thy cure:
To reule thame with thy miniftratiounis,
  And preif thame with the Croce at thy plefure,
  To purge thair flefhlie luft, and mak thame pure,
And for to rais thair myndis fpirituall,
To pryfe thy name now and perpetuall.

Heirfoir Kingis and Rewlaris now be war,
  Aduert till Goddis word and difcipline.
Reffaif his Sone, abone all thing prefar
  His godlie word, and keip weill his doctrine:
  Leir him to dreid, and traift in till him fyne,
Quhilk is the trew wirfhip and rychteoufnes,
That God requyris of mankynd mair and les.

Reffaif thairfoir his fweit correctioun,
  That he na mair with zow offendit be;
Befoir your eine with trew affectioun,
  And in zour hart ze haif him identlie.
  Obey his law, for quhen greuit is he,
Than quha dar his juft jugement abyde
Bliffit ar they, quhilk on him dois confyde.

FINIS.

Saluum me fac. Pfal. xj.

SAIF vs, gude Lord, and fuccour fend,
  For peryfit is halynes:

And

And treuth away from men is wend,
　　And fled fra thame is faithfulnes:
Diſſait amang thame ſa is ſawin,
The veritie may nocht be knawin;
　　Thair tungis ar full of feinzetnes.

Thair leing tungis, O Lord, cut out,
　　That ſpeikis in to thy contemptioun:
And ſayis in all place round about,
　　Our tungis hes ane exemptioun,
Euin as we pleis, our lippis may lie,
For we haue all authoritie;
　　Nane hes of vs dominioun.

Bot God hes ſaid, and will it keip,
　　I will ryſe vp incontinent,
For the oppreſt that ſair dois weip,
　　And murning of the indigent.
The pure that vexit is ſo ſoir,
I will them ſaue, and them reſtoir
　　Fra wickit toungis teichement.

And Goddis word and promit
　　Is trewar, cleirar, and mair pure,
Then ſiluer ſeuin tymes purifyit:
　　Sen that thow art in word ſa ſure,
Thow ſaue vs from ſic ſort of men,
And fra the doctrine that they ken
　　Eternally on vs tak cure.

Quhen hypocrites ar principall,
　　And hieſt in authoritie:
On force the pepill follow fall

Thair falset and hypocrisie.
The pepill follow mon, on neid,
Thir Prelatis and thair wickit deid,
Baith blindit from the veritie.
FINIS.

Vsque quo Domine. Psal. xxij. *with the tune of
Exaudi, Deus, orationem meam.*

O LORD, how lang for euer wil thow forzet,
And hyde thy face fra me, or zit how lang
Sall I reheirs thy counsell in my hart?
Quhen sall my hart ceis of this sorie sang?
O Lord, behald, help me, and licht my eine,
That suddand sleip of deid do me na teine.

Or ellis quhen my enemeis seis my fall,
We did preuaill, sone will thay say on me:
And gif thay se me be thame brocht in thrall,
Thay will reioyce into thair tyrannie
Bot I in God hes hope, and traist to se
His godly help, than sall I loue the Lord
Quhilk did me saue fra them that had me schord.
FINIS.

Domine, quis habitabit? Psal. xxiiij.

O LORD, quha sall in heuin dwell with thé,
In thy triumphant throne and tabernakil?
Or quha sall on thy haly hill sa hie
  Mak residence, and haue his habitakill?
    The innocent, that is ane spectakill
Of haly lyfe and conuersatioun,

And

And juft in all his operatioun.

And he quhilk on the treuth hes all his thocht,
 And with his toung the fame for till furthfchaw,
And quhais toung his nichtbour noyis nocht,
 And hurtis nane be boift, nor zit be blaw;
 And thocht his nichtbouris faute or vice be
He fcornis not: bot dois till his brother [knaw
As that he wald till him did ony vther.

He that hes in na reputatioun
 The wickit men, in nurifching thair vice,
With flatterie, and adulatioun;
 And all gude men he haldis into pryfe,
 And thay that dreidis God he countis wife.
Quhat euer he fweir to ony man, or say,
His promeis he will keip without delay.

Na occour will he vfe intill his lane,
 Bot frely with his nichtbour len and borrow;
Contrair the juft, rewaird he will tak nane,
 Bot him defend from fyre, fchame, and forrow.
 This will he do at midnicht and at morrow.
Quhat euer he be that weill obferuis this,
Sall neuer perifhe, but ring in heuinis blis.
FINIS.

Dominus regit me.   Pfal. xxiij.

THE Lord God is my Paftor gude,
 Aboundantly me for to feid;
Then how can I be deftitute
 Of ony gude thing in my neid?

He feidis me in feildis fair,
To riueris fweit, pure and preclair,
  He dryuis me but ony dreid.

My faull and lyfe he dois refrefche,
  And me conuoyis in the way
Of his juftice and richteoufnes,
  And me defendis from decay:
Not for my warkis verteoufnes,
Bot for his name fa glorious,
  Preferuis me baith nicht and day.

And thocht I wauer, or ga will,
  Or am in danger for to die,
Na dreid of deid fall cum me till,
  Nor feir of cruell tyrannie.
Becaus that thow art me befyde,
To gouerne me and be my gyde,
  From all mifcheif and miferie.

Thy ftaffe quhair of I ftand greit awe,
  And thy fcheip huke me for to fang;
Thay nurture me, my fautes to knaw,
  Quhen fra the hie way I ga wrang:
Thairfoir my spreit is blyith and glaid,
Quhen on my flefche thy fcurge is laid,
  In the richt way to gar me gang.

And thow ane tabill dois prouyde,
  Befoir me, full of all delyte,
Contrair to my perfewaris pryde,
  To thair difpleafure and difpyte.
Thow hes anointed weill my heid,

                    And

And full my coupe thow hes maid,
  With mony difches of delyte.
Thy gudnes and benignitie
  Let euer be with me thairfoir;
And quhill I liue, vntill I die,
  Thow lay them vp with me in ftoir;
That I may haue my dwelling place
Into thy hous, befoir thy face,
  To ring with thé for euer moir.
FINIS.

Exultate Jufti in Domino. Pfal. xxxiij.

ZE Richteous, rejoyce, and loue the Lord
  Juft men, to thank thair God, dois weil accord.
Play on zour lute, & fweitly to it fing,
  Tak harpe in hand with mony luftie ftring:
Tyrle on the ten ftringit inftrument,
  And prais zour God with hart, and hail intent:
Sing na auld thing the quhilk is abrogate,
  Bot fing fum new plefand perfite ballat:
Blaw vp organis with glaid and heuinly found,
  Joyfull in hart, quhilk all the fkyis refound:
For Goddis word is treuth and veritie,
  And dois all his deidis faithfullie.
The Lord lufis juftice and richteoufnes,
  And all the eird is full of his gudnes.
The heuinnis hie wer creat be the Lord,
  Thair ornamentis wer dreffit be his word.
He heipis vp the wateris lyke ane hill,
  Syne turnis them in deip quhen that he will.
Dreid ze the Lord, all dwelleris on the ground,
  And wirfchip him all hant the warld fa round.
F. j

Quhat God decretis is done incontinent,
  All creature obeyis his commandement.
The counsellis of the wickit and deuyse,
  He perturbis, appeirand euer sa wyse:
He scornis all thair consolatioun,
  And wicket pepillis imaginatioun:
Bot his counsell sall lest perpetuall,
  And sall indure till generations all.
Full happy is the pepill maist and leist,
  Quhilk in thair God & Lord hes all thair traist,
And quhome that God do cheis before all aige,
  Thame to posseid in proper heritage.
The Lord lukis furth of his heuinlie sait,
  And persauis all men of euerilk stait:
From his tryumphant throne he dois beholde
  All natiounis, and dwellaris on the molde:
For he allone did creat all thair hartis,
  And he allone dois knaw all thair warkis.
The King is not saif be his greit armie,
  Nor gyand saif be strenth of his bodie:
The bardit hors in neid sall men dissaif,
  And mony thousand hors may na man saif.
The eyis of the Lord thay do aduert
  To them that dreidis him with all thair hart,
Traisting his godly help with patience,
  To saif thair lyfe in tyme of pestilence;
And in the tyme of derth them for to feid;
  And be thair only help in all thair neid.
Thairfoir, my Saull, in God put thy beleif,
  Our strenth and targe to saif vs fra mischeif:
Our hart salbe into the Lord joyous,
  Sen we traist in thy name maist glorious.
                                    Assist

Aſſiſt to vs, O Lord, for thy gudnes,
  Euin as we traiſt in thy greit gentilnes.
FINIS.

Noli æmulari in malignantibus. Pſal. xxxvij.

THOW ſall not follow wickit menis wayis,
  Nor zit murne that ſinfull haue gude dayis;
For lyke the widderit hay ſone ſall thay faid,
  And as the graſſe that wallowis rute and blaid;
Bot in the Lord put thow thy haill beleif,
  And wirk his will, and not that may him greif;
And than the frutefull land thow ſall poſſes
  Aboundantlie, and ſall haue grit riches.
Into the Lord put all thy haill delyte,
  And he ſall grant thy hartis appetyte.
Schaw furth befoir the Lord thy mynd and will,
  And traiſt in him, he ſall it weill fulfill:
Than, as the goldin morning ſchynis bricht,
  Sa ſall thy juſtice ſchyne till euerie wicht;
And as the ſone in midday ſchawis fair,
  Sa ſall thy vertew knawin be alquhair.
Upon the Lord haue euer thyne intent,
  Befoir thyne eine, and haue him ay preſent;
And muſe thé not at thair proſperitie,
  That leuis all thair lyfe wrangouſlie.
Remoue rancour and ire furth of thy thocht,
  The ill exempill of the wickit follow nocht:
For cruell men ſall ſune deſtroyit be;
  Bot quha abydis the Lord pacientlie,
Sall bruke the land, and his poſſeſſioun
  Full peciabillie, without oppreſſioun.
Suffer a lytill quhile, and thow ſall ſe,

Thow sall not follow.

The wickit man perishe befoir thyne E:
Thow sall behald him, and his mansioun,
  Be brocht to nocht, and vtter confusioun.
But humbill men sall inherite the eird,
  And leif in peace fra wickit mens reird.
The sinful man with euill will await,
  The innocent that can mak na debait;
With countenance austeir sall on him gyrne,
  His irefull hart with baill sall euer byrne.
Bot thow, gude Lord, sall lauch thame all to scorne,
  And knawis the tyme that thay salbe forlorne.
The cruell men sall draw thair birnist brand,
  And haue thair bow bent reddy in thair hand,
For till slay the meik and innocent,
  That thay may cum to thair wicket intent.
Thair awin sword sall stryke thame throw the hart,
  And broken sall thair bow be in all part.
The lytill of the just is mair commendit,
  Sa that it be weill win, and better spendit,
Than is the grit ryches of wickit men,
  Quhair throw thay do baith God & man misken.
The power of the wickit sall decay;
  Bot God sall preserue the just man for ay:
The tymes of the just God dois record,
  Thair heritage salbe with God the Lord:
In tyme of perrell thay sall not be agast,
  And in grit derth thair fude salbe adrest.
Bot wickit men sall perishe in thair neid;
  And thay that of the gude Lord hes na dreid,
Lyke Sacrifice thay sall consumit be,
  Quhairof bot reik, thow can na mair se.
The wickit man will tak, and wil not pay,
                          The

Thow fall not follow.

The juft frelie wil gif without delay.
Quha luiffis him, and of him fpeikes gude,
  Sall bruke the land; bot quha will delude,
Or dois blafpheme the kynde and liberall,
  Sall ruttit be furth of memoriall.
The paithis of the juft God dois direct,
  He luiffis him and will him not neglect.
Suppofe he fall be fey, or zit be land,
  God will erect him with his helping hand.
I haue bene zung, and cum now to grit age,
  Zit faw I neuer the juft left in thirlage,
Nor zit haue fene his pofteritie,
  Beggand thair breid for grit neceffitie.
Bot he will giue and len his gude at large,
  Till thame that myfter hes, & will him charge,
Zit fall his feid leif into plenteoufnes,
  Aboundantly poffes grit riches
He leuis ill, and followis gude thairfoir,
  With God he fall ring euer moir.
The Lord luiffis juftice and equitie,
  And leuis not his Sanctis in miferie.
For he on thame perpetuallie hes cure,
  Bot wickit mennis feid fall not indure,
Juft men with joy the eird fall poffes,
  And dwell lang tyme on it, and haue fucces.
The juft mannis mouth exercis fapience,
  Of equitie ay fpeikand of prudence.
The law of God is in his hart fa haill,
  In all his wayis thairfoir he can nocht faill.
The wickit dois obferue the innocent,
  To feik to flay him with cruell intent.
Bot God will not him leif into his neid,

Bot will him faif fra tyrannis wickit deid.
Thay can not him condampne; quhen thay accufe
   Preferuit fall he be from thair abufe.
Traift in the Lord, and keip weill his command,
   And he fall thé exalt in euerie land.
Poffes the eird thow fall, and with thyne E,
   The wickit men deftroyit fall thow fe.
Sum tyme a tyrane flureis haue I fene,
   Lyke lawrel tre quhilk euer growis grene:
Bot in fchort tyme fune was he brocht to nocht;
   He was not found, nor that belangit him ocht.
Keip juftice, and haue E vnto the richt,
   That fal mak peace for euer with God of micht:
For wrangus men fall end mifcheuouflie,
   And wickit mennis fyne his miferie.
The juft all haill vpon the Lord dependis,
   Quhilk is his ftrenth, & all tyme him defendis,
God helpis him and fendis him fupplie,
   And fauis him fra tyrannis crueltie;
Becaufe in him he did put his traift,
   Into his trublis [nocht] culd him moleft.

FINIS.

Exaudi Deus orationem meam.   Pfal. lxiiij.

O LORD, aduert vnto my voce and cry,
   Now quhen I pray vnto thy Majeftie.
From dredour of my mortall ennemie,
   Defend my lyfe, and als delyuer me:
   Defend me from the fals fubtellitie
Of wickit men, and from the cruelnes,
Of thame that alwayis wirk vnrichteoufnes,

Fra

Fra thame that hes thair tungis fcharp & ground,
    And fcharper than ony twa edgeit fword,
Lyke deidly dartis thow geuis ftang & ftound.
    Rycht fa proceidis of thair mouth euerie word,
    Quhairwith to flay thay think it bot a bourd,
The innocent with fecreit diffemblance,
Without dredour of Goddis vengeance.

Thay haue deuyfit abbominatioun
    Amang thame felfis in thair malicioufnes.
Richt priuelie is thair communicatioun,
    To fet thair nettis with clokit craftines,
    With fic deuice as it war halynes,
That na man fuld thair violence efpye,
Quhilk wald reuenge thair fals hypocrifie.

Thair counfell is to feirche and to inquyre,
    The innocent with wrang for till accufe;
In all this warld thay haue na mair defyre,
    For euer in thair mynde of this thay mufe,
    Quha will delay it, thay will mak na refufe
Of fa or fule, and for fufpitioun,
Thay will bring men vnto confufioun.

Bot now na mair thair malice fall remaine,
    For God fall ftryke them in fchort fefoun,
Of quhome thay falbe plaguit with grit paine,
    And men fall hald thame in derifioun:
    Thair tungs falbe thair awin confufioun,
Quhilk was fa fcharp in contrair innocence,
That for thame felfis thay fall mak na defence.

Quhen men fall fe this haiftie fuddand change,

Than fall thay wonder and cleirlie vnderftand,
That it is God quhilk dois his awin reuenge,
   All men fal fe this wark of Goddis hand,
   And fall weill knaw, that nane can him withftand.
The juft fall traift in God, and als rejoyis,
And all trew hartis fall joy to heir this noyis.

FINIS.

Quam bonus Deus Ifrael.   Pfal. lxxiij.

TILL trew in hart God of Ifraell is fweit,
   Bot ftakerand almaift failzeit my feit,
Quhen I beheld thir peruerft wickit men
Profper alway, thocht thay did God mifken.

Thair is na zock thir wickit men may oppres.
Bot euer in welth, plefour and grit riches,
Quhen vther men ar trublit, and difefit,
With all paftime full plefandlie thay ar eafit.

Throw quhilk thay ar exaltit in to pryde,
Thair violence and wrang walkis full wyde
Throw thair grit micht in alkin luft thay leif,
Quhat thay can think vnto thair hart thay geif.

Quhat euer is done, thay think it vanitie,
Bot giue that thay the authoure of it be;
God of heuin thay blafpheme with thair mouth,
To curs all men thay think it na vncouth.

For this the peple dois flow to and fra,
Quhen thay the wickit with welth fe do fwa,
Thay dar be bald to dout giue God dois knaw,
Or vnderftand the breking of his law.

                                   And

And I alſo thocht thair proſperitie
Suld euer indure with thame eternallie;
And thocht vnto my ſelf I did offence,
That wuſche my handis, and leuit in innocence.

To thole diſtres, I thocht it was in vaine,
Baith day and nicht to tak on me ſic paine.
Quhen I had lang argound on ſic a kinde,
The sonnis of God I dampnit in my minde.

I tuke trauell on this to knaw the treuth,
Bot all for nocht, my laubour was bot ſleuth.
Quhen I ſall enter in Goddis ſecreit place,
Than ſall I ſe thair end befoir my face.

Full ſlydrie is the ſait that thay on ſit,
And for thair fault till hell ſune ſall thay flit:
For ſuddenlie thay ſall die with miſcheif,
Thair deſtructioun ſall be without releif.

As quhen ane man awalkis of his dreame,
Sa ſall the Lord deſtroy thair fuliſche fame:
Quhen I had this imaginatioun
My dullie ſpreit was in greit paſſioun.

Imprudently this brint I in my thocht,
In thy preſence as brutall beiſt of nocht,
Zit leit thow not me fall on ſic ane ſort,
Bot held my hand, and gaue me gude comfort.

With thy counſell thow ſall me weill conuoy,
And efter this reſſaue me to thy joy.
O Lord, quhat euer in heuin ordand for me,
Outher in eird, compair I not to thé.

Na thing am I, my body nor my hart:
God is my ſtrenth, and euer ſalbe my part.
Periſhe ſall thay, that fleis from thé far;
Loſte ſall thay be, that ocht to thé prefar.

To me, forſuith, I think it for the beſt,
To cleue to God, and on him put my traiſt,
And ſchaw the nobill warkis that He hes done,
To quhome be gloir ringand in his throne.
FINIS.

Deus quis ſimilis erit tibi. Pſal. lxxxiij.

GOD, for thy grace, thow keip no more ſilence:
[Ceiſs not, O God, nor hald thy peax no moir;]
Poſtpone it not, bot haiſt thy vengeance
  On hypocritis, humelie I thé exhort;
  For thay rebellis with rage do reſort,
And thay quhilk at thé haue mortall feid,
Contrair thy micht hes lifted vp thair heid.

And till oppres thy pepill do pretend,
  Under pretence and cloikit halynes:
With ſubtell flycht to ſlay vs thay intend;
  Conſiderat thay ar, baith mair and les,
  Contrair thy teſtament, our hope & richteouſnes:
Thay ſay, thay ſall vs rute from the ground,
That na mentioun of vs ſall mair be found.

Thay now conſpyre with cruell hart and fell,
  With ane conſent, togidder in ane band:
Quhilk neuer befoir culd gre amang thame ſell,
                    Stryuand

Stryuand for ſtait and hicht, in euerie land:
  Bot contrair thé togidder ſtife thay ſtand,
And faſt lyke burris thay cleif baith ane and all,
To hald, O God, thy word and vs in thrall.

Ze Edomeitis, idoll, with thrinfald croune,
  The crop and rute of pryde and tyrannie;
Ze Iſmalitis, with ſcarlat hat and gowne,
  Zour bludie boiſt na ſyith can ſatiſſie;
  Ze Moabitis, with hornis twa full hie,
Outwart lyke ſcheip, ze beir the beiſtis mark,
Inwart lyke tykis, ze byte, bot can not bark.

Of Agarins, quhat tung can tell the tryne,
  With hurklit hude ouir a weill nureiſt neck?
Jabell and Amon, als fat as ony ſwyne,
  Quhilk can not do, bot drink, ſing, jouk, and bek;
  The Amelekis, that leſingis weill can clek,
The Paliſtenis with dum doctouris of Tyre
Quhilk dar nocht diſpute, bot cryis, Fyre, fyre.

Aſſur, in harnes, is with thame euer moir.
  Companzeoun he is perpetuall
To Lotis ſonis, for to mantene thair gloir;
  He wate nocht ellis, for his conſcience is thrall
  To thame quhilk hes na hope celeſtiall,
Bot contrair God indurit hes thair hartis,
Syne [ſylie] Princes, blindly, tak thair partis.

O God of gloir, reſiſt thair cruelnes,
  As thow ſum tyme ouerthrew the Madionitis
And Sicera, with his malicioufnes.
  And Jabene, with his bludie hypocritis.

At Kyſon flude, as weill the ſtorie dytis;
Thay periſchit at Endor throw thy micht,
Syne mucke become, and fylth, for all thair hicht.

Thair gouernouris and gydis, gif ſiclike
  As Oreb, Seb, Seba, and Zelmanie.
Thair ſinnis ſhawis thay ar a bludie byke;
  And zit thay wald, throw thair hypocriſie,
  Poſſes the Kirk of God, throw tyrannie,
And will cüm to na Counſell Generall,
For feir thay loſe thair pompe Pontificall.

As quheill vnſtabill, and caffe befoir the wind,
  And as the wod conſumit is with fyre:
And as the flame burning quhair it can find
  The faggat, in the feild with grit impyre:
  Siclike perſew thame with thy greuous ire.
Lat thy tempeſt thair wraithfulnes reuenge,
And lat thy ſtorme thair pryde in purteth change.

Confound thame, Lord, that they may ſeik thy
  Perturbe thair minde with care continuall, [name,
And let thame periſche, and cum till vtter ſchame;
  Lat thame knaw thé for the God eternall,
  Allanerlie on thé allone to call:
And thé obey abone all eirdlie thing,
Maiſt michtieſt, maiſt hieſt in thy ring.

FINIS.

Qui habitat in Adiutorio. Pſal. lxxxxj.

QVHA on the Hieſt will depend,
  And in his ſecreit help will traiſt,
  Almichtie God ſall him defend,

And

Quha on the Hieſt will depend. 93

 And gyde him with his Haly Gaiſt.
  Thairfoir with mynde rype and degeſt,
Thow ſay to God, My trew releue,
  My hope, my God of michtis maiſt,
Onlie in him I will beleue.

He ſall delyuer thé at neid,
  And ſaue thy lyfe from peſtilence;
His wingis ar thy weirlie weid,
  His pennes ar thy ſtrang defence;
  And thow ſall haue experience,
That his trew promeis is thy ſcheild;
  His word of grit magnificence
Sall be thy buklar and thy beild.

Na wickit ſpreit ſall thé affray,
  Nor thé delude into the nicht;
The fleand dartis be the day,
  To trubill thé ſall haue na micht;
  Na ſuddand chance of vncouth flicht,
Sall cummer thé, nor mak thé red,
  Nor thé perturbe in mark nor licht,
Bot from all plague thow ſall be fred.

And thow ſall ſe at thy left hand,
  Ane thouſand haue ane ſuddand fall;
And als thow ſall ſe ten thouſand
  At thy richt hand, quhilk periſche ſall.
  Zit nocht to thé ſall cum at all:
Bot thow ſall with thine eine behald,
  Sinnaris put fra memoriall,
With plagues grit and monyfald.

O Lord, my hope and all my grace,
  Thow ſaue me for thy grit mercy;

Quha on the Hieſt will depend.

Thy gyrth is ſet in ſicker place,
   For he ſall ſaue thé michtfullie.
And na miſchance ſall cum to thé,
Nor maledie ſall thé moleſt;
   Na miſfortoun thy hous ſall ſe,
Bot all thingis wirk ſall for the beſt.

His Angellis he ſall giue ane charge,
   That thay on thé ſall take the cure,
In all thy wayis to be ane targe,
   To keip thé from miſauenture;
   And with thair handis thay ſall thé ſure,
That thow hurt nocht aganis ane craig
   Thy fute, bot ſall preſerue thé ſure
From perrellis, panis, and from plaig.

Thow ſall ſtrampe on the edderis ſtrang,
   And tred on the cruell cocketrice;
The lyonnis craig thow ſall ouer gang,
   The dreidfull dragoun thow ſall chace.
   Sen thow me traiſtis in all caſe,
Sayis God, I ſall thé ſaif from ſchame,
   And thé defend in euerie place,
For cauſe thow knew my godly name.

Quhen thow ſall call, I ſall thé heir,
   And in diſtres ſall be with thé.
I ſall reſtoir thé haill and feir,
   And als I ſall thé magnifie:
   With lang lyfe dotit ſall thow be,
And at the laſt I ſall thé bring
   Quhair thow eternall gloir ſall ſe,
For euer moir with me to ring.

FINIS.

Quhen fra Egypt.

In exitu Ifrael. Pfal. cxiiii.

QVHEN fra Egypt departit Ifraell,
And Jacobis hous fra pepill harbour fell,
To Juda, Lord, thow wes his Sauiour,
And to Ifraell ane gyde and gouernour:
Quhilk, quhen the fey had fene, for feir it fled,
  The flude Jordane zeid back, it was fa red.
The mountainis muifit, & ran athort lyke ramis,
  The hillis danfit, and lichtly lap lyke lambis.
Thow fwelland fey quhat muifit thé to fle?
  To gang abak, Jordane, quhat ailit thé?
Quhat gart zow, montanis, lyke ramis ftert and
  And, ze hillis, lyke lambis loup and bend? [ftend?
It was the Lordis feir that maid fic reird,
  And Jacobis God perturbit all the eird:
For God turnit the craig in frefche reueir,
  The barrane bra in fontane water cleir.

[*Non nobis Domine.* Pfal. cxv.]

Not vnto vs, not vnto vs, O Lord,
  Bot to thy fweit promeis, and to thy word,
And to thy name be gloir allanerlie,
  Quhilk keipis thy promeis faithfullie.
Thairfoir lat not our ennemeis blafpheme
  Thy Majeftie, for we may not fuftene
To heir thame fay, Quhair is thy grit afcence,
  Thy godly help of thy magnificence?
Our God forfuith ringis in heuin full hie.
  And quhat him liftis, or lykis, workis he.
Thir imagis of ftock, ftane, gilt with gold,
  Ar maid be men, and fyne for money fold:

Thay haue a mouth can nouther say nor sing;
　Thair eine ar blind, and thay can se na thing.
Thay can nocht heir, thocht men do cry and zell.
　Thair noisthirlis can nouther sauer nor smell.
Thay haue handis, can nouther feill nor grope:
　Thair fundyit feit can nouther gang nor loupe:
Thay can pronunce na voce furth of thair throtis:
　Thay ar ouergane with mouswobs & moitis.
Quha makis thame, or traistis in thair support,
　Ar lyke to thame in all maner of sort.
Bot thow, Israel, in God put thy traist,
　Thy protectour into thy myster maist.
Ze hous of Aaron, in God put zour beleif
　Zour defender, and na man can zow greif.
All worschippers of God, traist in his name,
　He is zour help and Sauiour allane.
The Lord hes mynde and mercy vpon vs,
　Will fauour vs, and bring vs to his blis.
Als feid the hous of Israel with his fude
　And to the hous of Aaron will be gude.
Thow sall do weill to them that dreidis thé,
　Baith zoung & auld, quhat stait that euer thai be.
God sall augment his pepill and incres,
　And eik thair sonnes and dochteris mair & les.
He is the Lord that creat heuin
　And eird, with his creatures, in dayis seuin.
The heuinnis ar the Lordis habitatioun;
　The eird he gaue to mannis propagatioun.
The deid may not thé loue among the laue,
　Nor thay that ar discendit in thair graue;
Bot we that ar on liue sall loue and sing
　To God for euer, vnto our lyues ending.

FINIS.

Except the Lord.

Nisi quia Dominus. Pſal. cxxiiii.

EXCEPT the Lord with vs had ſtand,
 Say furth, Iſraell, vnfenzeitlie,
Had not the Lord bene our warrand,
 Quhen men rais in our contrarie,
Thay had vs all on liue deuorit,
With ire ſa ſcharpelie thay vs ſchorit,
 Sa kendlit was thair crueltie.

For lyke the welterand wallis brym,
 Thay had ouerquhelmit vs with micht;
Lyke burnis that in ſpait faſt rin,
 Thay had ouerthrawin vs with flicht.
The bulrand ſtremis of thair pryde,
Had periſhit vs throw bak and ſyde,
 And reft fra vs our lyfe full richt.

Bot louing to the Lord, allone,
 That gaue vs nocht to be thair pray,
To be rent with thair teith anone,
 Bot hes vs fred full well thame fray.
Lyke to ane bird taine in ane net,
The quhilk the foullar for her ſet,
 Sa is our lyfe weill win away.

The net is broken in pecis ſmall,
 And we ar ſauit fra thair ſchame;
Our hope was ay and euer ſall
 Be in the Lord, and in his Name:
The quhilk hes creat heuin ſa hie,
And maid the eird ſa meruellouſlie,
 And all the ferleis of the ſame.

FINIS.
G. j

De profundis. Pſal. cxxx.

FRA deip, O Lord, I call to thé,
  Lord, heir my inuocatioun,
Thy eiris thow inclyne to me
  And heir my lamentatioun:
For gif thow will our ſin impute
Till vs, O Lord, that we commit
  Quha may byde thy accuſatioun?

Bot thow art mercyfull and kynde,
  And hes promittit in thy write,
Them that repent with hart and mynde
  Of all thair ſin to mak them quyte.
Thocht I be full of ſinfulnes,
Zit thow art full of faithfulnes,
  And thy promeis trew and perfyte.

My hope is ſteidfaſt in the Lord,
  My ſaull euer on him traiſt,
And my beleue is in thy word,
  And all thy promittis maiſt and leiſt.
My ſaull on God waitis and is bent,
As watcheman wald the nicht wer went,
  Bydand the day to tak him reſt.

Iſraell, in God put thy beleue,
  For he is full of gentilnes,
Fredome, gudnes, and ſall releue
  All Iſraell of thair diſtres:
He ſall delyuer Iſrael,
And all thair ſinneris ſall expell,
  And cleith them with his richteouſnes.

FINIS.

At the Riuers of Babylon.

Super flumina Babylonis. Pfal. cxxxviii.

AT the Riuers of Babylon,
 Quhair we dwelt in captiuitie,
Quhen we rememberit on Sion,
 We weipit all full forrowfullie.
On the fauch treis our harpis we hang,
Quhen thay requyrit vs ane fang,
 That held vs in fic thirldome;
Thay bad vs fing fum pfalme or hymne,
That we fum tyme fang Sion in;
 To quhome we anfwerit full fone:

How may we outher play or fing
 The pfalmes of our Lord fa fweit,
Intill ane vncouth land or reigne?
 My richt hand firft fall that forleit,
Or Jerufalem forzettin be;
Faft to my chaftis my toung fall be
 Clafpit, or that I it forzet.
In my maift glaidnefs and my game,
I fall remember Jerufalem,
 And all my hart vpon it fet.

O Lord, think on the Edometis,
 How thay did at Jerufalem;
Thay bad deftroy with cruelteis,
 Put all to fack, and it ouirquhelme:
Bot wrakkit fall thow be, Babylon;
And bliffit is that campion
 Sall ferue thé as thow feruit vs:
And he that fall thy barnis plaig,
And rafche thair harnis aganis a craig,

G. ij

Is happy and full glorious.
FINIS.

Exaltabo te. Pſal. cxliiii.

I WILL thé loue, my gracious Lord and King,
Thankand thy Name, for euer will I ſing;
All tyme I will rejoyce and ſing to thé,
   And pryſe thy name alſo perpetuallie.
Greit is the Lord, and all laude dois excell,
   And his greit micht quha can diſcryue or tell?
Ane generation thy warkis dois declair
   Unto ane vther, and als thy greit powair,
Thy gloir, thy greitnes, and thy magnificence,
   Thy nobill actis digne of rememberance,
I will furth ſchaw thy meruellis ſa greit,
   Thy magnitude I will it put in dyte.
Memorie als of thy greit gentilnes,
   We ſall ay ſing, and of thy richteouſnes.
The Lord is meik, and mercyfull is he,
   Slaw to reuenge, and to forgiue reddie;
Courtes and kynde till all men is the Lord,
   In all his warkis [he is] miſericord;
And all thy warkis do thank thé thairfoir,
   And all thy Sanctis to thy name gif gloir.
The glorioufnes of thy Kingdome [they] teiche,
   And with thair toung thy greit power preiche
Till all natiounis, thy magnitnde and micht,
   Of thy riche renoun the heuinly luſum licht.
Thy royall realme, is realme of realmes all
   And thy impyre indure for euer ſall.
The Lord is help to thame that ſlyde and ſtummer
   Them that troublit ar bringis out of cummer.
                                 All

All mennis eine, O Lord, do thé abyde,
  Thow feidis them in all tyme and tyde.
Thow oppinnis furth thy hand ful graciouslie,
  And satiffyis all flefhe aboundantlie.
In all his wayis the Lord is juft and richt,
  In all his warkis is sanctifyit his micht,
Till all call on the Lord, he is full neir,
  Sa that in trew beleif be thair prayer.
He grantis thair defyre that dreidis him,
  And heiris thame, and forgeuis thair sin.
All thame that luffis the Lord, he sauis thame,
  And he confoundis all fort of wickit men.
The louing of the Lord my mouth sall found;
  All louing men in to this warld sa round,
Sall loue thy name perpetuall, and moir,
  Gif moir may be, regnand into thy gloir.
    FINIS.

Deus venerunt gentes. Pfal. lxxvii.

THE Hethin folk, Lord, in thy heritage,
  Hes cum in til exerce thair tyrannie,
And hes defylit euer, to this aige,
  The Tempill quhilk was dedicat to thé,
  Quhilk haly was, and zit fall bliffit be.
Jerufalem, as appillis, lay in heip:
Bot thow, gude Lord, ryfe vp, and na mair fleip.
Thair tyrannie aganis thy commandis,
  Richt cruellie exerfit in difpyte,
Hes put to deid thy juft and trew feruandis,
  The foulis of the heuin with grit delyte
    Did eit thair flefhe, and beiftis fair culd byte
          G. iij

Thair bodyis, quhen thay lay in commoun ſtreit:
Jeruſalem thairfoir richt ſair did weip.

Thair blude was ſched, as riueirs of a well,
   That compaſt hes Jeruſalem about.
Nane was that micht thair tyrannie expell,
    Aganis them it was ſa ſtrang and ſtout:
    Thair bodyis, throw thair danger and greit dout,
Unburyit was, voide of all ſepulture,
That nane to bury them wald tak the cure.

Our nichtbouris, Lord, hes mockit vs with ſcorne,
    And leuch at vs with greit illuſioun:
Bot thow, gude Lord, let vs not be forlorne;
    How lang ſall we remaine in confuſioun?
    Will thow vs hald in thair abuſioun?
Vnto the end, ſall thy wraith burne as fyre?
Allace! gude Lord, remuſe fra vs ſic ire.

Rather caſt furth thy greif and cruelnes
   On wickit men, quhilk neuer will thé knaw;
And realmes quhilk miſknaw thy godlynes,
   Not hauand E vnto thy godly law.
   For Jacob and his hous thae ſair ouirthraw,
And hes vs left all follit into cair,
Beleuand for to bring vs to diſpair.

Auoyde, Lord, furth of thy remembrance,
   Our ſinfull lyfe that we haue ſleipit in:
Our will ſalbe thy mercy to aduance,
   For be the ſamin remittit is our ſin:
   And as water [that] faſt rinnis ouir ane lin,
Dois not returne againe to the awin place,

Sa thow, gude Lord, put our ſin from thy face.

Help vs, gude Lord, our gyde and gouernour;
    Delyuer vs for thy names faik glorious:
Thow art our hope, our help, and Sauiour,
    And als our ſinnis maiſt dangerous
    Dois put away, for that thow promeiſt vs.
Quhen we will turne to thé with a trew hart,
And fra our ſinfull lyfe to thé conuert.

For, ſchaw thow not thy mercy in diſtres,
    Our Enemeis ſall grow in tyrannie,
And ſall ſay, God hes left vs mercyles:
    Bot thow, gude Lord, exerce thy crueltie
    Upon our fais, that ſayis ſchamefullie
Quhair is thair God, in quhome thay did beleif?
He hes them left without help and releif.

The vengeance of the blude of thy feruandis,
    Mot cum into thy prefence and thy ſicht,
The greting of thy pure that ar in bandis,
    In priſoun pynde, of day wantand the licht:
    The voyce of them that to the deid ar dicht,
Heir now, gude Lord, and help them in thair neid,
And be thair ſtrenth at all tymes and remeid.

Rewaird thy fais according to thair wrang,
    Seuinfald thair ſin, gude Lord, mot puneiſt be,
For thay haue blaſphemit all to lang,
    Speikand contrair thy godly Majeſtie:
    Bot we, thy pepill and ſcheip, ſall magnifie,
And als exalt thy laude, thy name and gloir,
And ſall thé loue now and for euer moir.

FINIS.
G. iiij

104 *Haue mercy on me, God of micht.*

Miserere mei Deus. Psal. li.

HAVE mercy on me, God of micht,
  Of mercy Lord and King:
For thy mercy is set full richt
  Aboue all eirdly thing.
Thairfoir I cry baith day and nicht,
  And with my hart sall sing:
    To thy mercy with thé will I go.

Haue mercy on me, O gude Lord,
  Efter thy greit mercie:
My sinfull lyfe dois me remord,
  Quhilk sair hes greuit thé:
Bot thy greit grace hes me restord,
  Throw Christ to libertie:
    To thy mercy with thé will I go.

Et secundum multitudinem.
Gude Lord, I knaw my wickitnes,
  Contrair to thy command,
Rebelland ay with cruelnes,
  And led me in ane band
To Sathan, quha is mercyles:
  Zit, Lord, heir me cryand:
    To thy mercy with thé will I go.

Quhat toung can tell the multitude,
  Lord, of thy greit mercie:
Sen sinners hes thy celsitude
  Resistit cruellie.
Zit na sinner will thow seclude
  That this will cry to thé:
    To thy mercy with thé will I go.
    Amplius laua me.

Thow

Thow wuſhe me, Lord, quhen I was borne,
    From all my wickitnes,
Bot zit I did throw ſin forlorne
    Of heuin the richteouſnes.
Weſche me againe, and from thy horne
    Delyuer me in ſtres :
    To thy mercy with thé will I go.

And fra my ſin thow mak me clene,
    As thow maid Dauid King:
With Peter, Paule, and Magdalene,
    Quha now dois with thé reigne
In heuinly joy, fair and amene;
    And I ſall with thame ſing:
    To thy mercy with thé will I go.

    Quoniam iniquitatem.
Full weill I knaw my wickitnes,
    And ſin contrarious :
Blaſphemit hes thy gentilnes,
    With ſin maiſt dangerous,
And hes me led in heuynes,
    Zit, O God, maiſt gracious :
    To thy mercy with thé will I go.

I grant my ſinfull lyfe did vſe
    In ſenſualitie :
Zit thow, gude Lord, will nane refuſe,
    That will cum vnto thé :
Heirfoir I ſchairply me accuſe,
    Cryand for thy mercie :
    To thy mercy with thé will I go.

    Tibi ſoli peccaui.
Only to thé I did offend,

And mekill euill hes done,
  Throw quhilk appeirandly defence
    To me is nane abone:
Thus men will judge, thy juſt vengeance
  Hes put me from thy throne:
    Zit to thy mercy with thé will I go.

Thocht thow, gude Lord, be judgeit thus,
  Full fals and wrangouſlie:
O God, ſa gude and gracious,
  Let thair judgeing vincuſt be,
And ſchaw thy mercy plenteous,
  Quhilk mot vs juſtifie:
    To thy mercy with thé will I go.

[Ecce enim in iniquitatibus.]
Conſauit into ſin I am,
  My wickitnes thocht thow behald,
Quhilk I contractit of Adame,
  Sinnand richt monyfald.
My mother als·did eik the ſame,
  And I to ſin was ſald:
    To thy mercy with thé will I go.

Bot zit the Lord Omnipotent,
  My cairfull cace did cure,
At font quhen I was impotent,
  Fragill, vaine, vyle, and pure;
Than helpit me that King potent
  In my miſauenture:
    To thy mercy with thé will I go.

Ecce enim veritatem.
Behald thow luſis treuth, gude Lord,

Thow

Thow art the veritie:
This weill thy promeis can record,
   Quhair thow dois it schaw to me,
The hid thingis of thy godly word,
   That war vnsure to me:
   To thy mercy with thé will I go.

Thow hecht to Abraham anone,
   Isaack his eldest sone:
Thow promeist als that Salomone
   Suld bruik King Dauids throne.
To sinners als that callis thé one
   Grace cummis from abone:
   To thy mercy with thé will I go.

Asperges me.
With isope, Lord, thow sprinkill me,
   And then I sall be clene;
And clenar then maid sall I be
   Then euer snaw hes bene,
Zit of my clensen thy mercy
   The rute is euer sene:
   To thy mercy with thé will I go.

This isope is humilitie,
   Richt law in till assence;
The snaw sa quhyte in all degre,
   Betakinnis innocence.
For, and thir twa do gouerne me,
   I sall do nane offence:
   To thy mercy with thé will I go.

Auditui meo dabis.
Then joy and mirth thow sall me geue,

Thy mercy quhen I heir;
My bandis law thow ſall releue,
  And be my ſcheild and ſpeir:
Thy ſword alſo richt ſoir ſall greue
  My enemies with feir:
    To thy mercy with thé will I go.

My hope and traiſt hes bene to lang
  In mennis fals ſupplie,
Quhairfoir I grant I haue done wrang,
  Not hopeand help of thé;
Bot now with ſteidfaſt faith I gang
  Unto thy Majeſtie:
    To thy mercy with thé will I go.

Aduerte faciem tuam.

Fra my ſinnes aduert thy face,
  My wickitnes expell;
Sen I haue hoipit in thy grace
  Thow ſaue me fra the hell:
Thy mercy is ſet in ſicker place,
  Na ſinner can repell:
    To thy mercy with thé will I go.

The theif that hang on the richt hand,
  And ſufferit with thé deid:
In the laſt hour thy mercy fand,
  For ſin the haill remeid.
Siclyke, gude Lord, heir me cryand,
  And help me in my neid:
    To thy mercy with thé will I go.

Cor mundum.

Thow creat in me, O God, ane hart,
  Baith clene and innocent:

And

And let me not from thé depart,
  My God omnipotent:
Sen vnto thé I fchaw my fmart
  Richt pure and indigent:
    To thy mercy with thé will I go.

Renew me with thy Haly Spreit,
  To help my febilnes:
My teiris fall my cheikis weit,
  For my greit finfulnes:
Bot thow, gude Lord, my comfort fweit,
  Expell my wickitnes:
    To thy mercy with thé will I go.

Ne projicias me.

O gude Lord, caft me not away
  From thy perfite prefence,
Sen that I grant my finnes ay
  Hes done thé greit offence;
And I fall prais baith nicht and day,
  Thy greit magnificence:
    To thy mercy with thé will I go.

Tak not from me thy godly Spreit
  In my aduerfitie:
For till my faull it is full fweit,
  Quhen fin befettis me;
And thow fall mak my faull full meit
  Unto thy Majeftie:
    To thy mercy with thé will I go.

Redde mihi.

Giue me the blyithnes and the blis
  Of my fweit Sauiour:
For throw his bitter deid I mis

110 *Haue mercy on me, God of micht.*

Of hell the dyntis dour,
  And in this mortall lyfe, he is
    My ſtrang defence and tour:
    To thy mercy with thé will I go.
Conforme thy Spreit maiſt principal,
  Into me, throw thy grace:
For ſin richt lang held me in thrall,
  And put me from thy face:
Zit vnto thé, my Lord, I call,
  Into my heuie caſe:
    To thy mercy with thé will I go.

    Docebo iniquos.
Then I ſall teiche the wickit men
  Thy wayis juſt and richt:
And thay that did thé lang miſken,
  Sall knaw the God of micht.
Quhen thay ſall ryſe furth of the den
  Of ſin, and cum to licht:
    To thy mercy with thé will I go.

The ſinfull then to thé reuart,
  Sall into gudlie haiſt,
And rew thair ſinnes with thair hart,
  And thair auld lyfe deteſt:
And to them, Lord, thow ſall conuart,
  Quhen they thy mercy taiſt:
    To thy mercy with thé will I go.

    Libera me.
Delyuer me from blude ſchedding,
  For blude betakinnis ſin:
For puniſhment I ſerue conding,
  Zit efter thé I rin:
                      Grant

Grant me that I may with thé reigne,
  And at thy port get in:
To thy mercy with thé will I go.
Than fall my toung thy richteoufnes
  Extoll and magnifie,
Quhen gane is my greit finfulnes,
  And greit iniquitie.
God, for thy grace and gentilnes,
  Grant me thy greit mercie:
To thy mercy with thé will I go.

[*Domine libera mea.*]
My lippis, Lord, then loufe thow fall,
  Quhilk clofit lang haue bene;
From thy louing fair bound in thrall,
  Brekand thy fweit biddene;
And keip me from ane fuddand fall,
  For greit paine I fuftene:
To thy mercy with thé will I go.

And then my mouth fall do furthfchaw
  Thy louing glorious:
And I fall caus all finners knaw
  Thy micht, fa meruellous;
And fra thine furth fall keip thy law,
  Quhilk is fa precious:
To thy mercy with thé will I go.

Quoniam fi voluiffes.
Gif thé had plefit facrifice,
  I fuld them offerit thé:
Bot thow will not fic auarice,
  For thow art wonder fre;
And geuis vs thy benefites,

Throw Chriſtis blude frelie:
   To thy mercy with thé will I go.
Brint ſacrifice is na delyte,
   Unto thy Majeſtie:
Thow curis nocht of it ane myte,
   For ſin to ſatiſſie;
For only Chriſt did mak vs quyte
   Of all ennormitie:
   To thy mercy with thé will I go.

Sacrificium Deo.

Ane ſacrifice to thé pleſand,
   Is ane ſweit humbill hart,
Unto the quhilk, I vnderſtand,
   Thow dois the haill conuart;
Thairfoir, gude Lord, let thy command
   Na way from me depart:
   To thy mercy with thé will I go.

Ane contrite hart do not diſpiſe,
   God, for thy greit mercie:
Sen for thy grace ſa oft it cryis
   For ſuccour and ſupplie:
And it ſall thank ane thouſand fyſe
   Thy godly Majeſtie:
   To thy mercy with thé will I go.

Benigne fac Domine.

To Sion, Lord, be gude againe,
   Efter thy godly will;
And let thy louing thair remaine,
   Thy promeis to fulfill:
For Mont Sion, with greit diſdaine,
   In thrall is hiddertill:
               To thy

To thy mercy with thé will I go.

Jerusalem did get ane fall,
  Hir wallis war maid full law;
For scho miskennit the God of all,
  And daylie brak his law;
Bot thow sall put hir out of thrall.
  Quhen scho hir God dois knaw.
    To thy mercy with thé will I go.

Tunc acceptabis.

Then sacrifice thow sall accept,
  Of treuth and richteousnes,
Conforming to thy trew precept,
  And to they gentilnes:
For na man then sall thow except
  Into thair neid and stres.
    To thy mercy with thé will I go.

Then calfis and brint sacrifice
  Thy altar sall repleit,
Then greitar gloir and benefice,
  Thow sall mak for vs meit;
Quhair, day and nicht, we sall not ceis
  Ay singand Sanctus sweit.
    To thy mercy with thé will I go.

FINIS.

Beati omnes qui timent. Psal. cxxviii.

BLISSIT ar thay that sit in Goddis dreid,
  And liue in his commandement alway:
Of thy hand labour thow sall eit, be not feird,
  And fair weill thow sall euerie day.

Thy wyfe fall be as ane fruitefull wyne,
    And fall weill ay incres thy hous:
Thy barnis all fall to vertew inclyne,
    As fair oliue treis that be plenteous.

Quhen euer thow fittis at thy tabill,
    Thy barnis fall ftand round about thé;
Sa will the Lord mak thé abill,
    And fill thy hous with honeftie.

Sa fall God him euer blis,
    That dreidis him ay in his leuing;
Alway fall he be ficker of this,
    That is neidfull to want na thing.

Fra Sion fall the Lord blis thé,
    That thow may fe to thy greit weill,
How profperous Jerufalem fall be,
    And thow reffauit to greit heill.

Ane profitabill lyfe fall be giuen thé,
    And God alway fall be thy freind:
Thy childeris children, thow fall fe,
    And peace in Ifraell fall thow find.

FINIS.

FOR lufe of one I mak my mone,
    Richt fecreitlie,
To Chrift Jefu, that Lord maift trew
    For his mercy;
Befeiking that fré, grant grace to me,
    Or I be gone;
And to redres my heuines,
    And all my mone:

For lufe of one.

Or I be deid, send me remeid,
   For thy pietie,
O Lord, quhilk wrocht all thing of nocht,
   Grant me thy mercy.
We thé beseik, with wordis meik,
   O mercyfull Lord,
Thy humill word, with ane accord,
   Let be restord
To sinneris all, quhen they do call
   For thy mercy.
For quhilk on Rude thow sched thy blude
   Richt plenteouslie:
Sanct Johne did tell, thow heryit hell,
   And schew mercie;
Ane thousand scoir thow did restoir
   To thy glorie.
O King of peace, in quhome is grace
   Haboundantlie:
My miserabill life, and sinnis ryfe,
   Thow forgeue me.
Sen be na richt, I haue na micht,
   Me to defend
Fra hellis pane, bot giue thow plane
   Me succour send.
Be thy sweit word to me, O Lord,
   In my distres:
Ane thousand syse, than sall I pryse
   Thy halines:
Lat vs now sing, and loue the King,
   For his greit mercie:
And his greit grace, schawin vs the space,

    Sa plenteouſlie.
With ane accord, let vs thank the Lord
    Richt hartfullie:
With hart and ſpreit, ſing pſalmes ſweit,
    Richt pleſandlie.
As brether deir, in this lyfe heir,
    We may indure:
Baith nicht and day, to Chriſt lat vs pray,
    To mak vs ſure.

FINIS.

QVHO is at my windo? quho, quho?
Go from my windo, go, go!
  Quho callis thair, ſa lyke a ſtrangair?
    Go from my windo, go!

Lord, I am heir, ane wretchit mortall,
That for thy mercy dois cry and call
Unto thé, my Lord celeſtiall.
    Se quho is at my windo, quho.

How dar thow for mercy cry,
Sa lang in ſin as thow dois ly?
Mercy to haue thow art not worthy.
    Go from my windo, go.

My gylt, gude Lord, I will refuſe,
And the wickit lyfe that I did vſe,
Traiſtand thy mercy ſall be myne excuſe.
    Se quho is at my windo, quho.

To be excuſit, thow wald richt faine,
In ſpending of thy lyfe in vaine,
Hauing my Goſpell in greit diſdaine.

Quho is at my windo?

    Go from my windo, go.

O Lord, I haue offendit thé,
Excufe thairof thair can nane be:
I haue followit them that fa teichit me.
    Se quho is at my windo, quho.

Nay, I call thé nocht fra my dure, I wis,
Lyke any ftranger that unknawin is;
Thow art my brother, and my will it is,
    That in at my dure thow go.

With richt humbill hart, Lord, thé I pray,
Thy comfort and grace obteine I may:
Schaw me the paith and reddy way
    In at thy dure for to go.

I am cheif gyde to riche and pure,
Schawand the paithway richt to my dure,
I am thair comfort in euerie hour,
    That in at my dure will go.

Bot thay that walk ane other way,
As mony did teiche from day to day,
Thay wer indurit, my Gofpell did fay,
    And far from my dure fall go.

O gracious Lord, comfort of all wicht,
For thy greit power, and cheif excellent micht,
Sen thow art gyde, and verray licht,
    In at thy dure let me go.

    Man, I gaue thé nocht fre will,

H. iij

That thow fuld my Gofpell fpill;
Thow dois na gude bot euer ill;
 Thairfoir from my dure that thow go.

That will, allace, hes my begylit,
That will fa fair hes me defylit,
That will thy prefence hes me exilit;
 Zit at thy dure lat me go.

To blame that will, thow dois not richt,
I gaue thé reffoun, quhairby thow micht
Haue knawin the day by the dark nicht,
 In at my dure for to go.

Lord, I pray thé with all my hart,
Of thy greit mercy remufe my fmart,
Lat ane drop of thy grace be my part,
 That in at thy dure I may go.

I haue fpokin in my Scripture,
I will the deid of na creature;
Quha will afk mercy, fall be fure
 And in at my dure for to go.

O Lord, quhais mercy is but end,
Quhairin ocht to thé I did offend,
Grant me fpace my lyfe to amend,
 That in at thy dure I may go.

Remember thy fin, and als thy fmart,
And als for thé quhat was my part:
Remember the fpeir that thirlit my hart,
 And in at my dure thow fall go.

         And

And it wer zit till do againe,
Rather or thow fuld ly in paine,
I wald fuffer mair in certaine,
    That in at my dure thow micht go.

I afk na thing of thé thairfoir,
Bot lufe for lufe, to lay in ftoir:
Gif me thy hart, I afk no moir,
    And in at my dure thow fall go.

O gracious Lord celeftiall,
As thow art Lord and King eternall,
Grant vs grace, that we may enter all,
    And in at thy dure for to go.

Quho is at my windo? quho?
Go from my windo, go!
Cry na mair thair, lyke ane ftranger,
    Bot in at my dure thow go.
        FINIS.

Deus mifereatur. Pfal. lxvii.

O GOD, be mercyfull to vs,
    And fend to vs thy bliffing;
Thy face fchaw vs fa glorious,
    And be euer to us luiffing;
That men on eird may knaw thy way,
    Thy fauing heill and richteoufnes,
That they be nocht led nicht nor day
    Fra thy preceptis, and trew juftice,
    To feik faluatioun quhair nane is.

Thairfoir the pepill micht magnifie:
 O God, all folke, and honour thy Name;
Let all the pepill rejoyce glaidlie,
 Becaus thow dois richt without blame:
The pepill dois thow judge trewlie,
 And ordouris euerie Natioun:
Thow hes declarit the Eird juſtlie
 Euer ſen the firſt Creatioun,
 Throw thy godlie prouiſioun.

The pepill moſte ſpred thy name ſa hie,
 All pepill (O God) mon giue thé honour;
The eird alſwa richt plenteouſlie,
 Mot incres euer moir and moir;
And God, quhilk is our God ouer all,
 Mot do vs gude and pleſour.
God mot blis vs greit and ſmall,
 And all the warld him honour
 Alway, for his micht and power.

FINIS.

IN till ane mirthfull Maij morning
 Quhen Phebus did vp ſpring,
Walkand I lay, in ane garding gay,
 Thinkand on Chriſt ſa fre:
Quhilk meiklie for mankynde
Tholit to be pynde
 On croce cruellie.   La.   La.
And how he hes me wrocht,
And formit me of nocht,
Lyke his picture, the Lord maiſt ſure,
 In eird he hes me ſupport:
                              Syne

Syne me to hald in richt,
Hes send ane Angell bricht,
 To be my comfort. La. La.

O Sathan fals, vntrew,
Quhilk cruelly dois persew,
With violence, and greit defence,
 In eird to tempt mankynde,
With cruell Sinnis Seuin,
The saull to gyde from heuin,
 To hell for to be pynde. La. La.

Thairfoir (O gracious Lord)
Quhilk mercy hes restoird,
That sinfull wicht destroy his micht,
 Quhilk wirkis aganis thy gloir:
And send thy gracious word,
Thy pepill may be restoird
 We pray thé thairfoir. La. Lay.

 FINIS.

ALL my hart, ay this is my sang,
With dowbill mirth and joy amang;
Sa blyith as byrd my God to fang:
 Christ hes my hart ay.

Quha hes my hart bot heuinnis King:
Quhilk causis me for joy to sing,
Quhome that I lufe atouir all thing:
 Christ hes my hart ay.

He is fair, sober, and bening,
Sweit, meik, and gentill in all thing,

Chrift hes my hart ay.

Maift worthieft to haue louing:
   Chrift hes my hart ay.

For vs that bliffit barne was borne;
For vs he was baith rent and torne;
For vs he was crownit with thorne:
   Chrift hes my hart ay.

For vs he fched his precious blude;
For vs he was naillit on the rude;
For vs he in mony battell ftude:
   Chrift has my hart ay.

Nixt him, to lufe his Mother fair,
With fteidfaft hart, for euer mair;
Scho bure the byrth, fred vs from cair:
Chrift hes my hart ay.

We pray to God that fittis abufe,
Fra him let neuer our hartis remufe,
Nor for na fuddand warldly lufe:
   Chrift hes my hart ay.

He is the lufe of luifaris all,
He cummis on him quhen we call;
For vs he drank the bitter gall:
   Chrift hes my hart ay.
        FINIS.

MY Lufe murnis for me, for me;
   My lufe that murnis for me;
I am vnkynde, hes nocht in mynde,
  My Lufe that murnis for me,

Quha

Quha is my lufe, bot God abufe,
   Quhilk all this warld hes wrocht?
The King of blis, my lufe he is,
   Full deir he hes me bocht.

His precious blude he fched on rude,
   That was to mak vs fre:
This fall I preif, be Goddis leif,
   That fair my lufe murnis for me.

This my lufe come from abufe,
   And borne was of ane mayd;
For till fulfill his Fatheris will,
   Till fill furth that he faid.

Man haue in mynde, and thow be kynde,
   Thy lufe that murnis for thé,
How he on rude did fched his blude,
   From Sathan to mak thé fre.

FINIS.

TELL me now, and in quhat wife,
   How that I fuld my lufe forgo;
Baith day and nicht ane thoufand fyfe
   Thir tyrannis walkins me with wo.

At midnicht mirk thay will vs tak,
   And into prifone will vs fling:
Thair mon we ly, quhill we forfaik
   The name of God, quhilk is our king.

Then faggottis mon we burne or beir,
   Or to the deid thay will vs bring:

It dois them gude to do vs deir,
   And to confufioun vs doun thring.

Allace, zour Grace hes done greit wrang,
   To fuffer tyrannis in fic fort,
Daylie zour leigis till ouergang
   That dois bot Chriftis word report.

Chrift, fen zour Grace wald cry ane cry,
   Out throw the realme of all Scotland,
The man that wald liue faithfullie,
   Ze wald him fuffer in the land.

Then fuld we outher do or die,
   Or ellis our lyfe we fuld lay for it;
And euer to liue in cheritie,
   Be Chrift Jefus, quhilk is our Lord.

Pluk up zour hartis, and mak zow bowne,
   For Chriftis word fe ze ftand for it:
Thair crueltie it fall cum downe
   Be Chrift Jefus, quhilk is our Lord.

Thow King of gloir, grant vs thy blis,
   Send vs fupport and comforting,
Aganis our fais, that biffie is,
   That fchaipis till ftroy baith auld and zing.

In hour of deid grant vs thy ftrenth,
   Glaidly to thoill thair crueltie,
And that we may with thé at lenth,
   Reffaue thy joy eternallie.

FINIS.

Magnificat

My Saull dois magnifie the Lord.

Magnificat anima mea.

MY Saule dois magnifie the Lord,
   My spreit rejoycis gretumlie
In God my Sauiour, and in his word;
   For he hes sene the law degre
   Of me his hand-madin, trewlie:
Behald now, efter this day,
   All generations sall speik of me,
And call me blissit alway.

For he that is onlie of micht,
   Hes done greit thingis vnto me,
And haly is his name be richt:
   As for his endles mercie,
   It duris perpetuallie,
In euerie generatioun,
   And thay that dreidis him vnfenzeitlie,
Without dissimulatioun.

He schawis strenth with his arme potent,
   Declaris him self to be of power:
He scatteris all men of proude intent,
   Euin for thair wickit behauiour,
   Quhilk reignes in thair hartis euerie hour:
He puttis down the michtie
   From thair hie estait and greit honour,
Extolling them of law degre.

The houngrie feidis he with gude,
   And lettis the riche ga emptie:
Quhen his awin pepill wantis fude
   It thinkis vpon his greit mercie,

And helpis his feruandis ane and all,
Euin Ifrael he hes promyfit,
And to our fatheris perpetuall,
Abraham and to his feid.
FINIS.

Chrifte, qui luxes.

CHRIST, thow art the licht, bot & the day,
The mirknes of nicht thow puttis away:
We knaw thow art the verray licht,
That fchynis to vs baith day and nicht.

O haly Lord, we thé befeik,
This nicht vs to defend and keip,
Thy reft and peace be with us all,
Lat neuer na euill thing vs befall.

Na heuy fleip, nor deidly fin,
Lat not our ennemeis vs ouercum,
Nor zit our flefhe giue na confent:
Grant vs our faultis for to repent.

Lord, lat our eine fum fleip do take,
Our hartis all tyme on thé may waik,
Thy richt hand keip us from all euill,
Thy awin feruand that luffis thé weill.

Our defender, to thé we pray,
All ire and malice thow put vs fra,
Thy feruandis gouerne in the fteid,
For quhais ranfoun thow did fair bleid.

Haue mynde on vs, thow Lord Jefu,

In this

Christ is the onlie Sone of God.

In this fals warld that is vntrew;
Thow art defendar of our faule,
Lord, heir vs quhen we on thé call.

Gloir be to God, Father of micht,
And to Chrift Jefus, his Sone fa bricht:
The Haly Gaift that is fa fair,
Keep vs this nicht, and euer mair.

FINIS.

CHRIST is the onlie Sone of God,
    The Father eternall:
We haue in Jeffe found the rod,
    God and man naturall.
He is the morning Star;
His bemis fend he hes out far,
    Bezond vther fternis all.

He was for vs ane man borne,
    In the laft part of tyme;
Zit keipit fcho hir maidinheid vnforlorne
    His Mother that bure him, fyne
He hes hellis zettis brokin,
And heuin he hes maid oppin,
    Bringand vs life againe.

Thow onlie Maker of all thing,
    Thow euerlaftand licht,
From end to end all rewling,
    Be thy awin godly micht,
Turne thow our hartis vnto thé,
And lichtin thame with the veritie,
    That ar far from the richt.

Let vs incres in lufe of thé,
 And in knawledge alſo,
That we, beleuing ſteidfaſtlie,
 May in ſpreit ſerue thé ſo;
That we in hartis may ſauour
Thy mercy, and thy fauour,
 And traiſt efter no mo.

Awalk vs (Lord) we pray thé,
 The Haly Spreit vs geue,
Quhilk may our auld man mortifie,
 That our new man may leue:
Sa will we alway thank thé,
That ſhawis vs ſa greit mercy,
 And our ſinnis dois forgeue.

FINIS.

CHRIST Jeſus is ane A per C,
 And peirles Prince of all mercy;
For he fra me my ſin hes tane,
And is my Sauiour allane.

To ſaue bot he none is, nor ſall,
I out tak nane greit nor ſmall;
To him is na compariſoun:
He is my Sauiour allone.

I ſall him lufe with ſteidfaſt hart,
And for na cauſe fra him depart:
Bot him to ſerue, I me diſpone,
As to my Sauiour allone.

Sa on his grace I will depend,
Quhill Lacheſis draw my life till end;
Syne

Syne leue my saule, quhen I am gone,
To regne with thrinfald God in one.
FINIS.

ALLONE I weip in greit diſtres,
We ar exilit remediles,
  And wait nocht quhy,
Fra Goddis word, allace, allace,
  Uncourteſlie.
Quhair that we ſuld glaidlie behauld,
Our Sauiour, baith zoung and auld,
  Sa pleſandlie;
Now ar we baneiſt monyfauld,
  Uncourteſlie.
Thay may our body fra thé bind,
Sa can thay not our hartis and mynde
  Fixit on thé,
Howbeit we be with dolour pynde
  Maiſt cruellie.
O Antichriſt, we may thé call,
From Goddis word wald gar vs fall;
  Thy crueltie
Wald baneis vs from pleſouris all,
  Uncourteſlie.
Indurit ignorance hes ſlaine,
Thy hart and put vs to greit paine;
  Quhat remedie?
Sen we are baneiſt from Chriſt allaine,
  Uncourteſlie.
FINIS.

THE Lord ſayis, I will ſchaw
My will, and eik my mynde,

The Lord sayis, I will schaw.

Mark weill my Scripture, and my Law,
   Quhairin that thow sall find,
That with my faith I mak ane vow
   And knittis it with ane knot;
The treuth is sa, I lufe thé now;
   Be war I hait thé not.

It was my Fatheris will
   That I suld tak the cure,
For to cum downe in eirth thé till,
   And tak thy vyle nature.
To cleith my precious body pure,
   Sa clene from sin and spot,
For lufe of thé I mak thé sure;
   Be war I hait thé not.

I fand thé loist from blis,
   Throw Adamis sin and pleid:
And quha sa euer wrocht the mis,
   Was nane culd find remeid:
Quhill I my self did chose the deid,
   To saue thé from the pot.
I lufe thé weill, serue me in dreid;
   Be war I hait thé not.

For all the greuous sorrowis soir
   I sufferit, and paine,
To my rewaird I ask no moir,
   Bot thy trew lufe againe.
I am ane husband-man but weir,
   Quhilk labouris for my lot.
I lufe thé weill, I mak thé sure;
   Be war I hait the not.

                     My зock

My zock is wounder fweit,
   And als my burding licht;
All that be with my grace repleit:
   Sall go the way full richt.
I am the rute of all mercy,
   Quhilk neuer fall faid nor rot;
Sen nane thé luffit fa weill as I,
   Be war I hait thé not.

All ze that fair dois thrift,
   Throuch brukilnes of the flefche,
Cum vnto me quhen that ze lift,
   I fall zour faulis refrefche.
Call vpon me, and I fall heir,
   And faif thé from the fchot:
I lufe thé weill, I coft thé deir;
   Be war I hait thé not,

Attend, and tak gude keip,
   To thame that cumis to thé
Into the habite of ane fcheip,
   With fubtell fermonis flie:
For doubtles thay war inwartlie
   Fals wolfis vnder cot:
Renunce thair lawis, and cum to me,
   Trewlie I hait thé not.

Na man fall cum to me,
   Except my Father him draw;
Nor fe my Father in heuin fa hie,
   Bot be me and my law.
Quhairfoir, O man, prent in thy mynde,
   Thir wordis, and this knot,

And wirk as my word dois thé bind:
Be war I hait thé not.
FINIS.

GREVOVS is my forrow,
Baith euin and morrow;
Unto my felf allone,
Thus Chrift makis his mone:
Saying, Vnkyndnes hes killit me,
  And put me to this paine:
Allace, quhat remedie,
  For I wald nocht refraine.

My Father was fa mouit,
And with mankynde fa greuit;
Man was fa wylde and nyfe,
And rageing in all vyce,
That diftroyit he fuld be:
  Than for man I tuke paine;
Allace, quhat remedie,
  For I wald nocht refraine.

Than furthwith, for his faik,
I did his nature tak,
Within ane Virgin pure,
As fchawis my Scripture,
Quhais vnkyndnes dois kill me,
  And puttis me to greit paine:
Allace, quhat remedie,
  For I wald nocht refraine.

Quhen I was bot ane chylde,
With my Mother, maift mylde,

The Jewis did me difpyfe,
And euer mair furmyfe,
With vnkyndenes to kill me,
   And put me to greit paine:
Allace, quhat remedie,
   For I wald nocht refraine.

Thay lykit nocht my leuing,
Praying, fafting, not repreuing,
For quhen that they did fleip,
Than did I fich and weip,
That vnkyndnes fuld keill me,
   And put me to greit paine:
Allace, quhat remedie,
   Zit wald I nocht refraine.

Than at the laft thay tuke me,
And all my freindis forfuke me,
Bot my deir Mother allone,
And my coufing Sanct Johne,
Till vnkyndnes had killit me,
   And put me to this paine:
Allace, quhat remedie,
   Zit wald I nocht refraine.

Firft I was betin lang,
With fcurgis fcharp and ftrang,
And as ane fule mockit,
Euill totcheit and rockit
Till vnkyndnes fuld keill me,
   And put me to that paine:
Allace, quhat remedie,
   I thocht nocht to refraine.

Than to ane croce on hie,
Thay nalit my bodie,
And fyne between twa theifis,
They did me mony greuis,
Till vnkyndnes did keill me,
 And put me to greit paine:
Allace, quhat remedie,
 I thocht nocht to refraine.

And quhen I waxit dry,
And for drink lang did cry,
My comfort was bot fmall,
To fup the bitter gall,
With vnkyndnes thay feruit me,
 And put me to greit paine:
Allace, quhat remedie,
 Zit wald I nocht refraine.

Thus had I neuer reft,
Bot with panis oppreft;
And with ane fpeir full fcharp,
Thay peirfit my tender hart,
Sa that vnkindnes killit me,
 And put me to greit paine:
Allace, quhat remedie,
 For I wald nocht refraine.

For this my greit kyndnes,
Me think, of richt doutles,
Mannis faule fuld lufe me beft,
Sen it my deid hes dreft;
Quhais vnkyndnes hes killit me,
 And put me to this paine:
       Allace,

Greuous is my forrow.

Allace, quhat remedie,
   Zit wald I nocht refraine.

Gif ony ane be heir,
That will buy lufe ſa deir,
Nocht with ſiluer nor gold,
Bot with my blude, beholde
Thy vnkyndnes, man, has ſlaine me,
   And put me to this paine:
Behald this pieteous body
   Thus moſte vnkyndlie ſlaine.

O man, quhome I creat,
Quhy art thow ſa ingrait?
Seing how I am ſpilt,
All onlie for thy gilt;
And with vnkyndnes dois kill me,
   And put me to this paine:
Zit all thy vylanie
   Can nocht mak me refraine.

Quhat ſorrow culd be moir,
Than to ſuffer ſo ſoir,
Of them that knew my lawis,
And wiſt I gaue na caus,
Unkyndely thus to kill me,
   And put me to ſic paine:
Allace, quhat remedie,
   Zit wald I nocht refraine.

Father, forgiue Cayphas,
Pylate, Anna, and Judas;
Pardone all Jurie
           I. iiij

That cryit *Crucifige:*
Thocht vnkyndelie thay flew me,
   And put me to this paine:
Zit thair was na remedie,
   For I will nocht refraine.

My faull in thy handis fre,
My laft will fall be:
O Father, I commit
Into thy handis my fpreit.
Thocht-vnkyndely I die,
   And am put to greit paine,
Zit for mannis remedie,
   I fall ryfe vp againe.

I leue in Teftament,
My body in Sacrament,
For mannis faull to fupport,
And be his cheif comfort.
Thocht man vnkyndely haue left me,
   And flew me with greit paine:
Thair is na remedie,
   My hart will nocht refraine.

Go, hart, I thé bequyeth
To hir that was my deith,
Mannis faul is fcho trewlie,
My hart hir hart fall be:
Thocht fcho maift vnkyndely flew me,
   And put me to greit paine:
Zit thair is na remedie,
   My hart will nocht refraine.

                    The

The laudes of the Lord trewlie
Ze may fing mirrylie,
For all our faulis health,
In euerlafting wealth :
Thocht vnkyndelie ze flew my bodie,
    And did put me to paine;
Ze may perfaue daylie,
    My lufe dois nocht refraine.

My tumbe is frefhe and new,
In fauing I was trew ;
To put mankynde fra dout,
Thair fall be written about,
The Jewis King heir dois ly,
    Quhome vnkyndenes hes flaine;
And focht na remedie,
    For he wald nocht refraine.

O Father Imperiall,
I pray thé in fpeciall,
My deith mannis faull forgiue,
In heuin with me to liue :
Thocht vnkyndely fcho killit me,
    I wald fcho had na paine;
For I had rather die
    For hir faik anis againe.

Ane gentill Admonitioun of Chrift.

ALL pepill leirne of me
   Gentilnes and pietie :
Remember my fober bodie,
Sa woundit and bludie :
Kill na man vnkyndelie,

With sclander nor with paine:
Amend your faultis daylie,
   And from all vice refraine.
FINIS.

JOHNE, cum kis me now,
   Johne, cum kis me now;
Johne, cum kis me by and by
   And mak no moir adow.
The Lord thy God I am,
   That Johne dois thé call;
Johne representit man,
   Be grace celestiall.
For Johne, Goddis grace it is,
   (Quha list till expone the same):
Och Johne, thow did amis,
   Quhen that thow loist this name.
Heuin and eirth of nocht,
   I maid them for thy saik:
For euer moir I thocht
   To my lykenes thé mak.
In Paradice I plantit thé,
   And made thé Lord of all;
My creatures not forbidding thé
   Na thing bot ane of all.
Thus wald thow not obey,
   Nor zit follow to my will;
Bot did cast thy self away,
   And thy posteritie spill.
My justice condempnit thé
   To euerlasting paine,

Man

Man culd find na remedie,
   To buy man fre againe.
O pure lyfe, and meir mercy,
   Myne awin Sone downe I fend,
God become man for thé,
   For thy fin his lyfe did fpend.
Thy attonement and peace to mak,
   He fched his blude maift halie,
Suffering deith for thy faik,
   Quhat culd he do moir for thé?
It plefit Chrift, without defart,
   For his enemie to die,
Suffering a fpeir to peirs his hart,
   The caus was thy folie.
Beleue this, repent thy fin,
   His deith haue euer in mynde,
Remiffioun of fin lyis only thairin,
   To thy Lord be neuer vnkynde.
Quhen he afcendit [he] left him behind
   His word to reid and heir,
Quhen Antichrift wald thé blind,
   That thow fuld giue him na eir.
Bot quhen Sathan was lowfit out of hell,
   And had fet man in my place,
All that he did thow thocht it weill,
   At him thow focht for grace.
Na thing regarding how of me,
   All thing had thair creatioun;
Nor zit quhat Chrift fufferit for thé,
   To redeme thé from dampnatioun.
Bot the abhominatioun of defolatioun

Thow settis in the haly place,
  Be Antichristis sals perswasioun
    My Sonnis passioun to deface.
Quhairfoir my justice mouit me
    My word fra thé restraine,
And to thy lust to giue vp thé,
    To traist in thingis vaine.
In mannis warkis then did thow traist,
    Seiking helth thow wist not quhair,
At thy deith thow did mistraist
    And sa fell in dispair.
Quhen I did draw ony to me,
    My Gospell to profes,
Thow did them slay richt cruellie,
    Thinkand to do me seruice.
Thy seruice sall rewardit be
    With euerlasting paine,
And all that hait my word and me,
    Except thay do abstene.
Thus, quhen thow was in dangerous case,
    Reddy to sink in hell,
Of my mercy and speciall grace,
    I send thé my Gospell.
My Prophetis call, my preicheouris cry,
    Johne, cum kis me now,
Johne, cum kis me by and by,
    And mak no moir adow.
Ane Spreit I am incorporate,
    Na mortall eye can me se,
Zit my word dois intimate,
    Johne, how thow must kis me.

                                      Repent

Repent thy ſin vnfenzeitlie;
  Beleue my promeis in Chriſtis deith;
This kis of faith will juſtifie thé,
  (As my Scripture plainely ſaith.)
Mak na delay, cum by and by,
  Quhen that I do thé call,
Leſt deith do ſtryke thé ſuddanelie,
  And ſa cum nocht at all.
Gif thow cum nocht quhill thow hes ſpace,
  Bot my Goſpell dois contempne,
I will tak from thé my grace,
  And my word will thé condempne.
Of all that cum I will none reject,
  Na creature greit nor ſmall:
For Chriſtis ſaik I will them accept,
  And giue them lyfe eternall.

FINIS.

In te Domine ſperaui. Pſal. xxxi.

LORD, let me neuer be confoundit,
  That firmely do confyde in thé:
Bot let thy juſtice ay be groundit
  With mercy to delyuer me.

Inclyne thine reuthfull eiris in tyme,
  To me that am in miſerie:
And from all ſort of ſin and cryme,
  Thow bliſſit Lord, delyuer me.

Be my defendar, God of grace,
  My gyde, my gouernour, all thre;
And in thy heuinlie dwelling place,
  Of all refuge thow ſuccour me.

For fen thow art my ftrenth and force,
  My hope, fupport, and haill fupplie:
Be thy fweit name, and deid on Croce,
  Thow fall vpbring and nourifhe me.

Thow fall me gyde from gyrne and fnair,
  And byde in fecreit quhair nane may fe;
For thow art keipar lait and air,
  Protectour and defence of me.

My fpreit I rander in thy handis,
  Eternall God of veritie:
Quhilk hes from bailfull Baliallis bandis
  Redemit and delyuerit me.

FINIS.

GO, hart, vnto the Lamp of licht,
  Go, hart, do feruice and honour;
Go, hart, and ferue him day and nicht,
  Go, hart, vnto thy Sauiour.

Go, hart, to thy only remeid,
  Defcending from the heuinlie tour,
Thé to delyuer from pyne and deid;
  Go, hart, vnto thy Sauiour.

Go, hart, but diffimulatioun,
  To Chrift, that tuke our vyle nature,
For thé to fuffer Paffioun;
  Go, hart, vnto my Sauiour.

Go, hart, richt humbill and [full] meik,
  Go, hart, as leill and trew feruitour,

To him that heill is for all feik;
  Go, hart, vnto my Sauiour.

Go, hart, with trew and haill intent,
  To Chrift, thy help and haill fuccour;
Thé to redeme he was all rent;
  Go, hart, vnto thy Sauiour.

To Chrift, that rais from deith to lyue,
  Go, hart, vnto my latter hour,
Quhais greit mercy can nane difcryue;
  Go, hart, vnto thy Sauiour.

FINIS.

OVR Brother let vs put in graue,
And na dout thairof let vs haue
Bot he fall ryfe on Domifday,
And haue immortall lyfe for ay.

He is of eird, and of eird maid,
And mon returne to eird throw deid;
Syne ryfe fall fra the eird and ground,
Quhen that the laft trumpet fall found.

The faull regnis with God in gloir,
And he fall fuffer paine no moir;
For caus his faith was conftantlie
In Chriftis blude allanerlie.

His painefull pilgramage is paft,
And till ane end cummin at the laft,
Deand in Chriftis zock full fweit,
Bot zit is leuand in his Spreit.

The faull leuis with God, I fay,

144 *Our Brother let vs put in graue.*

The body sleipis quhill Domisday;
Then Christ sall bring them baith to gloir,
To ring with him for euer moir.

In eird he hed vexatioun,
Bot now he hes saluatioun,
Ringand in gloir and blis but weir,
And schynis as the sone sa cleir.

Ye faithfull, thairfoir let him sleip,
And nocht lyke Hethin for him weip;
Bot deiply prent into zour breist,
That deid to vs approchis neist.

Quhen cummin is our hour and tyme,
Then we mon turnit be in slyme;
And thair is nane vther defence,
Bot die in hope with pacience.

Thocht pest or sword wald vs preuene,
Befoir our hour to slay vs clene,
Thay can nocht pluke ane lytill hair
Furth of our heid, nor do vs deir.

Quhen fra this warld to Christ we wend,
Our wretchit schort lyfe mon haue end,
Changeit fra paine and miserie
To lestand gloir eternallie.

End sall our dayis, schort and vaine,
And sin, quhilk we culd not refraine;
Endit salbe our pilgramage,
And brocht hame to our heritage.

Christ,

Chrift, for thy micht and celfitude,
That for our finnis fched thy blude,
Grant vs in faith to leue and die,
And fyne reffaue our faulis to thé.
FINIS.

MVSING greitlie in my mynde,
The folie that is in mankynde,
Quhilk is fa brukill and fa blind,
   And downe fall cum, downe ay, downe ay.

Leuand maift part in all vice,
Nouther fa gracious, nor fa wyfe,
As out of wretchitnes to ryfe,
   Bot downe to cum, downe ay, downe ay.

And all this warld to weild thow had,
Thy body perfit and properlie maid,
Zit man, as floure, thow fall faid,
   And downe thow fall cum, downe ay.

Thocht thow war euer eternall,
As man that neuer fuld haue ane fall,
Zit doutles die thow fall,
   And downe fall cum, downe ay, downe ay.

Thocht thow war man neuer fa thrall
Remember zit that die thow fall;
Quha hieft clymmis gettis greiteft fall,
   And downe fall cum, downe ay, downe ay.

Thocht thow war neuer of fa greit degre,
In riches nor in dignitie,

Remember, man, that thow mon die,
  And downe fall cum, downe ay, downe ay.

Thair is na King, nor Empreour,
Duke, nor Lord of greit valure,
Bot he fall faid as lely floure,
  And downe fall cum, downe ay, downe ay.

Quhair is Adam, and Eve his wyfe,
And Hercules, with his lang ftryfe,
And Matuffalem, with his lang lyfe?
  Thay all ar cum downe ay, downe ay.

FINIS.

PRAY God for grace, my lufe maift deir,
  Quhilk bocht vs with his precious blude,
That we him lufe with hairt inteir,
  In welth and want, be land and flude.

Afk, and haue, fayis the Lord;
  Als geue, and geuin fall be to zow.
Quhat fweiter thing may we record,
  Nor thy word, Chrift, firmelie to trow?

Traift we alfwa, baith air and lait,
  With faithfull hope and efperance,
We fall reffaue, efter our eftait,
  All juft defyre but difcripance.

Thairfoir, I think we fuld rejoyis,
  And now greit myrthis mak from the fplene,
Sen we ar chofin to repois
  In faith of Chrift, and lyfe ferene.

Chrift

Chrift our onlie fuccour in diftres;
 In till his grace quha dois confyde,
His grace till him will ay incres,
   Quhen warldlie traift will faill at neid.
FINIS.

DOWNE be zone Riuer I ran,
  Downe be zone riuer I ran,
Thinkand on Chrift fa fre
That brocht me to libertie;
  And I ane finfull man.

Quha fuld be my lufe bot he,
That hes onlie fauit me,
  And be his deith me wan:
On the croce fa cruellie,
He fched his blude aboundantlie,
  And all for the lufe of man.

How fuld we thank that Lord,
That was fa mifericord,
  Be quhome all grace began!
With cruell paine and fmart,
He was peirfit throw the hart,
  And all for the lufe of man.

That gaue him in the Jewis handis,
To brek bailfull Baliallis bandis,
  Firft quhen he began:
Thair gaue him felf to die,
To mak vs catiues fre,
  Remember finfull man.
K. ij

Thay spittit in his face,
All for our lufe, allace!
   That Lord he sufferit than
The cruell panis of deid,
Quhilk was our haill remeid,
   Remember sinfull man.

Loue we that Lord allone,
Quhilk deit on the throne,
   Our sinnis to refraine:
Prayse him with all our micht,
Sing till him day and nicht,
   The gloir of God and man.

Do all that thow art abill,
Zit thow art vnprofitabill:
   Do all that thow can,
Except thow weschin be,
With Christis blude allanerlie,
   Thow art condampnit man.

And sa I mak ane end,
Christ, grant vs all to kend,
   And steidfast to remaine,
Into Christis passioun,
Our onlie saluatioun,
   And in nane vther man.
        FINIS.

WITH heuie hart full of distres,
   Lamenting my greit sinfulnes,
To thé, O Lord, quha may me cure,
Haue reuth on me thy creature.

With heuie hart full of diſtres.

The ſeiknes that is in my fleſche,
Thow may it, Lord, allone depeſche,
And purge it clene, and mak it pure,
And ſaue me thy creature.

For in this ſeiknes I was borne,
And my foirbearis me beforne.
Our ſeiknes on thy back thow bure,
To ſaue me, Lord, thy creature.

This ſeiknes, Lord, it is the ſin,
That I was borne and gottin in,
Proceiding of my vyle nature,
Zit ſaue me ſinfull creature.

Thow may me ſaue, thow may me ſpill,
Baith lyfe and deid lyis in thy will;
Thow art the chirurgiane ſure,
That haillis all eirdlie creature.

Lord, thair is na ſaluatioun,
Bot in thy bliſſit Paſſioun,
As witnes beiris the trew Scripture,
Thow ſaifis all eirdlie creature.

And for the ſame to mak remeid,
Thow ſuſſeit nocht to ſuffer deid,
And mekill mair thow did indure,
To ſaue thy ſinfull creature.

To thé, O Lord, thairfoir I call,
For thy remeid, and euer ſall,
Quhill I be laid in ſepulture,

K. iij

To faue thy finfull creature.

For all the trubill and the paine,
I neuer wrocht fa gude againe,
But was vnthankfull feruiture :
Haue reuth on me thy creature.

Swa onlie thow, gude Lord of peace,
I me fubmit into thy grace,
For of my feiknes, thow may me cure,
And faue thy finfull creature.
FINIS.

WELCVM, Lord Chrift, welcum againe,
   My joy, my comfort, and my blis,
That culd me faue from hellis paine :
  Bot onlie thow, nane was, nor is.

Thairfoir, I may richt baldly fay,
  Geue Chrift, the quhilk hes me redreft,
Be on my fyde, quhilk hes done pay
  My ranfoun, quha can me moleft?

Sen Chrift now hes maid me at one
  With God the Father, and did die
To mak me juft, to gloir is gone;
  Than quhat ar thay can condampne me?

Was neuer nane to me mair kynde
  Nor Chrift, thairfoir I will him pryfe,
Onlie with faule, body, and mynde :
  My hope and traift haill in him lyis.

Bot

O Chriſt, quhilk art the lycht.

Bot that quhilk Scripture hes expreſt,
    Ane ſacrifice Chriſt anis thairfoir
Offerit to God, quhilk ſmellit beſt,
    For my treſpas, I ſeik no moir.

My part is than from ſin to ceis,
    And cleif to Chriſt, quhilk hes ſuppreſt
Sin, deith, and hell, and maid my peace,
    Throw faith in him that I might reſt.
        FINIS.

O CHRIST, quhilk art the licht of day,
    The clude of nicht thow driuis away;
The beame of gloir beleuit richt,
Schawand till vs thy perfyte licht.

This is na nycht, as naturall,
Nor zit na cloud materiall,
That thow expellis, as I heir ſay,
O Chriſt, quhilk art the licht of day.

This nicht I call Idolatrie,
The cloude ouirſpred, Hypocriſie,
Send from the Prince' of all vnricht,
O Chriſt, for till obſcure thy licht.

Quhilk twa hes had dominioun,
Lang leidand to diſtructioun,
The maiſt part of this warld aſtray
Fra Chriſt, quhilk is the licht of day.

Turnand till Goddis infinite,
'Puttand thair hope and thair delyte

152 *O Chrift, quhilk art the lycht.*

In warkis inuentit with the flicht
Of Sathan, contrair to thy licht.

Sum makis Goddis of ftok and ftaine,
Sum makis Goddis of Sanctis baine,
Quhilk war thay leuand heir, wald fay,
Idolateris, do way, do way.

To vs gif nouther laud nor gloir,
O fulis, gif ze fpeir quhairfoir?
We had na thing throw our awin micht,
Bot all we had throw Chrift our licht.

To that exempill fall be Paull
At Liftra, quha rufufit all
Maner of gloir, and this did fay,
Geue gloir to Chrift, the licht of day.

Geue nane to vs, we ar bot men,
Mortall as ze zour felfis may ken;
O fulis, quhairfoir tak ze flycht,
Rinnand fra Chrift, the perfite licht?

Sum makis goddis of freiris caip,
Thay monftouris mot in gallous gaip;
For thay haue led vs lang aftray
Fra Chrift, quhilk is the licht of day.

Sum mumlit Aueis, fum crakit Creidis,
Sum makis goddis of thair beidis,
Quhilk wait nocht quhat thay fing nor fay:
Allace! this is ane wrangous way.

FINIS.

With huntis vp.

WITH huntis vp, with huntis vp,
   It is now perfite day,
Jesus, our King, is gane in hunting,
   Quha lykis to speid thay may.

Ane cursit fox lay hid in rox
   This lang and mony ane day,
Deuouring scheip, quhill he micht creip,
   Nane micht him schaip away.

It did him gude to laip the blude
   Of zoung and tender lammis;
Nane culd he mis, for all was his,
   The zoung anis with thair dammis.

The hunter is Christ, that huntis in haist,
   The hundis ar Peter and Paull,
The Paip is the foxe, Rome is the rox,
   That rubbis vs on the gall.

That cruell beist, he neuer ceist,
   Be his vsurpit power,
Under dispens to get our penneis,
   Our saulis to deuoir.

Quha culd deuyse sic merchandise
   As he had thair to sell,
Onles it war proud Lucifer,
   The greit maister of Hell.

He had to sell the Tantonie bell,
   And pardonis thairin was;
Remissioun of sinnis in auld scheip skinnis,

With huntis vp.

Our faulis to bring from grace.

With bullis of leid, quhyte wax and reid,
  And vther quhylis with grene,
Clofit in ane box, this vfit the fox,
  Sic peltrie was neuer fene.

With difpenfatiounis and obligatiounis,
  According to his law,
He wald difpens, for money from hence,
  With thame he neuer faw.

To curs and ban the fempill pure man,
  That had nocht to flé the paine;
Bot quhen he had payit all to ane myte,
  He mon be obfoluit than.

To fum, God wot, he gaue tot quot,
  And vther fum pluralitie;
Bot firft with penneis he mon difpens,
  Or ellis it will nocht be.

Kingis to marie, and fum to tarie,
  Sic is his power and micht,
Quha that hes gold, with him will he hold,
  Thocht it be contrair all richt.

O bliffit Peter, the foxe is ane lier,
  Thow knawis weill it is nocht fa,
Quhill at the laft, he falbe downe caft
  His peltrie, pardonis, and all.

FINIS.

BANEIST

Baneiſt is Faith.

Baneist is faith now euerie quhair,
　　And fair forthinkis me:
Baneiſt is faith now euerie quhair,
Be the ſchauin ſort, I zow declair.
Allace! thairfoir my hart is fair,
　　And blyith I can nocht be.

Quhair we war wount to go richt glaid,
　　Furth of captiuitie;
Quhair we war wount to go richt glaid,
Now haue thay vs with chargis ouerlaid,
Quhilk bene ſa dampnabill, and ſa ſad,
　　That blyith we can nocht be.

Thay keip the key from vs, allace,
　　Quhairby enter ſuld we:
Thay keip the key from vs, allace,
And puttis vs downe all mercyles;
We ar ouerthrawin in euerie place,
　　That blyith we can nocht be.

Ryſe vp, I pray thé now, ſweit Lord,
　　And from thair crueltie:
Ryſe vp, I pray thé now, ſweit Lord,
Defend vs according to thy word,
Or we ſall periſche be fyre and ſword,
　　That ſhawis the veritie.

　　　　FINIS.

Mvsing greitlie in my mynde,
　　The cruell kirkmen in thair kynde,
Quhilk bene indurit and ſa blind,
　　And trowis neuer to cum downe.

Thocht thow be Paip or Cardinall,
Sa heich in thy Pontificall:
Refift thow God that creat all,
   Than 'downe thow fall cum, downe.

Thocht thow be Archebifchop, or Deane,
Chantour, Chanflar, or Chaplane,
Refift thow God, thy gloir is gaine,
   And downe thow fall cum, downe.

Thocht thow flow in Philofophie,
Or graduate in Theologie,
Zit and thow fyle the veritie,
   Than downe thow fall cum, downe.

Thocht thow be of Religioun,
The ftraiteft in all regioun,
Zit and thow glaik or gagioun
   The treuth, thow fall cum downe.

Quhair is Chore, and Abirone,
Jamnes, Jambres, and Dathane, becum?
To refift God, quhilk maid thame bowne,
   Ar thay nocht all cumit downe?

And quhair is Balaamis fals counfell?
Quhair is the prophetis of Jefabell?
And Bellis preiftis? be Daniell
   Downe thay war all brocht, downe.

And mony ma I culd zow fchaw,
Quhilk of thair God wald ftand na aw,
Bot him refiftit and his law,
                          And

And downe thay ar cum, downe.

Thair is na king nor empriour,
Erle nor duke, of greit valure,
From tyme ze knaw thair fals errour,
   Bot he fall pluck thame downe.

Ophni and Phenis gat na grace,
Hely brak his nek, allace!
And his offspring put fra thair place:
   King Salomone put thame downe.

And king Achab and Helyas
The fals prophetis diftroyit hes;
And als the nobill Jofias,
   Put all fals prophetis downe.

Is thair na ma? quhy faid I all?
Zit mony thoufand fall haue ane fall,
Quhilk haldis Chriften men in thrall,
   Princes fall put thame downe.

Wald thay na mair impunge the treuth,
Syne in thair office be nocht fleuth;
Than Chrift on thame fuld haue fic reuth,
   That thay fall nocht cum downe.

I pray to God that thay and we
Obey his word in vnitie,
Throw faith warkand be cheritie,
   And lat vs neuer cum downe.

        FINIS.

THE Bifchop of Hely brak his neck,
　　Difherift of his benefice,
Caufe he the Preiftis wald not correct,
　　Corruptand Goddis Sacrifice.
　　Sen our Hely in his office,
Is lyke in preuaricatioun:
　　He fall reffaue fic lyke juftice,
Mak he nocht reformatioun.

The Leuittis, at thair awin hand,
　　Thay reft thair teind, and mekill mair,
Expres aganis Goddis command;
　　Thair huredome haitit he richt fair.
　　Thairfoir, God fend thame fic cruell weir,
Thay tint the feild, the Ark was tane:
　　Hely fell downe, throw fuddand feir,
And brak his neck and coller bane.

Ophni and Phenis, zour confcience remord,
　　Amend zour lyfe, or in the feild
Ze falbe flaine; and ze my Lord,
　　Quhilk hes the wyte that thay ar keild,
　　Helis jugement falbe your beild;
And als zour mortall ennemeis
　　Sall bruke, withouttin fpeir or fcheild,
Zour office, euin before zour eyis.

For zour abufe may be ane brother,
　　To Pharis als lyke in fimilitude,
As euer ane eg was lyke ane vther,
　　Of Goddis word baith deftitude;
　　And greit God of fanctitude,
Quhais power hes nocht tane ane end,

　　　　　　　　　　　　　　　　Sall

Sall fend with that fame fortitude,
Siclyke to zow, except ze mend.

All the exempillis of the Law
   Ar writtin with greit diligence,
For our faikis, that me ftand aw
   Of Goddis hie magnificence:
   Of this we haue experience,
Of diuers natiounis round about;
   For Inglis Prelatis, Duche, and Dence,
For thair abufe ar rutit out.

Reforme in tyme, leue zour tyrannie;
   Firft mend zour lyfe, fyne leirne to preiche,
Thocht wage our Freiris faine wald lie;
   The treuth will furth, and will nocht leiche;
   For euerie man dois vther teiche,
And countis nocht zour crueltie;
   Except ze mend, I will nocht fleiche,
Ze fall end all mifcheuouflie.
         FINIS.

I AM wo for thir wolfis fa wylde,
   Quhilk neuer will conuert
   Thair fals indurit hart;
Sa lang the warld thay haue begylde,
   And baneift vs from Jefus Chrift.

Greit caufe thay haue for till repent,
   Zit will thay nocht do fo,
   Nowther for weill nor wo:
Thair blindit mynde can nocht confent,
   That we are onlie fauit be Chrift.

160 *I am wo for thir wolfis sa wylde.*

Thair subtill slychtis now ar spyit
   Be Christ the veritie:
   Thair fals hypocresie
Throw all the warld'is now out cryit,
   Quhairwith thay baneist vs fra Christ.

Thay brint, and heryit Christen men,
   And flemit thame full far;
   And said, Thay did bot erre
That spak of the Commandementis ten,
   Or red the word of Jesus Christ.

Heretykis thay did vs call,
   Cursand vs nicht and day,
   The treuth durst na man say.
Trew preichouris war forbiddin all
   To schaw the word of Jesus Christ.

Thay baneist thame in vncouth land,
   Full mony hunder myle;
   Quhair thay in thair exile,
Leirnit better till vnderstand
   The trew word of Jesus Christ.

Nobill Lordis of greit renowne,
   That fauouris the treuth,
   On zour saulis haue reuth,
And put thir Antichristis downe,
   Quhilk wald suppres the word of Christ.

Under cullour of commounweill,
   Thair cloikit subteltie,
   And with greit crueltie,

Efter

I am wo for thir wolfis sa wylde.

Efter thay think to flay and keill
   All that confes the word of Chrift.

For fa thay think to bleir zour eye,
   And fyne at zow to hount,
   And do as thay war wount,
And will exerce thair tyrannie
   On zow, and all that luifis Chrift.

Scotland was neuer in harder cafe,
   Sen Fergus firft it wan:
   The preiftis we may fair ban,
Quhilk hes the wyte that brak the peace,
   For to put downe the word of Chrift.

Ane hundreth thoufand thay wald fe
   Zockit in till ane feild,
   Under their fpeir and fheild;
Bot with the wyfis thay wald be
   At hame, to fmoir the word of Chrift.

Defend na mair thir wolfis fa wylde,
   Sa full of cruelnes,
   Thair cloikit halynes,
Baith men and wyfis fa lang hes fylde,
   And ar the verray Antichriftis.

FINIS.

A LLACE, vnkyndlie, Chrift we haue exilit,
   And of thair fude his flock we haue begilit;
With vanities we haue thame lang deludit,
And in fals beleif hes thame includit:
   And euer this was the blating of our queir,

Fatheris of haly kirk this xv. hunder zeir.

The water of lyfe we gaue them neuer to drink,
Bot ſtinkand pulis of euerie rottin fynk;
For haly Scripture allutterlie we haue mockit,
And with traditionis of men we haue them zockit;
    And euer this was the blating of our queir,
    Fatheris of haly kirk this xv. hunder zeir.

Man befoir God ſa lang we haue preferrit,
Quhill we ſe now almaiſt that all is marrit;
And God him ſelf is greuit and diſpleſit,
And we thairby ar bot lytill eaſit;
    Althocht it be the blating of our queir,
    Fatheris of haly kirk this xv. hunder zeir.

Our blind deſyris ſen we may nocht fulfill,
Welcum, gude Lord, full fair aganis our will;
Zit nocht the les we ſall do as we may,
And efter this luke for ane better day;
    And zit ſalbe the blating of our queir,
    Fatheris of haly kirk this xv. hunder zeir.

We knaw, as did King Saull, our fatell fall;
Zit, quhill we die, Dauid perſew we ſall:
Suppoſe we ſuld wrack our ſelf, and tyne
The feild, and all our kin be hangit fyne,
    Zit ſall it be the blating of our queir,
    Fatheris of haly kirk this xv. hunder zeir.

Lat Moſes preiche to Pharao as he lykis,
Zit ſall the pepill be tormentit lyke tykis,
And neuer depart from Egypt: (giue we may)

We salbe cruellest on the hinmest day.
  Quhen we ar drownit, we sall blait on our beir,
  Fatheris of haly kirk this xv. hunder zeir.

O cankerit cariounis, and O ze rottin stakis,
O stangand edderis, and O ze poysound snakis,
Sen ze will not change zour indurit will,
Knawand zour fault, zit will continew still;
  Sing on guk, guk, the blating of zour queir,
  Fals fatheris of haly kirk, this xv. hunder zeir.

FINIS.

OF the fals fyre of Purgatorie
  Is nocht left in ane sponk:
Thairfoir sayis Gedde, Way is me,
  Gone is preist, freir, and monk.

The reik, sa wounder deir, thay solde
  For money, gold, and landis;
Quhill halfe the riches on the molde,
  Is scasit in thair handis.

Thay knew na thing bot couetice,
  And lufe of paramouris:
And lat the saulis burn and bis
  Of all thair Foundatouris.

At corps presence thay wald sing,
  For ryches to flokkin the fyre;
Bot all pure folk that had na thing
  Was skaldit baine and lyre.

Zit sat thay heich in Parliament,

L. ij

Lyke Lordis of greit renowne:
Quhill now that the New Teſtament
Hes it and thame brocht downe.

And thocht thay fuffe at it, and blaw,
　Ay quhill thair bellyis ryue:
The mair thay blaw, full weill thay knaw
　The mair it dois miſthryue.
FINIS.

WO is the Hirdis of Iſraell
　　That feidis nocht Chriſtis flock;
Bot daintelie thay feid thame ſelf,
　Syne dois the pepill mock.

The ſyllie ſcheip was all forlorne,
　And was the wolfis pray:
The hirdis teindit all the corne,
　The ſcheip culd get na ſtray.

Thay gadderit vp baith woll and milk,
　And tuke na mair cure,
Bot cled thame with the coiſtlie ſylk,
　And ſiclyke cled thair hure.

Thairfoir ſayis God, I will requyre
　My ſcheip furth of thair handis,
And giue thame hirdis at my deſyre,
　To teiche thame my commandis.

And thay ſall nouther feid them ſelf,
　Nor zit hounger my ſcheip:
I ſall them from my Kirk expell,
　　　　　　　　　　　And

And geue thame fwyne to keip.
FINIS.

GOD fend euerie Preift ane wyfe,
   And euerie Nunne ane man,
That thay micht leue that haly lyfe,
   As firft the Kirk began.

Sanct Peter, quhome nane can reprufe,
   His lyfe in mariage led:
All gude preiftis quhome God did lufe,
   Thair maryit wyfis had.

Greit caufe than, I grant, had thay,
   Fra wyfis to refraine:
Bot greiter caufis haue thay may
   Now wyfis to wed againe.

For than fuld nocht fa mony hure
   Be vp and downe this land;
Nor zit fa mony beggeris pure
   In kirk and mercat ftand.

And nocht fa mekill baftard feid
   Throw out this cuntrie fawin;
Nor gude men vncouth fry fuld feid,
   And all the fuith war knawin.

Sen Chriftis law, and commoun law,
   And Doctouris will admit,
That Preiftis in that zock fuld draw;
   Quha dar fay contrair it.
FINIS.

166 *The wind blawis cauld.*

THE wind blawis cauld, furious and bauld,
    This lang and mony day:
But Chriftis mercy we man all die,
    Or keip the cauld wind away.

This wind fa keine, that I of meine,
    It is the vyce of auld;
Our faith is inclufit, and plainelie abufit,
    This wind hes blawin to cauld.

This wind hes blawin lang the pepill amang,
    And blindit hes thair wit;
The ignorant pepill fa lawit bene and febill,
    That thay wat nocht quhome to wyte.

Goddis word and lawis, the pepill mifknawis,
    Na credence hes the Scripture;
Quha the fuith dois infer, preiftis fay thay erre,
    Sic bene thair bufie cure.

Quha dois prefent the New Teftament,
    Quhilk is our faith furelie;
Preiftis callis him lyke ane heretyke,
    And fayis, brunt fall he be.

This cryis on hie the Spiritualitie,
    As nane thame fuld defy:
Bot thair illufioun and fals abufioun
    The pepill dois now efpy.

Quhome fuld we wyte of this difpyte,
    That hid fra vs Goddis Law,
Bot Preiftis and Clerkis, and thair euill warkis,
                            Quhilk

Quhilk dois thair God miſknaw.

Their greit extortioun, and plaine oppreſſioun,
    Aſcendis in the air:
Without God puneis thair cruell vyce
    This warld ſall all forfair.

The theif Judas did greit treſpas,
    That Chriſt for ſiluer ſauld:
Bot preiſtis will tak, and his pryce mak,
    For les be mony fauld.

With wrang abſolutiouns, & deſaitfull pardonis,
    For lucre to thame geuin;
Thay blind vs now, and garris vs trow,
    Sic will bring vs till heuin.

Giue eirdlie pardonis micht be our ſaluatiounis,
    Than Chriſt deit in vaine:
Giue geir micht by Goddis greit mercy,
    Than fals is the Scripture plaine.

Syne for our ſchoir he deit thairfoir,
    And tholit pane for our mis;
Is nane bot he that may ſurelie
    Bring vs to heuinnis blis.

Than be na way, ſe that ze pray
    To Peter, James, nor Johne,
Nor zit to Paule, to ſaue zour ſaule;
    For power haue thay none.

Saue Chriſt onlie, that deit on tre,

  He may baith louse and bind.
In vtheris mo, geue ze traist so,
  On zow blawis cauld the wind.

Now se ze pray, baith nicht and day,
  To Christ that bocht vs deir:
For on the rude he sched his blude
  To saue our saulis but weir.

FINIS.

H AY now, the day dallis,
  Now Christ on vs callis,
Now welth on our wallis,
  Apperis anone:
Now the word of God regnis,
Quhilk is King of all kingis,
Now Christis flock singis,
  The nicht is neir gone.

Wo be vnto zow hypocritis,
That on the Lord sa loudlie leis,
And all for to fill zour foule belleis:
  Ze ar nocht of Christis blude nor bone;
For ze preiche zour awin dremis,
And sa the word of God blasphemis;
God wat sa weill it semis,
  The nicht is neir gone.

Wo be to zow Pharesians,
That regnis zit lyke hie capitanis,
And haldis Christis men in mony panis,
  Richt cairfull is thair mone:
I traist till God ze sall deir by it,
Becaus

Hay now, the day dallis.

Becaus zour falſet is now ſpyit,
And all Chriſtin men ſall cry it:
   The nicht is neir gone.

Wo be to zow, Paip and Cardinall,
I traiſt to God ze ſall get ane fall,
With Monkis, Preiſtis, and Freiris all,
   That traiſtis nocht in God allone:
For all zour greit pomp and pryde,
The word of God ze ſall nocht hyde,
Nor zit till vs na mair be gyde:
   The nicht is neir gone.

Ze gart vs trow in ſtok and ſtone,
That thay wald help mony one,
And nocht till traiſt in God allone;
   I ſay ze leit euerie one:
I wat Sanct Peter, nor Sanct Paule,
Nor zit na Sanct can ſaif zour ſaule,
Thocht mony leſingis mak mony braull:
   The nicht is neir gone.

Ze ſerue to ſtrickin be with roddis,
Becauſe of idolis ze mak goddis;
For all zour joukis and zour noddis,
   Zour hartis is hard as ony ſtone.
Ze will nocht leif zour hypocriſie,
Bot zour deſyris is ay for to lie,
And the Feind away with zow wald fle:
   The nicht is neir gone.

Ze begylit vs with zour hudis,
Schawand zour relykis and zour ruddis.

To pluk fra vs pure men our gudis,
   Ze fchaw vs the heid of Sanct Johne
With the arme of Sanct Geill;
To rottin banis ze gart vs kneill,
And fauit vs from neck to heill·
   The nicht is neir gone.

Requiem Eternam faft thay patter
Befoir the deid, with haly watter;
The lawit folkis trowis the heuin will clatter,
   Thay fing with fic deuotioun.
Ze fay that Saule ze fall gar fanct,
Bot and the money war neuer fa fcant,
Ane penny of zour wage ze will nocht want:
   The nicht is neir gone.

Syne to zow we mon offer
Pundis and penneis furth of our coffer,
And lay it downe vpon the alter
   For the deid of that one.
Anime Omnium, ze will fay,
Syne caft the corps into the clay,
Than haue ze done all that ze may:
   Now the nicht is neir gone.

FINIS.

PREISTIS, Chrift beleue,
   And onlie traift into his blude,
And not into zour warkis gude,
As plainely Paull can preue.
   Preiftis, leirne to preiche,
And put away zour ignorance;
Prais onlie God, his word auance,

                          And

And Chriſtis pepill teiche.
  Preiſtis, cut zour gowne,
Zour nukit bonet put away,
And cut zour tippet into tway:
Go preiche from towne to towne.
  Preiſtis, tak zour ſtaffe,
And preiche the Euangell on zour feit,
And ſet on ſandellis full meit,
Bot caſt zour pantounis of.
  Preiſtis, keip na gold,
Siluer, nor cunze in zour purs,
Nor zit twa coitis with zow turs,
Bot ſchone to keip zow from cold.
  Preiſtis, thoill to preiche,
Sen ze zour ſelfis can preiche na thing;
Or we zour brawling downe ſall bring,
And na mair with zow fleiche.
  Preiſtis, tak na teind,
Except the word of God ze ſchaw;
Thocht ze alledge zour vſe and law,
It is nocht as ze weind.
  Preiſtis, tak na kyis,
The vmeſt claith ze ſall quyteclaime
Fra ſex pure barnis with thair dame,
A uengeance on zow cryis.
  Preiſtis, burne no mo,
Of wrang delatioun ze may hyre,
And fals witnes na mair inquire,
And let abjuring go.
  Preiſtis, all and ſum
Suld call ane Counſell Generall,
And dres all thingis Spirituall;

Bot thair thay will not cum.
 Preiſtis, read and wryte,
And zour fals Cannoun law lat be,
Quhair Papis contrair Scripturis lie,
And contrair Doctouris dyte.
 Preiſtis, pryde zow nocht
Quhat zour Counſellis hes conclude
Contrair the writ and Chriſtis blude,
The quhilk ſa deir vs bocht.
 Preiſtis, curſe no moir,
And now zour hartis na mair indure;
Bot on zour flockis tak cure,
Or God ſall curſe zow ſoir.
 Preiſtis, leif zour pryde,
Zour ſkarlat and zour veluote ſoft,
Zour hors and mulis coiſtlie coft,
And jakmen be zour ſyde.
 Preiſtis, ſober be,
And fecht not, nouther boiſt nor ſchoir;
Miſreule the realme and court no moir,
And to zour kirkis fle.
 Preiſtis, mend zour lyfe,
And leif zour foule ſenſualitie,
And vylde ſtinkand chaiſtitie,
Ane ilk ane wed ane wyfe.
 Preiſtis, pray nae mair
To Sanct Anthone to ſaue thy ſow,
Nor to Sanct Bryde to keip thy cow;
That greuis God richt fair.
 Preiſtis, worſhip God,
And put away zour imagerie,
Zour pardonis and fraternitie,

            To

To hell, the way and rod.
   Preiſtis, ſell na mes,
Bot miniſter that ſacrament,
As Chriſt, in the New Teſtament,
Commandit zow expres.
   Preiſtis, put away
Zour paintit fyre of purgatorie,
The ground of zour idolatrie;
It is neir Domiſday.
   Preiſtis, change zour tone,
And ſing into zour mother tung
Inglis Pſalmes, and ze impunge,
Ze will dyne efter none.
   Preiſtis, preif zow men,
And now defend zour libertie;
For France, and for zour dignitie,
Ze brak the peace ze ken.
   Preiſtis, now confes,
How ze ſa lang did vs begyle,
With mony haly bellie wyle,
To leue in idilnes.
   Preiſtis, I zow exhort,
Zour office to do perfyte;
For I ſay nathing in diſpyte,
Sa God mot me ſupport.

FINIS.

Till our Gude-man, till our Gude-man,
Keip faith and lufe till our Gude-man.

FOR our Gude-man in heuin dois ring
  In gloir and blis without ending,

Quhair angellis singis euer Osan
In laude and praise of our Gude-man.

Our Gude-man desyris three thingis:
Ane hart quhair fra contritioun springis,
Syne lufe him best our saullis that wan,
Quhen we war loist fra our Gude-man.

And our Gude-man that euer was kynde,
Requyris of vs ane faithfull mynde,
Syne cheritabill be with euerie clan,
For lufe only of our Gude-man.

Zit our Gude-man requyris moir,
To giue na creature his gloir;
And gif we do, do quhat we can,
We sall be loist fra our Gude-man.

And our Gude-man he promeist sure,
To euerie faithfull creature
His greit mercy, that now or than
Will call for grace at our Gude-man.

Adam, that our foirfather was,
He loist vs all for his trespas;
Quhais brukkill banis we may fair ban,
That gart vs lois our awin Gude-man.

Zit our Gude-man, gracious and gude,
For our saluatioun sched his blude
Upon the croce, quhair thair began
The mercyfulnes of our Gude-man.

This is the blude did vs refresche;
This is the blude that mon vs wesche:
The blude that from his hart furth ran,

Maid vs fré airis till our Gude-man.

Now let vs pray, baith day and hour,
Till Chrift our onlie Mediatour,
Till faue vs on the day that quhen
We fall be judgeit be our Gude-man.
FINIS.

REMEMBER, Man, remember, man,
That I thy faull from Sathan wan,
And hes done for thé that I can:
   Thow art full deir to me.
Is, was, nor fall be none,
That may thé faue, bot I alone:
Onlie thairfoir beleue me on,
   And thow fall neuer die.

Wolfis, quhome of my Euangeliftis wryte,
And Paull and Peter did of dyte,
Allace, haue zow diffauit quyte
   With fals hypocrifie!
My New Teftament, plaine and gude,
For quhilk I fched my precious blude,
Zour only hope and faullis fude
   Thay hald for herifie.

And hes fet up the fals doctrine,
For couetife, in fteid of mine,
With fyre and fword defendis it fyne,
   Contrair my word and me.
The Antichrift is cummin but dout,
And hes zow trappit round about;
Furth of his gyrne thairfoir cum out,

Gif ze wald lauit be.

His pilgramage and purgatorie,
His worſchipping of imagerie,
His pardounis and fraternitie,
   With zeill and gude intent,
The quhiſperit ſinnis callit eir confeſſioun,
With his Preiſtis mummillit abſolutioun,
And mony vther fals abuſioun,
   The Paip hes done inuent.

With Meſſis ſauld be Preiſt and Freir]
For land and money wounder deir,
Quhilk is the ground-ſtane of thair Queir,
   And rute of all thair pryde;
His Pater-noſteris bocht and ſauld,
His numerat Aueis, and Pſalmes tauld,
Quhilk my New Teſtament, nor my Auld,
   On na wayis can abyde.

Thair half hag matines faſt thay patter,
Thay geue zow breid, and ſellis zow watter;
His curſingis on zow als thay clatter,
   Thocht thay can hurt zow nocht.
Giue ze will geue thame caip or bell,
The clink thairof thay will zow ſell,
Suppoſe the ſaule ſuld ga to hell,
   Ze get na thing vnbocht.

Thay ſell zow als the Sacramentis ſeuin,
Thay micht haue maid aſweill aleuin,
Few or mony, od or euin,
   Zour purſis for to pyke,

Wald

Wald thay let bot twa vſit be,
Of Baptiſme, and of my Bodie,
As thay war inſtitute be me,
   Men wald thame better lyke.

Mariage is ane bliſſit band,
Quhilk I gaue man in my command
To keip, bot thay my word withſtand,
   Ane Sacrament it maid:
Unto thair vther Sacramentis fyue,
Our Saluatioun thay aſcryue,
Fra my trew faith zow for to dryue,
   In vaine to mak my deid.

Thair tryflis all ar maid be men,
Quhilk my Goſpell did neuer ken;
My Law and my Commandementis Ten
   Thay hid from mennis eine.
My New Teſtament thay wald keip downe,
Quhilk ſuld be preichit fra towne to towne,
Cauſe it wald cut thair lang tailit gowne,
   And ſchaw thair lyues vnclene.

And now thay ar with dolour pynde,
And lyke to raige out of thair mynde,
Becauſe fra thame ze ar declynde,
   And will na leſingis heir.
Thairfoir, thay mak ſa greit vproir,
Contrair thy flock of Chriſtis ſtoir,
Determit, or thay will geue it ouer,
   To fecht all into feir.

Bot hald zow at my Teſtament faſt,

And be na quhit of them agaft,
For I fall bring doun at the laft
   Thair pryde and crueltie.
Than cleirly fall my word be fchawin,
And all thair falfet fall be knawin,
That thay into all landis haue fawin,
   Be thair Idolatrie.

And ze fall leue in reft and peace,
Inftructit with my word of grace;
For I the Antichrift deface
   Sall, and trew Preichouris fend.
Repent zour fin with all zour hart,
And with trew faith to me conuert;
And heuinly gloir fall be zour part,
   With me to bruik but end.

We pray thé, Jefus Chrift, our Lord,
Conforme our lyues to thy word,
That we may liue with ane accord
   In perfite charitie.
And forgiue vs our finfulnes,
And cleith vs with thy richteoufnes;
Of thy fauour and gentilnes,
   We pray thé that fo be.

        FINIS.

THE Paip, that pagane full of pryde,
   He hes vs blindit lang;
For quhair the blind the blind dois gyde,
   Na wonder thay ga wrang:
Lyke prince and king he led the ring
   Of all iniquitie:

                    Hay

Hay trix, tryme go trix.

Hay trix, tryme go trix,
   Vnder the grene [wod-tree.]
Bot his abominatioun
   The Lord hes brocht to licht;
His Popifche pryde, and thrinfalde crowne,
   Almaift hes loift thair micht;
His plak pardounis, ar bot lardounis
   Of new found vanitie:
Hay trix, tryme go trix, &c.

His Cardinallis hes caus to murne,
   His Bifchoppis borne aback:
His Abbottis gat ane vncouth turne,
   Quhen fchauelingis went to fack:
With burges wyfis thay led thair lyfis,
   And fure better nor we:
Hay trix, tryme go trix, &c.

His Carmelites, and Jacobinis,
   His Dominiks had greit ado;
His Cordeleiris, and Auguftinis,
   ·Sanct Frances ordour to;
Thay fillie Freiris, mony zeiris,
   With babling blerit our ee:
Hay trix, tryme go trix, &c.

The Sifteris gray, befoir this day,
   Did crune within thair cloifter;
Thay feit ane freir thair keyis to beir,
   The Feind reffaue the fofter;
Syne in the mirk, fa weill culd wirk,
   And kittill thame wantounlie:
Hay trix, tryme go trix, &c.

       M. ij

The blind Bifchop he culd nocht preiche,
    For playing with the laffis;
The fyllie Freir behuffit to fleiche,
    For almous that he affis;
The Curat his creid he culd nocht reid,
    Schame fall the cumpanie:
Hay trix, tryme go trix, &c.

The Bifchop wald nocht wed ane wyfe,
    The Abbote not perfew ane,
Thinkand it was ane luftie lyfe,
    Ilk day to haue ane new ane,
In euerie place, ane vncouth face,
    His luft to fatiffie:
Hay trix, tryme go trix, &c.

The Perfoun wald nocht haue ane hure,
    Bot twa, and thay war bony;
The Vicar (thocht he was pure),
    Behuiffit to haue als mony;
The pareis Preift, that brutall beift,
    He polit thame priuelie:
Hay trix, tryme go trix, &c.

Of Scotland Well, the Freiris of Faill,
    The lymmerie lang hes leftit;
The Monkis of Melros maid gude kaill
    On Frydayis quhen thay faftit;
The fyllie Nunnis caift up thair bunnis,
    And heifit thair hippis on hie:
Hay trix, tryme go trix, &c.

Of lait I faw thir lymmaris ftand,

Lyke mad men at mifcheif,
Thinking to get the vpper hand,
   Thay luke efter releif:
Bot all in vaine, go tell thame plaine,
   That day will neuer be:
Hay trix, tryme go trix, &c.

O Jefus! gif thay thocht greit glie,
   To fe Goddis word downe fmorit,
The Congregatioun maid to flie,
   Hypocrefie reftorit;
With Meffis fung, and bellis rung,
   To thair Idolatrie;
Marie, God thank zow, we fall gar brank zow
   Befoir that tyme trewlie.

FINIS.

SAY weill is throuchlie a worthy thing;
Of Say weill, greit vertew furth dois fpring;
Say weill, from Do weill, differis in letter;
Say weill is gude, but Do weill is better.

Say weill is repute be man fum deale;
Bot do weill onlie to God dois appeale:
Say weill fayis godlie, and dois mony pleafe;
Bot do weill leuis godlie, and dois this warld eafe.

Say weill, mony vnto Goddis word cleuis;
Bot for laik of do weill, it quicklie leuis:
Bot gif fay weill & do weill war joynit in a frame,
All war done, all war won, gottin war the game.

Say weill in danger of deith is cauld,

Say weill, and Do weill.

Do weill is harneft, and wondrous bauld;
Than fay weill for feir fall trimbill and quaik;
Do weill fall be jocund, and joly cheir mak.

Say weill is flipper, and makis mony wylis;
Do weill is femely, without ony gylis;
Quhen fay weill at fum tymes falbe brocht bafe,
Do weill fall tryumphe in euerie place.

Say weill to filence fum tyme is bound;
Do weill is fre in euerie ftound:
Say weill hes freindis baith heir and thair;
Bot do weill is welcum euerie quhair.

Say weill mony things in hand dois tak;
Do weill ane end of them dois mak:
Quhen fay weill with mony is quyte downe caft;
Do weill is truftie and will ftand faft.

Say weill him felf will fum tyme auance;
Bot do weill dois nouther jet nor paunce:
Bot do weill dois profite this warld moir,
Then fay weill and his ane hundreth fcoir.

Say weill in wordis is wondrous trick;
Bot do weill in deidis is nymbill and quick:
Lord, quick and trick togidder knit,
And fa fall thay pype ane mirrie fit.

Say weill, mony will thay be sa kynde;
Bot Do weill, few will vnto thair freind:
May Say weill, than do weill, I tell zow in deid,
Bot Do weill is mair honeft in tyme of neid.

FINIS.

KNAW

KNAW ze not God Omnipotent;
　　He creat man, and maid him fre,
Quhill he brak his commandement,
　　And eit of the forbidden tre:
Had not that bliſſit Barne bene borne,
　　　　Sin to redres,
Lowreis, zour lyues had bene forlorne
　　　　For all zour Mes.

Sen we war all to ſin made ſure,
　　Throw Adamis inobedience:
(Saif Chriſt), thair was na creature
　　Maid ſacrifice for our offence;
Thair is na Sanct may ſaue zour ſaull
　　　　Fra ze tranſgres,
Suppois Sanct Peter and Sanct Paull
　　　　Had baith ſaid Mes.

Knawing thair is na Chriſt bot ane
　　Quhilk rent was on the rude with roddis:
Quhy giue ye gloir to ſtock and ſtane,
　　In worſchipping of vther goddis?
Thir idoles that on alteris ſtandis,
　　　　Ar fenzeitnes.
Ze gat not God amang zour handis,
　　　　Mumling zour Mes.

And ſen na Sanct zour ſaull may ſaue,
　　Perchance, ze will ſpeir at me than,
How may the Paip thair pardounis haue
　　With power baith of beiſt and man?
Throw nathing bot ane fenzeit faith
　　　　For halynes;

M. iiij

184 *Knaw ze not God Omnipotent.*

    Inuentit wayis to get thame graith,
        Lyke as the Mes.

Of mariage ze maid zow quyte,
    Thinking it thraldome to refraine:
Wanting of wyiffis is appetyte,
    That curage micht incres againe:
Thay hony lippis ze did perſew,
        Grew gall, I ges,
Thinking it was contritioun trew
        To dance ane Mes.

Giue God was maid of bittis of breid,
    Eit ze nocht ouklie ſax or ſeuin,
As it had bene ane mortall feid,
    Quhill ze had almaiſt heryit heuin:
Als mony Deuillis ze man deuoir,
        Quhill Hell grow les.
Or doutles we dar nocht reſtoir
        Zow to zour Mes.

Giue God be tranſubſtantiall
    In breid with *Hoc eſt corpus meum*,
Quhy war ze ſa vnnaturall
    As tak him in zour teith, and ſla him?
Tripairtit and deuydit him
        At zour dum dres;
Bot God knawis how ze gydit him,
        Mumling zour Mes.

Ze partit with dame Pouertie,
    Tuke Propertie to be zour wyfe;
Fra Charitie and Chaſtitie

With licharie ze led zour lyfe:
That raifit the mother of mifcheif,
   Zour gredynes,
Beleuing ay to get releif
    For faying Mes.

O wickit, vaine Veneriens,
 Ze ar not Sanctis (thocht ze feme haly);
Proude poyfonit Epecuriens,
 Quhilk had na God bot zour awin bellie;
Beleue ze, lownis, the Lord allowis
   Zour idilnes?
Lang or the fweit cum ouir zour browis
    For faying Mes.

Had not zour felf begun the weiris,
 Zour ftepillis had bene ftandand zit;
It was the flattering of zour Freiris
 That euer gart Sanct Frances flit;
Ze grew fa fuperftitious,
   In wickitnes,
It gart vs grow malitious
    Contrair zour Mes.

Our Bifchoppis ar degenerate
 Thocht thay be mountit vpon mulis,
With huredome clene effeminate;
 And Freiris oft tymes preuis fulis:
For Duftifit and Bob at euin,
   Do fa incres,
Hes dreuin fum of them to teine,
    For all thair Mes.

Chriſt keip all faithfull Chriſtianis
  From peruerſt pryde and Papiſtrie:
God grant thame trew intelligens
  Of his law, word, and veritie:
God grant thay may thair lyfe amend,
    Syne blis poſſes;
Throw faith on Chriſt all that depend,
    And nocht on Mes.

Sen Mes is na thing ellis to ſay,
  Bot ane wickit inuentioun,
Without authoritie or ſtay
  Of Scripture or fundatioun:
Giue Kingis wald Mes to Rome hence dryue,
    With haiſtines,
Suld be the meane to haue belyue
    Ane end of Mes.
          FINIS.

WAS not Salomon, the king,
    To miſerie be wemen brocht?
Quhilk wiſdome out of frame did bring,
  Till he maiſt wickitly had wrocht:
A thouſand wemen he did keip,
    Allace, allace!
Quhilk drownit him in ſin ſa deip,
    As come to pas.

Was not Paris maiſt wickitlie
  Be Venus led to Helenis luſt?
For quhilk ſin and adulterie,
  The plagues of Troy war efter juſt:
The ſturdie ſtormis he did indure,
                    Allace,

Allace, allace!
His lufting lyfe was nathing fure,
   As come to pas.

Thocht Troylus Creffed did enjoy,
   As Paris Helene did lykewife;
Zit leuit he not lang in Troy,
   Bot that fortoun did him difpife:
Quha wald then wirk accordinglie,
   Allace, allace!
Sic plefure bringis miferie,
   As come to pas.

Thocht Ouid fayne that Leander
   Aduenterit mekill his lufe to gaine:
Zit dois the poet Menander
   Aduertife vs for to refraine;
For lufting lyfe is nathing ftayed,
   Allace, allace!
Ilk man thairfoir may be afrayed,
   Quhilk is bot gras.

Quhat fall we fay to Pyramus,
   Sic wretchit wo did him affail?
His end in deid was dolorus,
   Quhen fulifche frenfie did preuaill.
Quhat wife man wald his fact commend,
   Allace, allace!
Quhilk brocht his lyfe vnto ane end,
   As come to pas.

Thocht Hercules for Exionie
   A michtie monfter did fubdew;

Ane diſſwatioun from vaine luſt.

Zit endit he in miſerie,
    Gif poetis faining may be trew;
His minſing mate Abderitus,
    Allace, allace!
Ane deith ſuſtenit meruellous,
    As come to pas.

Anaxaretus ſum do ſay,
    Entiſed Iphis outwardlie,
And than withdrew hir lufe away,
    And he him ſelf ſlew wilfullie:
Traiſt the vntraiſtie quha that will,
    Allace, allace!
For ſic my ſelf I will not kill
    As his lufe was.

Thocht Jupiter tranſformit him
    Alcumena for to defile;
The fenzeit goddis thay ſcornit him
    For lyke offence within a quhyle;
For quhen he lay in Venus lap,
    Allace, allace!
Vulcanus tuke him in ane trap,
    As come to pas.

Thus, bewtie breidis bitternes,
    And bringis baill to mony men;
Quha is led be wilfulnes,
    Sall feill the force of bewtie then:
For ſum being taken in the traine,
    Allace, allace!
Ar led to penurie and paine,
    As come to pas.

                                      Thocht

Thocht Cato, prince of prudent price,
  In welthie ſtate did lang remaine;
Zit be the chance of Fortounis dice,
  Mekill miſerie he did ſuſtaine.
His weddit wyfe did wirk him wo,
        Allace, allace!
Mekill mair thir beiſtis quhilk cum and go,
        Pas and repas.

Tiberius the empriour,
  Be his wyffis greit adulterie,
Loſte his pompe and puiſſant power,
  Ending his lyfe in miſerie.
Cheis weill thairfoir, leiſt ze do ſay:
        Allace, allace!
Lat thir and vther[is] at this day,
        Be as thy glas.

Althocht Marcus Antonius
  Was ſene in Coſmographia;
Zit was his end maiſt dolorus,
  Be that fals harlot Fauſtina:
Tak heid, thairfoir, of this be war,
        Allace, allace!
Be thow not ſnaird in Venus ſnair,
        In ony caſe.

Althocht Sextus Tarquinius
  Defylit chaiſt Lucreſia,
He, and his father Superbus
  From Rome war baniſchit away;
A juſt rewaird for ſic offence:
        Allace, allace!

Lyke punifchment for lyke offence,
    Oft cummis to pas.

Thocht fubtill Sardanapalus,
    A Prince was picht to rewle and reigne;
Zit, war his factis fa licharus,
    That euerie man micht fe them plaine:
At Babylon he did defyre,
    Allace, allace!
To fet the haill Caftell on fyre,
    Quhair brunt he was.

Ptholomeus Philopater,
    The michtie king of Egypt land,
Being a michtie conquerer,
    His luft vnto a wenche did ftand;
His weddit wyfe he put to deith,
    Allace, allace!
Thus Princes oft do fpend thair braith,
    As come to pas.

Phifco, lykewife, the lychorus,
    Quhilk children be his fifteris had,
That gat Heliogabalus,
    Quhais lyfe in luft was fpent to bad:
Defyling mayd and wyfe alfo,
    Allace, allace!
Harlottis with him micht ryde and go,
    Quhair he did pas.

Althocht Caius Caligula
    All his awin fifteris did defyle;
And thocht him felf in quyet ftay,
                             Poffeffing

Poſſeſſing pleſure for ane quhyle:
Zit his men did his deith conſpyre,
   Allace, allace!
This wretchit man he had his hyre,
   As come to pas.

Exampillis takin out of the Bybill.

WITH Bybill materis to begin,
   Hiſtoryis mony we may find,
How luſting lufe, that laithſum ſin,
   The oppin eyis of ſum do blind.
Thocht Sichem Dina had defylde,
   Allace, allace!
Baith he and Heymor war begylde,
   As come to pas.
Did not daintie Dalilay
   The michtie Sampſon bring to nocht?
Quhen he his ſecreit heid did wray,
   In Venus ſnair ſcho had him caucht.
Did not Apame, in lyke caſe,
   Allace, allace!
Straik that greit king vpon the face,
   As come to pas.
Thocht Ammon did his mynde fulfill
   Upon his ſiſter Thamar deir,
Zit Abſolon his blude did ſpill
   Schortly efter, as dois appeir.
Thocht Dauid was the Lordis elect,
   Allace, allace!
With Bethſabe he was infect,
   As come to pas.

192 *Exampillis takin out of the Bybill.*

Thocht Holofernes luſtit lang,
 To haue to do on Judethis bed;
His luſting lyfe did happin wrang,
 And ſcho did ſone ſtryke of his heid.
Quhat wyne and women do zow ſe,
 Allace, allace!
Walk and wander with modeſtie,
 In ony caſe.

Thocht Judas did with Thamar ly,
 Quhilk was his dochter be the Law;
The Geneſis dois teſtifie,
 Juſt Joſephis gude and godlie aw,
Quhen his lordis wyfe wald him conſtraine,
 Allace, allace!
He maid her purpois haillely vaine,
 As come to pas.

Of him let vs exampill tak,
 And never think on Cupides dart:
Venus can nouther mar nor mak,
 Gif vnto God we joyne our hart;
And leif this airt of langing luſt,
 Allace, allace!
And in the Lord haue hope and truſt,
 Quhilk is and was.
 F I N I S.

ALL my Lufe, leif me not,
 Leif me not, leif me not;
All my Lufe, leif me not,
 Thus myne alone:
With ane burding on my bak,

 I may

All my Lufe, leif me not.

I may not beir it I am fa waik;
Lufe, this burden from me tak,
   Or ellis I am gone.

With finnis I am ladin foir,
   Leif me not, leif me not;
With finnis I am ladin foir,
   Leif me not alone.
I pray thé, Lord, thairfoir
Keip not my finnis in ftoir,
Lowfe me or I be forloir,
   And heir my mone.

With thy handis thow hes me wrocht,
   Leif me not, leif me not;
With thy handis thow hes me wrocht,
   Leif me not alone.
I was fauld, and thow me bocht,
With thy blude thow hes me coft,
Now am I hidder focht
   To thé, Lord, alone.

I cry, and I call to thé,
   To leif me not, to leif me not;
I cry, and I call to thé,
   To leif me not alone.
All thay that ladin be,
Thow biddis thame cum to thé;
Than fall thay fauit be,
   Throw thy mercy alone.

Thow faues all the penitent,
   And leifis them not, and leifis them not;

All my Lufe, leif me not.

Thow saifis all the penitent,
  And leifis thame not allone:
All that will thair sinnis repent
Nane of thame salbe schent;
Suppose thy bow be reddy bent,
  Of thame thow killis none.

Faith, Hope, and Cheritie,
  Leif me not, leif me not;
Faith, Hope, and Cheritie,
  Leif me not allone:
I pray thé, Lord, grant me,
Thir godly giftis thre;
Than sall I sauit be,
  Dout haue I none.

To the Father be all gloir,
  That leifis vs not, that leifis vs not;
To the Father be all gloir,
  That leuis vs not allone.
Sone and Haly Gaist, euer moir,
As it was of befoir;
Throw Christ our Sauiour,
  We are saif euerie one.

FINIS.

Of the Day of Judgment.

ALL Christin and faithfull in hart, be joyfull;
  Rejoyce, and mak gude cheir;
Be merie and glaid, and be no moir sad,
  The day of the Lord drawis neir.
Under protestatioun, with line and correctioun,
                                                That

That nane be offendit heir,
I will fpeik planelie, to rais zour hartis quiklie;
The day of the Lord drawis neir.

All Paipis and Prelatis, and Spirituall eſtaitis,
  That thinkis ze haue na peir,
Caſt away zour wairis, zour princelie effairis;
  The day of the Lord drawis neir.

O hirdis of Iſrael, heir ze the Lordis bell
  Knelland faſt in zour eir,
Quhilk biddis in plaine, leue zour triffillis vane;
  The day of the Lord drawis neir.

Perſonis that hes cure to preiche vnto the pure,
  Ze haue zour waigis to deir;
The layit ze will not teiche, nor zit Goddis word [will preiche;
  The day of the Lord drawis neir.

I will zow exhort, in termis richt ſchort,
  Baith Preiſt, Channoun, Monk, and Freir,
To ſlaik of zour ſleuth, & ſchaw furth the treuth;
  The day of the Lord drawis neir.

And ze Brethren all, Eccleſiaſticall
  Serue zour Lord God in feir,
Leue zour ceremonyis of zour awin fund gyis;
  The day of the Lord drawis neir.

Zour coiſtlie reparationis, zour offeringis and ob-
  Zour curious notis in the queir,   [latiounis,
On the day of dreid, ſall ſtand in litill ſteid,
  Quhen the Lordis ſentence drawis neir.

All Chriſtin and Faithfull.

Princes and kingis that ſa ryall ringis,
  That ſuld haue all rewle and ſteir,
Do juſtice equall, baith to greit and ſmall;
  The day of the Lord drawis neir.

On the pure Commounis ſuffer na oppreſſiounis,
  Bot humblie thair plaintis heir,
With extreme juſtice treſpaſſouris puniſche;
  The day of the Lord is neir.

Syne with zour ſword, let furth Goddis word,
  Our heuinly mirrour cleir,
And anker zow ſure on Haly Scripture;
  For the day of the Lord drawis neir.

Erlis, Lordis, and Barrounis, hurt not zour com-
  In body, gudis, nor geir: [mounis,
Do ze the contrair, zour houſis will miſſair;
  The day of the Lord drawis neir.

Be trew to the Crowne, defend zour Regioun,
  That zour foirbearis coft ſa deir,
And euer haue eye vnto zour libertie;
  The day of the Lord drawis neir.

I cry, in generall, on Spirituall & Temporall,
  This lection that ze leir:
Remember alwayis, that ſchort be zour dayis;
  The day of the Lord drawis neir.

That day ſall horribill be, and eik terribill,
  Quhen that juſt Judge ſall appeir,
In his birnand ire, to judge the warld with fyre;
                                            The

The day of the Lord drawis neir.

At ane trumpet blaſt, we ſall be all agaſt,
   Heuin, Hell, Eird, ſall it heir;
Syne ſtand befoir the Juge without ony refuge;
   The day of the Lord drawis neir.

We ſall giue rekning, of our ſinfull leuing,
   We haue ſpendit in all maneir:
As we haue deſeruit, ſa ſall we be ſeruit;
   The day of the Lord drawis neir.

That day the faithfull ſalbe richt joyfull,
   Befoir Chriſt quhen thay compeir;
Bot the vnfaithfull ſalbe richt wofull,
   Quhen the Lordis ſentence drawis neir.

To vnbeleuaris all, this ſentence giue he ſall,
   With ire and awfull cheir,
Pas ze to the Hell, with Deuillis to dwell,
   The Heuin ze ſall neuer cum neir.

The juſt ſall all ſtand, euin at his richt hand,
   Defendit from all dangeir;
To quhome he ſall ſay, richt ſweitly that day,
   The ſentence quhilk drawis neir.

Cum heir my elect, and my awin ſweit ſect,
   Zour hyre ſall not be in weir;
Baith ſaull and body, in heuin eternallie,
   Thay ſall dwell with me richt neir.

Quhairfoir, I do call on all men mortall,

To ryis and be neuer sweir,
  Bot euer be war of the wofull snair;
    The day of the Lord drawis neir.

Awalk ay, and pray, baith in nicht and day,
  To Christ, that coft vs all deir,
To be our Mediatour in that feirfull hour,
  Quhen the day of the Lord drawis neir.

FINIS.

BLENK in this Mirrour, man, and mend,
  For heir thow may thy exempill se;
To all mankynde it is weill kend,
  That euer come hidder, that he mon die:
  And fra this dome he may not fle,
Suppois he haue land and gold to spend;
  Array zow all, and reddy be:
Blenk in this Mirrour, man, and mend.

Heir is the ressoun, quha lykis to reid,
  This day thow was ane King with croun,
The morne cummis Deith withouttin dreid,
  Commandis thé to his presoun:
  Richt suddanely he drawis thé doun,
Thow wait that thow mon with him wend;
  Thairfoir, leif weill, be reddy bowne:
Blenk in this Mirrour, man, and mend.

Thair is nane in stait sa hie,
  Prince, King, nor Empreour,
Fra this dome ane fute may fle,
  For all his gold and his valour:
  Thairfoir, thow blenk in this Mirrour,
                                    That

That is graciouſlie to thé ſend;
 Think on the ſweit, and als the ſour:
Blenk in this Mirrour, man, and mend.

Behald now to thir men of micht,
 That mekill hes, and wald haue mair,
And to thair ſembling tak gude ſicht,
 How that thay pas away ſa bair;
 And ſet not by how that we fair,
That winnis all that thay ſpend,
 Richt buſilie baith late and air:
Blenk in this Mirrour, man, and mend.

Sen thow wait that thow mon pas,
 And thow wait nouther quhen nor quhair,
And thy body ſall turne in aſſe,
 That thow now feidis vp ſa fair;
 Confes thy ſinnis les and mair
Unto thy God, or thow hyne wend,
 And till him leyne for euer mair:
Blenk in this Mirrour, man, and mend.

FINIS.

O MAN, ryſe vp, and be not ſweir,
 Prepair aganis this gude New Zeir.
 My New Zeir gift thow hes in ſtoir,
Sen I am he that coft thé deir:
 Gif me thy hart, I aſk no moir.

Gif me thy hart, for I ſuld haue it;
It is my richt, thairfoir I craif it:
 To win the ſamin, I ſufferit ſoir,
And now am reddy to reſſaue it:

N. iiij

200 *O Man, ryse vp, and be not sweir.*

Gif me thy hart, I ask no moir.

I am the Lord maid thé of nocht,
Lyke my awin image hes thé wrocht;
 Thé to all frelage I did restoir:
Sen my hart blude thy hart hes bocht,
 Gif me thy hart, I ask no moir.

I come in eirth, and thair did dwell,
I send na message bot my sell,
 Thé to relief of deidly soir:
Sen I haue fred thé from the hell,
 Gif me thy hart, I ask no moir.

I haue thé fred from all thirlage,
And hes preparit thyne heritage,
 Quhair deith sall neuer thé deuoir:
And now am cummin to craif my wage;
 Gif me thy hart, I ask no moir.

Be war, I am ane jelous God,
I am na image, stock nor wod;
 Thairfoir giue nane of thay my gloir,
Sen I to heuin mon be the rod:
 Gif me thy hart, I ask no moir.

Let be thy sculptill honouris vaine,
Quhilkis ar confoundit and prophaine,
 And swa ar all dois them adoir,
As testifyis Dauid in Scripture plaine:
 Gif me thy hart, I ask no moir.

Sen this last zeir thow hes offendit,
Contrair

O Man, behald this warldis vaniteis.

Contrair my law thy lyfe hes fpendit,
  My mercy is reddy zit as of befoir:
In this New Zeir all may be amendit:
  Gif me thy hart, I afk no moir.

FINIS.

O MAN, behald this warldis vaniteis,
  The joy of it I wait is fantafie;
Thairfoir be war, my counfell now it is:
  Be glaid in God, for doutles thow mon die.

Think thow art cum, and wait not quhen to pas;
  Think thow mon change, & wait not quhair to be:
Think quhy thow come, & quhat thy erand was:
  Be weill auyfit, for doutles thow mon die.

Auife thé weill, quhill thow hes tyme & fpace,
  Exempill tak daylie, as thow may fe;
Quhen deith cummis thair is na vther grace,
  Bot zeild thé than, for doutles thow mon die.

Zeild thé to God, with humbill hart contrite,
  In cheritie, lufe as thow wald lufit be;
Gif thow wald leif without this warldis defpite,
  Remember on this, for doutles thow mon die

Remember vpon thy God Omnipotent,
  That is, and was, and euer moir falbe;
And for thy fin he faikleflie was fchent;
  Be kynde againe, for doutles thow mon die.

Be kynde againe for heuin celeftiall,
  Quhair gloir and joy without end fall be;

Be kynde, and dreid the cruell paine of hell;
   Cheis thee the ane, for doubtles thow mon die.
FINIS.

SEN throw Vertew increſſis dignitie,
   And vertew is flour and rute of Nobles ay,
Of ony wit, or quhat eſtait thow be,
   His ſteppis follow, and dreid for none effray:
   Eject vice, and follow treuth alway;
Lufe maiſt thy God that firſt thy lufe began,
And for ilk inche he will thé quyte ane ſpan.

Be not ouir proude in thy proſperitie,
   For as it cummis, ſa will it pas away;
The tyme to compt is ſchort, thow may weill ſe,
   For of grene greſs ſone cummis wallowit hay.
   Labour in treuth, quhilk ſuith·is of thy fay;
Traiſt maiſt in God, for he beſt gyde thé can,
And for ilk inche he will thé quyte ane ſpan.

Sen word is thrall, and thocht is only fre,
   Thow dant thy toung, that power hes and may,
Thow ſteik thy ene fra warldis vanitie:
   Refraine thy luſt, and harkin quhat I ſay:
   Graip or thow ſlyde, and keip furth the hie way,
Thow hald thé faſt upon thy God and man,
And for ilk inche he will thé quyte ane ſpan.
FINIS.

Quod King James the Firſt.

THE TABILL

A.

ALL meit and drink was creat	16
All Chriſtin men tak tent and leir	22
Allace, that ſame ſweit face	56
At the Riuers of Babylon	99
All my hart, ay this is my ſang	121
Allone I weip in greit diſtres	129
All pepill leirne of me	137
Allace, vnkyndlie, Chriſt we haue exilit	161
All my Lufe, leif me not	192
All Chriſtin and faithfull	194

B.

BLISSIT is he quhome God dois correct	28
Be blyith, all Chriſtin men, and ſing	40
Blis, bliſſit God	65
Bliſſing, gloir, wiſdome	66
Bliſſit ar thay that ſit in Goddis dreid	113
Baneiſt is faith now euerie quhair	155
Blenk in this Mirrour, man, and mend	198

C.

CHRIST baptiſt was be Johne	12
Cum heir, ſayis Goddis Sone to me	25
Chriſt gaue him ſelf to deid	52
Chriſt, thow art the licht	126
Chriſt is the onlie Sone of God	127
Chriſt Jeſus is ane A per C	128

D.
DOWNE be zone Riuer I ran . . 147

E.
EXCEPT the Lord with vs . . 97

F.
FAITHFVLL in Chriſt, vſe zour riches 35
Fra deip, O Lord, I call to thé . . 98
For lufe of one I mak my mone . . 114
For our Gude-man in heuin dois ring . 173

G.
GIF ze haue riſſin from deid againe . 69
God, for thy grace, thow keip no more 90
Greuous is my ſorrow 132
Go, hart, vnto the Lamp of licht . . 142
God ſend euerie Preiſt ane wyfe . . 165

H.
HELP, God, the formar of all thing . 37
Hay, let vs ſing, and mak greit mirth 61
Haue mercy on me, God of micht . . 104
Hay now, the day dallis . . . 168

I.
I COME from Heuin to tell . . . 43
In dulce jubilo 47
I call on thé, Lord Jeſus Chriſt . . 57
In Burgh and Land 62
I will thé loue, my gracious Lord and King 100

The Tabill. 205

In till ane mirthfull Maij morning . .	120
Johne, cum kis me now . · . .	138
I am wo for thir wolfis fa wylde . .	159

K.
KNAW ze not God Omnipotent .	183

L.
LORD God, thy face and word of grace	48
Lord, let thy feruand now depart .	51
Lord, Father, God that gaif me lyfe .	65
Let vs rejoyce and fing	73
Lord, let me neuer be confoundit . .	141

M.
MOYSES vpon the Mont Sinay . .	6
My lufe murnis for me . . .	122
My Saull dois magnifie the Lord . .	125
Mufing greitlie in my mynde . . .	145
Mufing greitlie in my mynde . . .	155

N.
NOW let vs fing, with joy and mirth .	66

O.
OVR Father God Omnipotent . .	10
Our Sauiour Chrift, King of grace .	15
Onlie to God on heich	47
Of mercy zit he paffis all . . .	59
Of thingis twa I pray thé, Lord . .	64

O Lord, how lang for euer will thow forzet	78
O Lord, quha fall in heuin dwell with thé	78
O Lord, aduert vnto my voyce	86
O God, be mercyfull to vs	119
Our Brother let vs put in graue	143
O Chrift, quhilk art the licht of day	151
Of the fals fyre of Purgatorie	163
O Man, ryfe vp, and be not fweir	199
O Man, behald this warldis vaniteis	201

P.

PRAY God for grace, my lufe maift	146
Preiftis in Chrift beleue	170

Q.

QVHA can difcriue or put in write	68
Quha fuld my melodie amend	72
Quhat is the caus, O God omnipotent	74
Quha on the Hieft will depend	92
Quhen fra Egypt departit Ifraell	95
Quho is at my windo? quho	116

R.

RICHT foirly mufing in my mynde	54
Richt foir oppreft I am	55
Remember, Man	175

S.

SORE I complaine of Sin	19
Sinners, vnto my fang aduert	30
Saif vs, gude Lord	76
Say weill is throuchly a worthie	181
Sen throw Vertew	202

T.

TO vs is borne ane barne of blis	45
Till Chrift, quhome I am haldin	52
The grace of God appeiris now	63
The Lord is my Paftor	79
Thow fall not follow	83
Till trew in hart God of Ifrael	88
The Hethin folk, Lord	101
Tell me now, and in quhat wife	123
The Lord fayis, I will fchaw	129
The Bifchop of Hely brak his neck	158
The wind blawis cauld	166
The Paip, that pagane full of pryde	178

W.

WE trow in God allanerlie	9
We thank thé God, of thy gudnes	18
We wretchit finneris pure	21
We fuld into remembrance	60
We fuld beleue in God abufe	63
With heuie hart full of diftres	148
Welcum, Lord Chrift	150
With huntis vp	153
Wo is the Hirdis of Ifraell	164
Was not Salomon, the king	186
With Bybill materis	191

Y. Z.

ZE Richteous, rejoyce	81

FINIS.

I  R

NOTES AND GLOSSARY.

NOTES.

T is stated in the Preface that we have no information when this collection of "Godlie Ballates" originally appeared. That any edition was printed in Scotland prior to 1560 is extremely unlikely; but wherever it was first printed, it was probably enlarged by Henry Charteris, in 1569 or 1570, with an "augmentation," as the title of 1578 expresses it, " of sindrie Gude and Godlie Ballatis, not contenit in the first editioun." But this is mere conjecture. The earliest intimation of the book in a printed form occurs in the passage quoted, *supra*, p. xlvii., from James Melville's Diary, under the year 1570. He was then a scholar at Montrose, and speaks of his great delight when a travelling chapman or carrier (whom he calls a post), among other novelties from Edinburgh, brought him a copy of "Wedderburn's Songs." But no copy of that edition has reached our times. As for the words, "augmentation," &c. repeated on the titles, it was not unusual for the old Scottish printers to retain such an intimation, although the edition was a mere reprint of one of a previous date.

Of the edition now reprinted, the identical copy appears in the Sale Catalogue of Sir James Mackenzie's Library, sold by auction at Edinburgh in 1746, when it may have been bought by John Maule, one of the Barons of Exchequer, as it has his book-plate and autograph. His books were disposed of by auction at Edinburgh in 1782; but the volume was lost sight of, until it was accidentally acquired by Mr Thomas Jolley, an English collector, probably for a small sum, in one of his annual commercial visits to Scotland and Ireland. The title-page is mutilated at the front margin, and it wants two leaves of the Calendar and the last leaf of the Table. At the sale of his extensive collection, it was purchased at an extravagant price for the late William Henry Miller, Esq. of Craigentinny, and is now in the library at Britwell, Buckinghamshire.

The Almanack, for nine years from 1578 (which fixes the date), and Calendar, are not contained in the later editions. The two leaves, with the months of January and February—July and August, being deficient in the original, have been supplied chiefly from the Calendars prefixed to the old Psalm Books of that date.

The next edition known to be extant is that of 1600, of which a fac-simile title is given on the opposite page. This volume is a small 8vo, in black letter, signatures A to O in eights. I have not had any recent opportunity of collating it, but it corresponds very closely with that of 1621. In both editions, the orthography of 1578 is somewhat modernised.

ANE
compendius
Buik of Godly and Spirituall Sangis.

Colle[c]tit out of sundrye partes of the Scripture, with sundrye vther Ballatis changeit out of prophaine sangis in godly sangis, for auoyding of sin and harlatry, with augmentation of syndry gude & godly ballatis not contenit in the first Edition.

Exactly correctit and newlye Prented at Edinbrugh be Robert Smyth dwelling at the nether bow. 1600.

Herbert, in his enlarged edition of Ames, mentions the book as having been first printed at Edinburgh in 1597, in small 8vo. He gives no reference for his authority, and the date may have been mistaken for 1567. No such edition at least is known; and notwithstanding diligent research of more than half a century, when such books have been so eagerly sought after, and fetching high prices, only one copy of Smyth's edition of 1600, and two of Hart's of 1621, have yet been discovered. Many years ago, I obtained a fragment of an edition, smaller, I think, in size, than either of these, but, unluckily, I cannot ascertain what became of the leaves.

The copy of the 1600 edition, at the Duke of Roxburghe's sale in 1812, fetched £21; and it was resold with the library of George Chalmers in 1842, when it was bought for £15 for the Rev. Thomas Corser, Rector of Stand, Manchester.

Mr Corser, in his valuable collection of early poetical literature, also possesses the copy of Hart's edition 1621, with the date cut off. This copy formerly belonged to an old Edinburgh collector, George Paton, at whose sale, in March 1809, it sold for £6, 18s. In Bright's sale, one, described as imperfect, fetched £11, 10s.; while another copy of Hart's 1621 edition, at the sale of the Rev. John Brand's Library in May 1807, only produced £4, 4s. If I mistake not, Mr George Chalmers received in exchange from Mr Constable the 1600 edition, already mentioned, for that of 1621, which was transferred to the Advocates Library. It is in blue morocco, with the Roxburghe arms impressed on the side, which renders it probable that the Duke, on acquiring the earlier edition, had given away or exchanged this as a duplicate.

ANE
COMPENDIOVS
BOOKE, OF GODLY
AND SPIRITVALL SONGS

Collectit out of sundrie partes of the Scripture, with sundrie of other Ballates changed out of prophaine sanges, for avoyding of sinne and harlotrie, with augmentation of sundrie gude and godly Ballates, not contained in the first Edition.

Newlie corrected and amended by the first originall Copie.

EDINBVRGH,
Printed by *Andro Hart.* 1621.

The two collections of German Psalms and Hymns, from which I have given a few selections in the following Notes, are entitled:

1. Kirchengesanng Teutsch vnd Lateinisch, dauon in Newburgischer vnd Zweybruckischer gleichförmiger Kirchenordnung meldung geschicht. M.D.LXX.—Gedruckt zu Nürmberg, durch Dieterich Gerlatz. (Subjoined to Hertzog Wolffgangs (von Baiern's) Kirchenordnung) folio.

2. Das Deutsche Kirchenlied von Martin Luther bis auf Nicolaus Herman und Ambrosius Blaurer, von Dr. K. E. P. Wackernagel. Stuttgart, 1841, royal 8vo.

NOTES.

"The Lamentation of a Sinner," *O Lord, in Thee is all my trust.* These verses are omitted in the later editions of the Godlie Ballates. It was one of the Hymns subjoined to the metrical version of the Psalms by Sternhold and Hopkins, when completed in 1562. It is not unlikely, as suggested by Warton, that William Whittingham may have been the author.[1] Whittingham was Knox's colleague, both at Frankfort and Geneva.[2] In 1563 he obtained the Deanery of Durham, and died in 1579.

In the editions of the Psalms printed in England, only the first, second, and sixth verses are given, with the music, and the following rubric:—"Through perfect repentance, the sinner hath a sure trust in God that his sinnes shall be washed away in Christe's blood." On the other hand, in nearly all the editions of the Psalms in metre, "according to the form used in the Kirk of Scotland," from the one printed at Edinburgh by Thomas Bassandyne, 1575, to that by Robert Bryson, 1644, the six verses occur with the same music, and the above rubric.

In the rare edition of the English Psalms, harmonized in four parts, and printed at London by John Daye, the tune is given with the name of M. Tallis.

Page 3. In Hart's edition, 1621, the word "Followes" is prefixed to the two titles on this page.

[1] History of English Poetry.   [2] Knox's Works, vol. iv. p. 5, &c.

Page 9, line 11. "Of our Beleif." The title in edit. 1621 is, " Followes of our Creid." The word "Followes" is joined in that edition with most of the titles in the earlier part of the collection. In the present version of the Creed, the third stanza, p. 10, has only nine lines, instead of eleven. The lines wanting apparently are 6 and 9.

Page 10, line 11. "The Lordis Prayer," is given as a title in edit. 1621.

Page 12. "Of our Baptisme." *Christ baptist was be Johne in Jordan flude.* This is a version of Luther's hymn, "Ein geistlich lied, Von vnser heiligen Tauffe." It begins:

  Christ vnser Herr zum Jordan kam,
   nach seines Vaters willen,
  Von S. Johans die Tauffe nam,
   sein werck vnd ampt zur füllen.
  Da wolt er stifften vns ein bad
   zu waschen vns von sünden,
  Erseuffen auch den bittern tod,
   durch sein selbs blut vnd wunden,
  Es galt ein newes leben.

Wackernagel, No. 218, gives it entire in seven stanzas from the Wittenberg Gesangbuche, 1543; and so it appears in the Appendix to Professor's Mitchell's Lecture, which shows that the third, ninth, and tenth of Wedderburn's stanzas had been taken from a different copy.

Page 15. "The Supper of the Lord." *Our Saviour Christ, King of grace.* This is taken from Luther's German translation of the Latin hymn by John Huss. It extends to ten verses, and begins:

  Jesus Christus, vnser Heiland,
   der von vns den Gottes zorn wand,

> Durch das bitter leiden sein,
> halff er vns aus der Hellen pein.

Wackernagel gives it as No. 194 from the Erfurdt Euchiridion, 1524; and Professor Mitchell prints it (p. 57) alongside of Wedderburn's translation.

I prefer to give, for its beautiful cadence, and as superior to the translations, the original Latin hymn by John Huss. He is said to have also composed the tune, which was so much admired by Luther:

CARMEN QUODDAM JOANNIS HUS,
DE CŒNA DOMINI.

1.

Jesus Christus nostra salus,
Quod reclamat omnis malus,
Nobis in sui memoriam,
Dedit hanc panis hostiam.

2.

O quam sanctus panis iste,
Tu solus es Jesu Christe,
Caro, cibus, Sacramentum,
Quo non majus est inventum.

3.

Hoc donum suavitatis,
Charitasque Deitatis,
Virtutis Eucharistia,
Communionis gratia.

4.

Ave Deitatis forma,
Dei unionis Norma,
In te quisque delectatur,
Qui te fide speculatur.

5.

Non est panis, sed est Deus,
Homo liberator meus,
Qui in Cruce pependisti,
Et in carne defecisti.

6.

Non augetur consecratus,
Nec consumptus fit mutatus,
Nec divisus in fractura,
Plenus Deus in statura.

7.

Esca digna Angelorum,
Pietatis Lux sanctorum,
Lex moderna approbavit,
Quod antiqua figuravit.

8.

Salutare medicamen,
Peccatorum relevamen,
Pasce nos, a malis leva,
Duc nos, ubi est lux tua.

9.

Caro, panis, sanguis, vinum,
Est mysterium divinum,
Huic laus et gloria,
In sec'lorum secula.   AMEN.[1]

Page 15, line 23. *Repentand sair:* in edition 1621, *Repentand fore.*

[1] Historiæ et Monumentorum Joannis Hus atque Hieronymi Pragensis. *Novmbergensem* 1715, folio, vol. ii. p. 520.

Page 17, line 21. *For Kingdom*, &c. After this line the edition 1621 has this Conclusion:
"For ay. Amen. Lat it be sa ever, we Thee pray."
And line 28 is followed by the words, *Say the Lordis Prayer, above written, befoir Supper.*

Page 18, line 12. [Deo Gratias]. *We thank thee God, of Thy gudnes.* This grace is from the German of Nicolas Boie, beginning:

O Godt, wy dancken dyner gűde
dorch Christum vnsen Heren.

Wackernagel, No. 453, gives it from the Magdeburg Hymn Book, 1543: and also in Professor Mitchell's Lecture, p. 59.

Page 18, after line 7. The edition 1621 has the words, *Say the Lordis Prayer, or ane part of the Catechisme, efter Supper.*

Page 19. "Ane Confession of Sin." *Sore I Complaine of Sin.* In the edition 1621 the title reads "Followes Spirituall Sangis, and ane Confessioun of Sin, with ane Prayer. Line 12, *vyle*, is *vyld*.

The first three verses of this Confession, along with some other "Godlie Ballates," not included in the present collection, formed the fly-leaves of an old volume of the Kirk-session Records of Inverness. The volume contains the register from 1604 to 1616. For a transcript of the religious verses, or "ballatis," in their present mutilated state, I was indebted some years ago to the Rev. Hew Scott, D.D., author of the "Fasti Ecclesiæ Scoticanæ."

Page 21. "Ane Sang of our Corrupt Nature," &c. *We wretchit sinners pure.* These verses would read better, by having the third and sixth lines of each stanza divided into short lines, for the sake of the metre. This is from the German hymn by Hermann Bonn, which begins:

>Och wy armen sünders!
>vnse missedadt,
>Dar wy ynne entfangen
>vnd gebaren sint.
>Helft gebracht vns alle
>yn sulcke grote nodt,
>Dat wy vnderworpen sint
>dem ewigen dod.
>Kyrieleyson, Christeleyson, Kyrieleyson!

printed by Wackernagel, No. 451, from the Magdeburg Geystliche Leider vnd Psalmen, 1543; and by Professor Mitchell, p. 59.

Page 22. "Ane Sang of the Flesche and the Spreit." *All Christin men tak tent and leir.* The author of this poetical dispute or controversy was Hans Witzstat von Wertheim. It occurs as No. 276 in Wackernagel, with the title, "Der geystlich Buchsbaum, Von dem streyte des Fleysches wider den Geyst," and at p. 61 of Professor Mitchell's Lecture. Of a still earlier date, the Wedderburns might have found poems of a similar cast in the "Ressoning betwixt Aige and Yowth," or the "Ressoning betwixt Deth and Man," by Henryson, or in "The Merle and the Nychtingaill," by Dunbar.

This poem, "Ane Sang of the Flesche and the Spreit," and those in the preceding pages of the Godlie Ballates, are given as the "METRICAL CATECHISM," by the Rev. Dr H. Bonar, in the Appendix to his valuable collection of "Catechisms of the Scottish Reformation," Lond. 1866, post 8vo, pages 301-323. Whether under this title we should recognise an early printed edition mentioned by Ames in his Typographical Antiquities, 1749, p. 585, but of which no copy has been discovered, I will not pretend to say. Calvin's Catechism, in prose, was often reprinted. The title, as given by Ames, may be quoted.

"The Catechisme in two partes; the first in Scotch poetry, having a kalender before it. The second part in Latin and Scottis prose, entituled, Catechismus ecclesiae Geneuensis, hoc est, formula erudiendi pueros in doctrina Christi. Authore Johanne Calvino. Ubi colloquuntur praeceptor, et discipulus, vel minister, et puer. ¶ The Catechisme, or maner to teiche children the Christiane religioun. Wherein the minister demandeth the questioun, and the chylde maketh answer; made by the excellent doctour and pastour in Christis kirk, Johne Calvin. The first question is, Quhat is the principal and cheif end of mannis Lyfe? The chyld: To knaw God. Edinburgh. Imprinted by John Ross, for Henrie Charteris, 1574." 12mo.

Page 25. "Ane Sang of the Croce." *Cum beir, sayis Goddis sone to me.* Another composition by the same author, Hans Witzstat von Wertheim. Wackernagel, No. 275, gives two different sets,

Kompt her zu mir, spricht Gottes Son,
with considerable variations; the second of these is contained in Professor Mitchell's Appendix, p. 64.

Page 26, line 24. "Gais out his end" (edit. 1621.)

Page 27, line 1. "Than sa unthankfullie deceist" (edit. 1621.)

Page 27, line 5. *Thocht ane,* &c. In the old copies, the two lines that follow are evidently transposed, as both the sense and the metrical arrangement require that they should read thus—

> Thocht ane had all this warld sa wyde,
> With golde, and precious stanis of pryde,
> Yit he sall die, with dule and pyne.

Page 28, line 4. " And quhen this schort pyne do you greif" (edit. 1621.)

Page 29, line 8. *Said* is a mistake for *sad;* and *persevir* in the next line should have been corrected *perseveir.*

Page 35, line 28. "And syne efter" (edit. 1621.)

Page 36, line 14. "Wrytes Esay" (edit. 1621.)

Page 37. "The principal pointis of the Passion," &c. *Help, God, the former of all things.* From the German

> " Hilff, Gott, das mir gelinge."

It has thirteen stanzas. The last two lines, which mention the author's name, are not translated.

> 13. Recht last vns alle bitten
> Christum für öberkeit,
> Ob wir schön von in lidten
> gewalt, auch für all feind,
> Das in Gott wöll genedig sein:
> Hat HEINRICH MULLER gesungen
> in dem gefengnis sein.

See Wackernagel, No. 294. In place of these lines, it will be seen that Wedderburn has simply

> In prison, for the Veritie,
> Ane faithfull BROTHER maid this Sang.

Professor Mitchell, who gives the entire hymn, adds this note: "As stated in this last verse, Henry Muller was the author of this hymn, and composed it while in prison. His name is left out in the Scottish version, and

Sir J. Dalyell seems to have supposed the reference in it was to the imprisonment of the Scottish poet. The German appears first in the Magdeburg Hymn Book of 1540," (p. 70.)—It was quite natural, however, from the above words, to draw such an inference.

Page 39, line 4. "Him" is here repeated by mistake.

Page 40. " Ane Sang of the Euangell," &c. *Be blyith all Christin men, and sing.* The original hymn by Luther begins

>Ny freud euch, lieben Christen g'mein,
> vnd lasst vns frölich springen;
>Das wir getrost vnd all in ein
> mit lust vnd liebe singen;
>Was Gott an vns gewendet hat,
>Vnd seine susse wunderthat,
> Gar thewr hat er's erworben.

It consists of ten seven-line stanzas—(See it in Wackernagel, No. 184, and in Professor Mitchell's Lecture, p. 70). It has more than once been translated into English; and is reckoned to have been the first hymn which Luther published in 1524.

Page 42, line 20. "Saif thou man bee" (edit. 1621.)

Page 43. "Ane Sang of the Birth of Christ, to be sung with the tune of Balulalow." In the edition 1621, "with the tune of Baw lulalaw." *I come from Heuin to tell.* This may be called a literal translation of Luther's celebrated Christmas Carol or Hymn for Christmas Eve. Each of them contains 15 four-line stanzas. It forms No. 214 in Wackernagel, and is also printed in full by Professor Mitchell, p. 25. The first three may be quoted as a specimen of the versification.

P

*Ein Kinderlied, auff die Weihenachten,
vom Kindlein Jhesu.*

Von Himel hoch da kom ich her,
Ich bring euch gute newe mehr,
Der guten mehr bring ich so viel,
Dauon ich singen vnd sagen will.

Euch ist ein Kindlein heut geborn,
Von einer Jungfraw auserkorn,
Ein Kindelein so zart vnd fein,
Das soll ewr freud vnd wonne sein.

Es ist der Herr Christ vnser Gott,
Der will euch fürn auss aller not,
Er will ewr Heiland selber sein,
Von allen sunden machen rein. (Fol. xlvi.)

The same verses from Miss Winckworth's translation may also be quoted. She says this carol or hymn was written (in 1535) by Luther, for "his little boy Hans, when the latter was five years old, and it is still sung from the dome of the Kreuzkirche in Dresden before day-break on the morning of Christmas day. It refers to the custom then and long afterwards prevalent in Germany, of making at Christmas-time representations of the manger with the infant Jesus."—(Lyra Germanica, p. x.)

From heaven above to earth I come
To bear good news to every home;
Glad tidings of great joy I bring,
Whereof I now will say and sing:

To you this night is born a child
Of Mary, chosen mother mild;

This little child, of lowly birth,
Shall be the joy of all your earth.

'Tis Christ our God, who far on high,
Hath heard your sad and bitter cry;
Himself will your Salvation be,
Himself from sin will make you free.

Page 45, line 10. " Sall I bow" (edit. 1621.)

Page 45. [A Christmas Sang.] *To us is born a Barne of bliss.* Wackernagel, No. 666, includes this among the productions of unknown authors, "Unbekannte Dichter," from the Strassburg Psalter, 1539. Professor Mitchell also prints it in his Lecture, p. 25. It begins:

Ein Gesang auff Weihennachten.
Ein kindelin so lobenlich
  ist vns geboren heute,
Von einer Jungfraw seiberlich
  zü trost vns armen leute.
Wer vns das kindlin nicht geborn
So weren wir all z'mal verlorn,
  das heil ist vnser allen!
Oy du süsser Jesu Christ,
  Das du mensch geboren bist,
Behüt vns vor der hellen.

Page 47. "In dulci jubilo." In all the editions of the Godly Ballads this is inaccurately printed *in dulce;* and the next line has *in principio,* an evident typographical mistake for, *in præsepio* (in the manger or stable). The lines also run on, giving it a very unintelligible appearance. I have followed the form of the original.

This strange mixture of two languages is an exact

translation, in the same style, of the old German hymn which belongs to the fifteenth century. Wackernagel has given it in two different forms, in Nos. 125 and 791. The latter, he says, is from the "Geistlichen Liedern, gedruckt zu Wittemberg, 1535," and is similar to the following copy, taken from the Nuremberg collection, printed in 1570:—

Ein ander altes Weihenachten Lied (or, another old Song or Carol for Christmas Eve).

In dulci jubilo,
Nun singet vnd seid fro,
Vnsers hertzen wunne,
Leit in præsepio,
Vnd leuchtet als die Sonne,
Matris in gremio,
Alpha es & O; Alpha es & O.

O Jesu paruule,
Nach dir ist mir so weh,
Tröst mir mein gemüte,
O Puer optime,
Durch alle deine güte
O Princeps gloriæ,
Trahe me post te; Trahe me post te.

O Patris charitas,
O Nati lenitas,
Wir weren all verloren,
Per nostra crimina.
So hat er vns erworben,
Cœlorum gaudia,
Eia wer wir da; Eia wer wir da.

> Vbi sunt gaudia,
> Nirgend mehr denn da,
> Da die Engel singen,
> Noua Cantica,
> Vnd die Schellen klingen
> In Regis curia,
> Eia wer wir da; Eia wer wir da.   (Fol. xlix.)

Another and similar Song on the Nativity in Latin and German occurs in the Nuremberg volume, 1570, fol. 50. It begins:

> Puer natus in Bethlehem, in Bethlehem
> Ein kind geborn zu Bethlehem, zu Bethlehem.
> Unde gaudet Jerusalem, Halle Halleluia!
> des frewet sich Jerusalem, Halle Halleluia!
>
> Hic jacet in præsepio, præsepio,
> Hic light er in dem Krippelein, Krippelein,
> Qui regnat sine termino, Halle Halleluia!
> On ende ist die Herschafft sein, Halle Halleluia!

Line 7. "Alpha es et O," or Omega, the first and last letters of the Greek Alphabet. In the words of Scripture: "I am Alpha and Omega, the beginning and the ending." (Revel. ch. i. v. 8.)—"I am Alpha and Omega, the first and the last"—(*Ib.* v. 13). See also ch. xxi. v. 6.

Page 47. [Gloria in excelsis Deo.] *Onlie to God on heich, be gloir.* The author of the German original was Nicolaus Decius, and it appeared in the "Geystliche Leider vnd Psalmen," at Magdeburg, 1540. It is here copied from Wackernagel, No. 420.

> Allein Gott inn der höhe sey ehr,
> Vnd danck fur seine gnade,

> Darumb das nu vnd nimermehr
>   Vns ruren kan eine schade!
> Ein wolgefallen Gott an vns hat,
> Nu ist gros fried on vnterlas,
>   All fehde hat nu ein ende.
>
> Wir loben, preisen, anbeten dich
>   Fur deine ehre, wir dancken,
> Das du, Gott Vater, ewiglich
>   Regierest on alles wancken.
> Gantz vngemessen ist deine macht,
> Fort g'schicht, was dein will hat erdacht,
>   Wol vns des feinen Herren!
>
> O Jhesu Christ, Son eingeborn
>   Deines himlischen Vaters,
> Versöner der, die warn verlorn,
>   Du stiller vnsers haders.
> Lam Gottes, heiliger Herr vnd Gott
> Nim an die bitt von vnser noth
>   Erbarm dich vnser, Amen!
>
> O heiliger Geist, du gröstes gut,
>   Du aller heilsampst Tröster;
> Furs Teuffells g'walt fort an behut
>   Die Jhesus Christ erlöset
> Durch grosse marter vnd bittern tod!
> Abwend all vnsern jamer vnd noth,
>   Dazu wir vns verlassen.

The translation by Coverdale may also be quoted for comparison. He certainly exhibits less skill than Wedderburn in versification.

GLORIA IN EXCELSIS DEO.

To God the hyghest be glory alwaye,
   For his great kyndnesse and mercy;
That doth provide both nyght and daye
   Both for oure soule and oure body.
To mankynde hath God great pleasure
   Now is great peace everywhere;
God hath put out all emmyte.

Ad Patrem.

We love and prayse and honoure thé,
   For thy great glory; we thanke thy grace,
That thou, God, Father eternally,
   Art oure defender in every place.
Thou art to us a mercyfull Father,
   And we thy chyldren altogether;
Therefore we geve the thankes alwayes.

Ad Filium.

O Jesu Christ, thou onely Sonne,
   Of God Almyghty thy heavenly Father,
Our full and whole redempcyon.
   Thou that hast stilled God's displeasure;
O God's Lambe, thou takest synne awaye,
   When we have nede, helpe us alwaye;
Graunt us thy mercy altogether.

Ad Spiritum Sanctum.

O Holy Ghost, our confortoure
   In all oure trouble and hevynesse;
Defende us all from Sathan's power,
   Whome Christ hath bought from wofulnesse;

> Kepe oure hertes in the verite,
>   In oure tentacyon stonde us by,
>   And strength alwaye oure weake bodies.[1]

Page 48. "Of the greit louing and blyithnes of Goddis word." *Lord God, thy face and word of grace.* This hymn should be printed in short lines, thus—

> Lord God, thy face
> and word of grace
> Hes lang been hid be craft of men;
>   Quhill at the last
>   the nicht is past,
> And we full weill thair falset ken.

It is evidently founded upon a German hymn, contained in the Gesangbuch, printed at Wittenberg, 1535. As Coverdale has given a more literal translation in seven stanzas, the first three may be quoted for comparison, arranged in short lines for the rhyme:

> O Hevenly Lorde,
>   thy godly worde
> Hath longe bene kepte alwaye from us;
>   But thorow thy grace,
>   now in oure dayes,
> Thou hast shewed thé so plenteous,
>   That very well
>   we can now tell
> What thy Apostles have written al;
>   And now we se
>   thy worde openly
> Hath geven Anthyechrist a great fall.

[1] Works of Bishop Coverdale, p. 564. Camb. 1846. Parker Society.

Notes.

> It is so cleare,
> as we may heare,
> No man by ryght can it deny,
> That many a yeare
> thy people deare
> Have bene begyled perlously
> With men Spirituall,
> as we them call,
> But not of thy Spirite truly:
> For more carnall
> are none at all,
> Than many of these spirites be.
>
> They have been ever
> sworne altogether,
> Theyr owne lawes for to kepe alwaye:
> But, mercyfull Lorde,
> of thy swete worde
> There durst no man begynne to saye.
> They durst them call
> great heretikes all,
> That dyd confesse it stedfastly;
> For they charged,
> it shulde be hyd,
> And not be spoken of openly.

The original German, "Vom Evangelischen Glauben," of eight stanzas of eight lines, has been ascribed to Paulus Speratus; but Wackernagel, No. 637, classes it with others by unknown writers ("Lieder von Unbekannten Dichtern.") It begins—

> O Herre Gott, dein Göttlich wort
> ist lang verdunkelt blieben.

Professor Mitchell, at p. 73, gives the first, third, and fourth verses of Wedderburn's, with the same in German; and at p. 39, the second and third verses, with the similar version by Coverdale, remarking that "it is a translation which breathes quite as kindly and compassionate a spirit towards the deluded Papists as the original, and displays a tone and temper considerably different from that which even Coverdale has managed to throw into his version of the same hymn."

Page 52. "Ane Sang of the Resurrection." *Christ gaue him self to deid.* This appears to have been translated from the Latin, which is here copied from Professor Mitchell's Lecture, p. 27:—

> DE MORTE ET RESURRECTIONE CHRISTI.
>
> > Christus pro nobis passus est
> >   et immolatus, agnus est,
> > Effuso suo sanguine
> >   in ipsa Crucis arbore;
> > Et mortuus imperium
> >   devicit Diabolicum.
> >
> > Nam resurgens ex mortuis
> >   Victor redit ex inferis,
> > Delevit et chirographum
> >   nobis quod est contrarium,
> > Exspoliato Satana,
> >   reclusa Cœli janua.
> >
> > Habemus ergo liberum
> >   jam nos ad Patris aditum,

>   Per Christum Dei filium
>   pro nobis morti traditum.
>   Alleluia, Alleluia!
>   Benedicamus Domino!

Page 53, line 1. "That drerie difference" (edit. 1621).

Page 54, line 8. "From thyne to Ynde." The edit. 1621 corrects this to "from Thyle to Inde." *Thyle* is a name occurring in Solinus, as the *Ultima Thule*. (See Proceedings of the Society of Antiquaries of Scotland, vol. i. p. 16.) Lines 14 and 15 are omitted in edit. 1621.

Page 55, line 16. "I have faultit sore" (edit. 1621).

Page 57. *I call on thee, Lord Jesus Christ.* The original German hymn, with title, "Ein Geistlich lied, zu bitten vmb glauben, lieb vnd hoffnung," is printed by Wackernagel, No. 226, and ascribed to Paulus Speratus.

>   Ich ruff zu dir, Herr Jhesu Christ,
>   ich bit, erhör mein klagen;

in five stanzas of nine lines. It is given by Professor Mitchell at p. 73.

This is one of the four poems or psalms, common both to Coverdale and Wedderburn. The following various readings may be noticed:

Line 4. Tyll thy swete worde have conforted me.
    13. Excepte thou with thy grace oppresse.
    15.   Cause me therefore
        to hope evermore
    On thy mercy and swete promises.
    23.   unthankfully departe.
    38. Followe upon me where I go.
    Therefore wolde I
    Now fayne delyvered be.

In Coverdale's volume, the seventh line of each stanza is divided into two short lines, as above, line 15, &c.

Page 60, line 19. *Gloir*, for the sake of the rhyme, should be read *glorie*. The edition 1621 has *glore*.

Page 62, line 11. "Of Christ forsuith no thing wee knaw" (edit. 1621).

Page 63, line 22. "Our heill," edit. 1621; but *heill* and *helth* are synonymous.

Page 64. *Of thingis twa, I pray thee, Lord.* These verses are a paraphrase of the words of Agur, recorded in the Book of Proverbs, ch. xxx. v. 7, &c.

Page 64, line 21. "Puirteith" (edit. 1621).

Page 65, line 14. "Wald diuert;" and line 20, "As into deid" (edit. 1621).

Page 73, line 3. "Lat us rejoyce" (edit. 1621).

Page 74. Psalm ii. Coverdale's version of this Psalm consists of six verses. The first is as follows:

> Wherfore do the heithen now rage thus,
>   Conspyryng together so wyckedly?
> Wherfore are the people so malicious,
>   Vayne thynges to ymagyn so folyshly?
> The kynges of the earth stonde up together,
> And worldly rulers do conspyre [ever]
>   Agaynst the Lorde and his Christ truly.

Page 74. Psalm vi.—*Quhat is the caus, O God omnipotent*—is from the German,

> Hilff Gott, wie geht das imer zu,
>   dass alles volck so grimmet?

attributed to Andrew Knöpken, and said to have appeared in one of the *Enchiridions* of 1528. Wackernagel, No.

272, gives it in two texts of eight seven-line stanzas. Professor Mitchell, at p. 75, says, "It is found in the Magdeburg and in the Strasburg Hymn-books."

Page 75, line 4. "Yow hes send," read "Thow hes send;" and in line 13, "Thow makis," or "thou makes," in the old copies, is an evident misprint for "Thow mockis."

Page 76. Psalm xi. Coverdale's version of this Psalm is in six verses, with the following title. The first verse may serve as a specimen:

AGAYNST FALSE DOCTRYNE AND YPOCRITES.

> Helpe now, O Lorde, and loke on us,
> How we are brought in lowe degre.
> Thy sayntes are dryven from every house,
> Where are fewe faythfull lefte truly:
> Men wyll not suffre thy trueth to be known,
> Thy fayth is almost overthrowen
> Amonge men's chyldren piteously.

Page 76. Psalm xii. *Saif us, gude Lord, and succour send.* Or Psalm xi., as here, according to the numbering of the Vulgate. Luther's German version,

> Ah! Gott von himel, sich darein
> und las dich des erbarmen,

as given by Wackernagel, No. 185, was used by Wedderburn.

Page 78. Psalm xiii.—xxii. is a typographical mistake in the old copies for xii. according to the Vulgate, and line 5 is evidently wanting.

> Ach Got, wie lang vergissest mein
> gar nocht bis an das ende!

Professor Mitchell, p. 77, gives three verses of the German, and thus supplies the defective line,

> [Mine enemie exalted be, how lang?]

Wackernagel (No. 279) prints this version of "Der Zwelfft Psalm," under the name of the author, Mattheus Greiter.

Page 78. Psalm xv. is also wrong numbered xxiiij. *O Lord, quha sall in heuin dwell with Thee.* This Psalm was derived from the German of Wolfgang Dachstein,

> O Herr, wer wirt wonunge hon
> in deinen zelten klüge.

See Wackernagel, No. 263.

Page 79, line 6. "Be knaw," a mistake for "he knaw." Line 19. "From fyre," in edit. 1621, "from sinne."

Page 79. Psalm xxiii. *The Lord God is my Pastor gude*, is line for line with the German version of Wolfgang Meüszlin, or Wolfgang Musculus,

> Der Herre ist mein trewer hirt,
> Helt mich in seiner hüte.

See Wackernagel, No. 268, and the Appendix of Professor Mitchell's Lecture, pp. 79–80.

Page 80, line 11. "And thocht I wauer, or ga will;" in edit. 1621, "And though I wander, or goe will." *Go will* means to go astray.

Page 81, last line. "And worship him all haunts" (edit. 1621).

Page 86, line 7. "The wickit man;"—line 15, "Fyne (or end) is miserie" (edit. 1621).

Page 88, line 8. " Bot stakerand:" in edit. 1621, "But stagger, and almaist."

Page 90, line 18. For *flycht*, read *slicht;* and in the same line, Hart's edit. 1621 repeats the word *pretend* from 16, in place of *intend*.

Page 90. Psalm 83. *God, for thy grace.* An earlier version of this Psalm, without the translator's name, occurs in Bannatyne's MS., 1568. It consists of seven stanzas. The first line, and some others, are the same as Wedderburn's, the second line of which, being defective in the printed copies, is supplied from that MS., although the rhyme does not suit. In the MS. it begins

God, for thy grace, thow keip no moir silence,
   Ceiss not, O God, nor hald thy peax no moir,
For lo thy fois with crewall violence,
   Confiderat ar, and with ane hiddeous roir,
   In this thair rage, thaye ribbalis, brag, and schoir,
And thay that hait thé most maliciously
Aganis thy micht, thair heidis hes raisd on hie.

For to oppress thy pepill thay pretend
   With subtill slicht, and moue conspiracie
For sic as on thy secreit help depend,
   Go to, say thay, and latt us utterlie.
   This natioun rute out from memorie,
And of the name of Israelitis, lat nevir
Forther be maid mentioun for euir.

Conspyrit ar, with crewall hairtis and fell,
   Thus aganis Thé togidder in ane band.

   .   .   .   .

Page 91, line 25. In Hart's edit. 1621, "Syne sylie Princes," supplying the word omitted in edit. 1578.

Page 94, line 15. Read, as in edit. 1621, "edderis stang."

Page 95. Psalm cxiiii.—*Quhen fra Egypt departit Israell;* and Psalm cxv.—*Not unto us.* In the old copies, these two Psalms (cxiv. and cxv.) are printed as one, without any division, as in the Vulgate, but numbered lxxxj. Line 2, *harbour* is a mistake for *barbour* (barbarous).

Page 97, line 8. "For like the watter and walles (waves) bryme" (edit. 1621).

Page 97. Psalm cxxiv. *Except the Lord with us had stand.* Professor Mitchell extracts this along with Coverdale's version of the same Psalm, to shew that Wedderburn "was not a mere versifier like Myles Coverdale, but a true poet, whose words were fitted to go deep into the hearts of his countrymen, to rouse them to deeds of noble daring, and sustain them even under severest suffering."—(P. 43.)

Coverdale's version of this Psalm may be here given in full:

THE CXXIII. (CXXIV.) PSALME OF DAVID.

Nisi quia Dominus.

"Except the Lorde had bene with us,
  Now maye Israel say boldly;
Excepte the Lorde had ben with us,
  When men rose up agaynst us fearsly;
They had devoured us quyck doutlesse,
And had overwonne us confortless,
  They were so wroth at us truly.

> The waves of waters had wrapped us in;
>   Oure soule had gone under the floode.
> The depe waters of these proude men,
>   Had ronne oure soules over where they stode.
> The Lorde be praysed every houre,
> That wolde not suffre them us to devoure,
>   Nor in theyr tethe to sucke oure bloude!
>
> Our soule is delyvered from theyr power,
>   They can not have that they have sought.
> As the byrde from the snare of the fouler,
>   So are we from theyr daungers brought.
> The snare is broken, and we are fre;
> Oure helpe is in the Lorde's name truly
>   Which hath made heaven and earth of nought.

Page 98. Psalm cxxx. *Fra deip, O Lord, I call to thee.* This Psalm was also translated by Coverdale, and is given by Professor Mitchell, p. 34, as "one of the most favourable specimens of Coverdale's powers as a translator." It begins:

> Out of the depe crye I to Thé,
>   O Lorde! Lorde! hear my callynge;
> O let thyne eares enclyned be
>   To the voyce of my complaynynge.
> Yf thou, Lorde, wylt deale with stratenesse,
> To marke all that is done amysse,
>   Lorde, who may abyde that rekenynge?

Page 99. Psalm cxxxvii. in the old copies is numbered cxxxviii. by mistake. This Psalm occurs in Coverdale's collection in five stanzas, of which the first may be given:

> At the Ryvers of Babilon,
>   There sat we downe ryght hevely;
> Even whan we thought upon Sion,
>   We wepte together sorofully;
> For we were in soch hevyrtes,
> That we forgat all our merynes,
>   And lefte of all oure sport and playe.
> On the willye trees that were thereby
> We hanged up our harpes truly,
>   And morned sore both nyght and daye.

Page 101, line 14. *All loving*, a mistake in the old copies for *All leving*.

Page 102, line 22. "All foldit" (edit. 1621).

Page 104. Psalm li. *Have mercy on me, God of micht.* See Preface, p. xl., respecting the supposition of this metrical version having been sung by George Wishart the night before his apprehension in 1546, Knox quoting the lines

> Have mercy on me now, good Lord,
>   After thy great mercy.

There were, however, other translations, particularly two by Coverdale, which undoubtedly existed at that time in a printed form. A specimen of each may be subjoined from his "Ghostly Psalmes and Spirituall Songs:"—

> THE L. (LI.) PSALME OF DAVID.
> *Miserere mei Deus.*
> O Lorde God, have mercy on me,
> After thy marvelous great pitie:
> As thou art full of mercy,
> Do away all my iniquite;

And washe me from all fylthynesse
Of my great synnes and wantonesse;
For they are many within me,
And ever I fele them hevye:
My synne is alwaye before myne eye;
I have alone offended thé;
Before thé have I lyved synfully;
In thy worde stondest thou stedfastly,
Thoughe thou be judged wrongfully.

THE SAME PSALME.
Miserere mei Deus.

O God, be mercyfull to me,
Accordynge to thy great pitie;
Washe of, make clene my iniquite:
I knowlege my synne, and it greveth me;
Agaynst thé, agaynst thé only
Have I synned, which is before myne eye;
Though thou be judged in man's sight,
Yet are thy wordes founde true and ryght.

Page 107, line 18. "Zit of my cleneness" (edit. 1621).

Page 108, lines 14 and 15. *Aduerte*, and *aduert*, so in the old copies, in place of *Auerte*, and *auert* (turn away.)

Page 110, line 5. "Conforme" should be, as in edit. 1621, "Confirme thy Spreit."

Page 113, line 21. "Ay singand Sanctus sweit." In the edit. 1578, "Sanctis;" in that of 1621, "Ay singand with sainctes sweit." But the word evidently is *Sanctus*, from the *Ter Sanctus* (Thrice Holy) in the words of the Seraphim, in the magnificent description by Isaiah of his heavenly vision (ch. vi. 3), in the ascription of praise to the Almighty—SANCTUS, SANCTUS, SANCTUS, DOMINUS SABAOTH, PLENA EST OMNIS TERRA GLORIA EJUS; and of St John (Revel. iv. 8)—SANCTUS, SANCTUS, SANCTUS, DOMINUS DEUS OMNIPOTENS, QUI ERAT, ET QUI EST, ET QUI VENTURUS EST.

Sir David Lyndsay, in his Dreme, says the glorious Spirits of the Angelic Host were divided into Nine Orders,

——————— the quhilkis excellentlye
Makis loving (praise) with sound melodious
Syngand SANCTUS rycht wounder ferventlye.

So also Dante, before reaching the ninth heaven, says—

Si com'io tacqui, un dolcissimo canto,
Risonò per lo Cielo; e la mia donna[1]
Dicea, con gli altri, SANTO, SANTO, SANTO.

Page 113. Coverdale has two versions of this Psalme, cxxviii., the one being an alteration of the other; but neither of them need be quoted.

Page 114, line 25. "Beseikand that hee grant mee grace" (edit. 1621).

Page 116. "Quho is at my window, quho? quho?" In Chappell's Popular English Song and Ballad Music, vol. i. p. 140, the tune of this song, as it occurs in various early collections, is given to the words

Go from my window, love, go;
Go from my window, my dear.
The wind and the rain
Will drive you back again,
You cannot be lodged here.

Page 117, line 7. "Like a stranger" (edit. 1621).

[1] *Mia Donna*, my Lady Beatrice.—(PARADISO, canto xxvi.)

Page 118, line 5. "Sa farre has;"—line 7, "In at thy doore" (edit. 1621).

Page 119. Psalm lxvii. "Deus misereatur." *O God be mercifull to us.* This version is common both to Coverdale and to Wedderburn. The chief variations are the following lines:

    Line 1. God be mercyfull unto us,
           And sende over us his blessynge;
           Shewe us his presence glorious,
           And be ever to us lovynge.
      7. That they be not led by nyght nor day
           Throwe the pretexte of trewe justice.
     16. Thou haste directe the earth justly.
     19. O God, let the people prayse thé;
           All people, God, mought geve thé honoure.
     27. Fearynge alwaye his myght and power.

Page 122, line 25. "I am not kinde" (edit. 1621).

Page 124, lines 3 and 7. "Your Grace" evidently applies to James Hamilton, Earl of Arran, created Duke of Chatelherault, who was appointed Governor of Scotland, and filled the office from 1542 to 1554.

Page 125, line 13. "It indureth" (edit. 1621).

Page 125. "Magnificat anima mea." *My Saul dois magnifie the Lord.* This, the Song of the Virgin Mary, is Coverdale's translation, as given in his "Ghostly Psalmes and Hymns." The original German "Das Lobgesang Marie," by Symphorianus Pollio, in 1524, begins—

        Meyn seil erhebt den Herren meyn,
           Meyn geyst thut sich erspringen.
        In dem, der sol meyn heyland sein!
           Maria al thut singen:

Printed in 1570 volume, fol. lxii.: and in Wackernagel, No. 521. The chief variations in Coverdale are—

Line 17. He sheweth strength with his great arme,
Declarying hymselfe to be of power;
He scatereth the proude to theyr own harme,
Even with the wicked behavioure.
24. Exaltynge them of lowe degre.
29. And helpeth his servaunt truely
Even Israel, as he promysed
Unto oure fathers perpetually,
Abraham and to his sede.

An anonymous "Song of the Virgin Mary," in ten stanzas, is preserved in George Bannatyne's MS. 1568.

Page 126. "Christe, qui lux es." *Christ, thow art the licht*, &c. The original was one of the beautiful old Latin hymns of the early Christian Church. It may be quoted in full, although Wedderburn was probably indebted to the old German translation, which Wackernagel, No. 138, gives from the "Salus Animæ," Nurnberg, 1503, 16mo. He also, as No. 21, gives the Latin verses, in the "Interpretatio Theotisca," ed. Jac. Grimm. It wants the concluding doxology.

HYMNUS. AD COMPLETORIUM.

1.

Christe, qui Lux es et dies,
Noctis tenebras detegis,
Lucisque lumen crederis,
Lumen beatum prædicans.

Notes.

2.
Precamur, sancte Domine,
Defende nos in hac nocte;
Sit nobis in Te requies,
Quietam noctem tribue.

3.
Ne grauis somnus irruat,
Nec hostis nos surripiat;
Nec caro illi consentiens,
Nos Tibi reos statuat.

4.
Oculi somnum capiant,
Cor ad Te semper vigilet;
Dextera Tua protegat
Famulos, qui Te diligunt.

5.
Defensor noster, aspice,
Insidiantes reprime;
Guberna Tuos famulos,
Quos sanguine mercatus es.

6.
Memento nostri, Domine,
In graui isto corpore;
Qui es defensor animæ,
Adesto nobis, Domine.

7.
Deo Patri sit gloria,
Ejusque soli Filio,
Cum Spiritu Paraclito
Et nunc, et in perpetuum.   Amen

The above hymn is given from the old Salisbury Missal. See the Hymnarium Sarisburiense, p. 64, Lond. 1851, 8vo, where it is printed with the music, and collated with the best MSS. It is also in the "Kirchengesanng Teutsch vnd Lateinisch," &c., fol. lxxiiij., printed at Nuremberg, 1570, folio, which also has at fol. li. the old German translation, beginning

> Christe der du bist tag vnd liecht,
> Für dir est Herr verborgen nichts
> Du Vaterliches liechtes glantz,
> Lehr vns den weg der warheit gantz.

An English version, by Coverdale, in a different kind of metre, is contained in his Ghostly Psalms and Spiritual Songs. It begins

> O CHRIST, that art the lyght and daye,
>   Thou discoverst the darkness of nyght;
> The lyght of lyghtes thou art alwaye,
>   Preaching ever the blessed lyght.
>
> Thou holy Lorde, to thee we praye
>   Defende us all in this darke nyght,
> Let us have rest in thee alwaye,
>   And graunt us all a quyet nyght.

In Bannatyne's MS., 1568, fol. 21, is an older metrical version, in seven stanzas of eight verses, the first and last of each having the corresponding lines of the Latin original. The first verse may serve as a specimen:

> Christe, qui lux es et dies:
> O Jesu Chryst the verry licht
> And daye that undois all dirknes
> Uncovering mirknes of the nicht

> The licht of licht, belevit richt,
> Thow grant us all, but disperance,
> Of thy visage to haif a sicht,
> > Lumen beatum predicans.

Page 126, line 6. "The night;"—line 17, "To take;"—line 20, "Loues full weill" (edit. 1621).

Page 127. *Christ is the onlie Sone of God.* This is the fourth poem in the present collection which belongs to Coverdale. The only variations worth noticing are

> Line 12. He hath Hell gates broken.
> 21. That they erre not from the ryght.
> 28. And to thyrst after no mo.

It is nearly a literal version of the "Geistlich Lied von Christo." The first and second of five verses of the original may be quoted, from the 1570 collection, fol. xl. Wackernagel, No. 236, inserts it from the earlier "Geystliche Gesangbüchlin," Wittenberg, 1525, 12mo (No. xxxv. in his Descriptions, p. 727), and ascribes its composition to Elisabeth Creutziger:

> Herr Christ der einig Gotts Son,
> Vatters in ewigkeit,
> Auss seim hertzen entsprossen,
> Gleich wie geschriben steht:
> Er ist der Morgensterne,
> Sein glantz streckt er sehr ferne,
> Für andern Sternen klar.
>
> > Für vns ein mensch geboren,
> > Im letzten theil der zeit.
> > Der Mutter vnuerloren,
> > Ir junckfrewlich keuscheit.

> Den tod für vns zubrochen,
> Den Himel auffgeschlossen,
> Das leben, widerbracht.

Page 128, line 8. "Awake, O Lord" (edit. 1621).

Page 128. *Christ Jesus is ane A per C:* that is, *A per se.* The letter *A, by itself,* as the first in the alphabet, is applied by the old Scottish poets—by Dunbar, Douglas, and others—to denote a person or thing incomparable. (Alex. Scott's Poems, 1568, p. 91.)

Page 132. *Grevous is my Sorrow.* The original of this may have been an English song of the latter part of the Fifteenth Century, preserved in a MS. of Sloane's—British Museum, No. 1584, fol. 85. It has fourteen stanzas of eight lines, and is printed, with the title, "The Dying Maiden's Complaint," in Ritson's Ancient English Songs, 1790, p. 93, and as "A Song of Love-Longing," in Wright and Halliwell's Reliquiæ Antiquæ, 1841, vol. i. p. 70. The first verse may be quoted—

> Grevus ys my sorowe,
> Both evyne and moro!
> Unto my selfe alone
> Thus do I make my mowne:
> That unkyndnes hath kylled me,
> And put me to this peyne;
> Alas! what remedy?
> That I can not refreyne.

Page 136, line 14. "My Testament" (edit. 1621).

Page 137, line 23. "For I had lever die;"—line 24, "For hir saull" (edit. 1621).

Page 138, line 10. "Represents man;"—line 15, "Oh Johne" (edit. 1621).

Page 138. "Johne, cum kis me now." The old and popular English tune, with this name, is found in Queen Elizabeth's Virginal Book, and in various printed collections. Mr Chappell, in his "Popular Music of the Olden Time," vol. i. p. 147, has collected numerous allusions to it by the old dramatists and other writers. One of these is from Burton's Anatomy of Melancholy. I do not find the words in the edit. Lond. 1632; but they occur in the fifth and augmented edition, p. 532, 1638, folio—"Yea, many times this love will make old men and women, that have more toes than teeth, dance,—*John, come kiss me now.*"

In Greaves's Songs, London, 1604, folio, No. v., as quoted by Mr George Chalmers (MS. collections, in my possession), we find

    I pray thee, sweet John,
    Gentle John, come quickly kisse me;
    Come quickly kisse me;
    Quick, quick, quick, quick, and let me be.

Mr C. adds, "Query if this be not a ridicule of 'John, come kiss me now,' in the Godlie Ballates?"

Page 139, line 3. "O pure lyfe" probably should be "Of pure luif (love);"—line 19, "He left behinde" (edit. 1621).

Page 141, line 12. "Thus contende" (edit. 1621).

Page 142, line 6. "And bid;"—line 8, "Defender;" —line 25, "And full meike" (edit. 1621). *Byde*, in line 6, is a mistake for *hyde*.

Page 143, line 1. "That health is for all flesh;"—line 2, "Thy Saviour;"—line 16, "Returne to earth againe" (edit. 1621).

Page 143. *Our Brother let us put in graue.* This func-ral hymn I printed in the Wodrow Miscellany, 1844, along with "The Forme and Maner of Buriall used in the Kirk of Montrois" (pp. 291–300), from a MS. of the latter part of the 16th century. I was not aware at the time of the German original; nor indeed till I met with Miss Winckworth's English translation, accompanied with the notice that it was written by Michael Weiss. When the dawn of the Reformation was hailed with joy by the Bohemian Church, Weiss was one of two messengers deputed in 1522 to see Luther, and to entreat his advice. In 1531, Michael Weiss published the Hymns of the Bohemian Brethren, translated into German, with the addition of several written by himself, of which this was one. Luther introduced several of these into his own Hymn-book. The original words of this hymn are here subjoined from the Nuremberg collection, 1570, which also has the music. The English translation alluded to above will be found in the Lyra Germanica, Second Series, p. 117; and reprinted in "The Chorale Book for England," No. 96, Lond. 1863, 4to, having the original tune harmonised. In this excellent collection, the Hymns are from the Lyra Germanica, by Miss Winckworth, accompanied with "the Tunes from the Sacred Music of the Lutheran, Latin, and other Churches, for four voices, compiled and edited by Professor W. Sterndale Bennett and Otto Goldschmidt," London, 1863, small 4to.

Geseng zum Begrebnuss.

Nun lasst vns den Leib begraben,
Daran gar kein zweiffel haben,
Er werd am Jüngsten tag auffstehn,
Vnd vnuerwesslich herfür gehn.

Erd ist er, vnd von der erden,
Wird auch zu erd wider werden,
Vnd von der erd wider aufferstehen,
Wenn Gottes posaun wird angehn.

Sein Seele lebt ewig in Gott,
Der sie allhie auss lauter gnad,
Von aller sünd vnd missethat,
Durch seinen Son erlöset hat.

Sein jammer, trübsal vnd ellend,
Ist kommen zu eim seligen end,
Er hat getragen Christus joch,
Ist gestorben vnd lebt doch noch.

Die Seele lebt on alle klag,
Der Leib schlefft biss an Jüngsten tag,
An welchem Gott er verkleren,
Und ewiger freud wird gewehren.

Hie ist er in angst gewesen,
Dort aber wird in genesen,
In ewiger freud vnd wonne,
Leuchten wie die helle Sonne.

Nun lassen wir in hie schlaffen,
Vnd gehn allheim vnser strassen,
Schicken vns auch mit allem fleiss,
Denn der Todt kombt vns gleicher weiss.

Das helff vns Christus vnser trost,
Der vns durch sein blut hat erlost,
Vons Teufels gwalt vnd ewiger pein,
Im sey lob, preiss vnd ehr allein.

                Folio, 1570, fol. lxv.

In Wackernagel, No. 373, we find a somewhat different text. He omits the last four lines. It only remains to observe, that four of Wedderburn's stanzas (the 8th, 9th, 10th, and 11th)—

   Quhen commin is our hour and tyme,

are probably original, as they have no counterpart in the German texts.

 Page 148. *With hevie Hart full of Distres.* This poem occurs in the Inverness Manuscript (see p. 221). The following variations may be noted:

  Line 8. And salve (save) me sinfull creature.
   14. That I was gottin and borne in.
   20.   healls all earthlie.
   23. The haill Scriptoure.

The concluding lines after 28 are lost.

 Page 151. *O Christ, quhilk art the licht of day.* The similarity in the first verse renders it not unlikely that it may have been suggested by the older hymn, *Christ, thou art the licht*, printed at page 126.

 Page 152, line 6. "Idolatrie;"—line 13, "Sum raknit Creids" (edit. 1621).

 Page 152. "With huntes up, with huntes up." The popular English song, which was a favourite of Henry the Eighth, is said to have been written by William Gray, who wrote a ballad on the downfall of Thomas Earl of Cromwell. It begins

   The hunt is up, the hunt is up,
    And it is well-nigh day;
   And Harry our king is gone hunting,
    To bring his deer to bay.

But a similar Song was known in Scotland at a much earlier date. See note in Henryson's Poems and Fables, p. 295. Also Chappell's Popular Music of the Olden Time, &c., vol. i. p. 60; and Dr Rimbault's Little Book of Songs and Ballads, p. 67, Lond. 1851, post 8vo. Alexander Scott, in his poem " Of May " (before 1568), has

With hunts up, every morning plaid.

Page 153, line 19. " Our pence; "—line 25, " Tantonie Bell," evidently the Bell of St Anthony, although Dr Jamieson explained it as " a small bell," from the Fr. *tinton-er*, to resound; but in the Supplement to his Dictionary he admitted that it might refer to St Anthony.

Page 154, line 13. " Absolued" (edit. 1621).

Page 159, line 10. " Are rutted out;"—line 13, " Thocht vagant Freiris" (edit. 1621).

Page 160, line 8. " They said, Thay did botterre" (edit. 1621).

Page 161, line 21. " Sa lang hes sylde" (edit. 1621).

Page 162, line 1. " Fatheris of haly kirk, this xv. hunder zeir." In the edit. 1621, this and the last line of the other stanzas are changed to "the xvi. hunder zeir."

Page 163, line 12. "Therefore, sayes Gedoe, woes mee" (edit. 1621).

Page 164, line 4. "They snuffe at it;"—line 8, " Way is the hirdis" (edit. 1621).

Page 166. "The wind blawis cauld." This is the burden of an English song in praise of Christmas, entitled " A pleasant countrey new ditty; merrily shewing how to drive the Cold Winter away." See Chappell's Popular Music of the Olden Time, vol. i. p. 198.

It will be observed that in this set of verses there is a double rhyme in lines 1 and 3 of each stanza.—Line 6. "This is the vyce" (edit. 1621).

Page 168, line 2. "Traist to;"—lines 12 and 25, "Rings" (reigns) (edit. 1621).

Page 168. *Hay now, the day dallis.* Dallis is the same as *dawis,* or dawns. Dunbar and Gawyn Douglas, in the reign of James the Fourth, mention the tune, *Now the day dawis,* and *The joly day now dawis,* as one that was well known to the common minstrels. Alexander Montgomery, who flourished in the reign of James the Sixth (1580 to 1598), has, in the MS. collection of his minor poems, an imitation of the old ballad. See it printed in his Poems in 1821. I may take this opportunity to add, that the note at p. 315 contains an evident mistake in supposing Montgomery's song to have been anterior in date to that in the present collection. The first verse of Montgomery's, correcting the orthography, may be here quoted, as suggesting that both imitations had one common source:—

> Hay! now the day dawis,
> The jolie cok crawis,
> Now shroudis the shawis
>   Throw Nature anone:
> The thrissell-cok cryis
> On luvaris quha lyis:
> Now skaillis the skyis,
>   The nicht is neir gone.

The only resemblance in the remaining verses is the burden—
    The nicht is neir gone.

Page 170, line 3. "The Arme of Sanct Geill." The arm-bone of St Giles was regarded as a relique of inestimable value, when brought to this country by William Prestoun of Gourtoun, who bequeathed it "to our mother kirk of Sant Gele of Edynburgh," 11th of January 1454-5. See facsimile of the Charter, and an account of the fate of this far-famed relique, in the Historical Notices (p. xvi.) prefixed to the volume of Charters of the Collegiate Church of St Giles, printed for the Bannatyne Club, 1859, 4to.

Page 170, line 5. "And sauit" (so also in edit. 1621, but should be "sanit").

Page 172, line 3. "Common lawes;"—line 27, "Saue" (edit. 1621); but *saue* should be *sane* (bless).

Page 175, line 14. "Woluis;"—line 22, "Their false doctrine" (edit. 1621).

Page 175. "Remember, man," &c. Dr Rimbault, in his Little Book of Songs and Ballads, p. 79, gives this Christmas Carol from the collection entitled "Melismata: Musicall Phansies fitting the Court, Citie, and Countrey Humours," Lond. 1611, 4to, but says it is much earlier than the date of the book. It is also to be found in the Aberdeen Cantus, 1662, 1666, and 1681, No. ix., as a religious song, in nine verses, of which the first runs thus—

> Remember, O thou man, Remember, O thou man,
>   Remember, O thou man, thy time is spent;
> Remember, O thou man, how thou was dead and gone,
>   And I did what I can; therefore repent.

Page 176, line 18. "The haly hag matines" (edit. 1621).

Page 178. "Hey trix," &c. In this satirical effusion,

R

the expressions used evidently refer to events when the Protestants, under the name of The Congregation, had taken matters into their own hands, or, to the year 1559.

Page 180, line 15. "The parson" (edit. 1621).

Same page, line 19. "The parish priest;"—line 20, "He polit thame wantonly" (edit. 1621).

Same page, line 22. "Scotland Well" the name of an hospital or religious house in the shire of Kinross, founded in the year 1238, and afterwards bestowed upon the Red Friars. "Faill" is in Kyle, one of the subdivisions of Ayrshire: it was a cell or priory depending upon the Abbey of Paisley.

Page 181. "Say weill, and Do weill." This anonymous poem occurs in Bannatyne's MS. 1568, fol. 83. There are a few verbal discrepancies, but not worth pointing out, excepting that the MS. has 82 lines: the last two, not in the printed text, are as follows:—

Say weill and Do weill ar thingis twane,
Thryse happy is he quhome in thay do remane.

Page 182, line 17. "Nouther sect nor prance" (edit. 1621).

Page 185, line 22. "Your bishops;"—line 26, "For Dustifit," &c. (edit. 1621). *Dustyfoot*, a name given to a pedlar; but here, as Dr Jamieson suggests, it has an evident application to revelry.

Page 186. "Ane Disswation from vaine Lust." *Was not Salomon the King*. A similar poem in ten stanzas, the examples adduced corresponding with the first portion of the present one, occurs among "The Ballatis of Luve," in the fourth part of George Bannatyne's MS. 1568, fol. 215. It is signed, "Finis, quod ane Inglisman." The first two verses of the MS. may serve for comparison. There is this difference, however, that the one is a prolix Dissuasion from Love, while the other is the entreaty of a Lover to his Lady.

> Was nocht gud King Salamon
>   reuisit in sindry wyiss
> With very lufe of paragon
>   glistering befoir his eis?
> Gif this be trew, trew as it was,
>   Lady! Lady!
> Suld nocht I serwe yow, alace!
>   My fair Lady!
>
> Quhen Paris wes inamorit
>   of Helena dame bewteis speir,
> Than Venus first him promisit
>   to venter on, and nocht for to feir:
> Quhat sturdy stormes indurit he,
>   Lady! Lady!
> To win her lufe, or it wald be,
>   My deir Lady!

The tenth or concluding stanza in the MS. may be added, as it has no counterpart in the present volume.

> Now gif all thir Wechtis of wirdines
>   indiuorit sic panis to tak,
> With wailzeant deidis and sturdines,
>   in ventering for thair ladeis saik,
> Quhy suld nocht I, puir sempill man,
>   Lady! Lady!
> Lawbour and serwe yow the best that I can,
>   My deir Lady!

It may be noticed that *King Salomon* was a popular tune in England. In 1561-2, John Tesdale, among other ballads, obtained a license for printing " a new ballatt after the tune of *Kynge Salomon*." In the remarkable collection of Black-letter Ballads and Broadsides in the collection of Henry Huth, Esq., recently published, there is one entitled, " A proper new Balad of the Bryber Gehesie—*to the tune of King Salomon*," licensed to Thomas Colwell in 1566-7. In the same collection is, " A godly ballad declaring by the Scriptures the plagues that have insued whordome," printed by John Allde, 1566. It is of a similar import with the *Dissuasion* in the Gude and Godlie Ballates, but in a different measure.

Page 187, line 20. "To Paramours" (edit. 1621).

Page 188, line 7. "Anaretus" (edit. 1621). This refers to Anaxarete, who despised the addresses of Iphis.—See Ovid, Metamorph. lib. xiv.

Page 202. "Sen throw Vertew incressis dignitie." This is the only authority for attributing these verses to KING JAMES THE FIRST of Scotland (1406—1437). In Bannatyne's MS. 1568, fol. 58, they occur anonymously, with numerous verbal differences. In neither copy do we find the language of the early part of the fifteenth century.

GLOSSARY.

Abak, page 95, *back*.
Abbominabill, 71, *abominable*.
Abbottis, 179, *abbots*.
Abill, 114, *able*.
Abirone, 156, *Abiram*.
Abone, 76, *above*.
Aboue, 30, *above*.
Aboundantlie, 147, *abundantly*.
Abrogate, 81, *abrogated*.
Abstene, 140, *abstain*.
Abufe, 63, *above*.
Abusioun, 176, *abuse*.
Abusit, 166, *abused*.
Abyde, abydis, 64, 83, *abide, abides, waits for*.
Achab, 157, *Ahab*.
Acknawledged, *acknowledged*.
Actis, 100, *acts*.
Adamis, 183, *Adam's*.
Adoir, 200, *adore*.
Adorne, 63, *adore, worship*.
Adow, 138, *ado*.
Adrest, 84, *provided*.
Aduance, 65, *advance*.

Aduance, 102, *promote*.
Aduenterit, 187, *adventured*.
Aduersitie, 109, *adversity*.
Aduert, 30, 108, *advert, turn away*.
Aduerteis, 36, *inform*.
Aduertise, 187, *advise*.
Aduocate, 61, *advocate*.
Affray, 93, *frighten*.
Afrayed, 187, *afraid*.
Againe, 30, *again*.
Againe, 75, *against*.
Aganis, 94, *against*.
Agast, 84, *aghast*.
Aige, 82, *age*.
Ailit, 95, *ailed*.
Aind, 26, *breath, spirit*.
Air, 24, *early*.
Air and lait, 67, *early and late*.
Air, 75, *heir*.
Airis, 175, *heirs*.
Airt, 192, *way*.
Alanerlie, 56, *only*.
Aleuin, 176, *eleven*.
Aliue, 24, *alive*.
Alkin, 88, *each*.

Glossary.

Allace, 102, *alas.*
Allaine, 124, *alone.*
Allalua, 52, *halleluiah.*
Allane, 47, *alone.*
Allanerlie, 92, *only.*
All haill, 86, *wholly.*
Allone, 59, *alone.*
Allowis, 185, *allows.*
Alluterlie, 162, *utterly.*
Almaist, 179, *almost.*
Almichtie, 92, *almighty.*
Almous, 180, *alms.*
Alquhair, 83, *everywhere.*
Als, 24, *as;* 35, *also.*
Alswa, 42, *also.*
Alteris, 183, *altars.*
Alwayis, 61, *always.*
Amang, 44, *among.*
Amendit, 201, *amended.*
Amene, 105, *pleasant.*
Amis, 72, *amiss, wrong.*
Ane, 40, *a.*
Ane, 57, *one.*
Aneuch, 23, *enough.*
Angell, 73, *angel.*
Angellis, 47, *angels.*
Anis, 57, *once.*
Anis, 153, *one's.*
Anker, 196, *anchor.*
Anone, 33, *anon.*
Answerit, 36, *answered.*
A per C, 128, *A per se.*
Appeir, 29, *appear.*
Appeirand, 55, *apparent.*
Appeirand, 82, *appearing.*
Appeirandly, 106, *apparently.*
Appeiris, 63, *appears.*
Appeirit, 39, *appeared.*

Apperis, 168, *appears.*
Appetyte, 83, *desire.*
Appetyte, 65, *appetite.*
Appillis, 101, *apples.*
Approchis, 144, *approaches.*
Apostillis, 38, *apostles.*
Ar, 21, *are.*
Archebischop, 156, *archbishop.*
Areird, 50, *disordered.*
Argound, 89, *argued.*
Arme, 170, *arm.*
Armes, 32, *arms.*
Articklis, 2, *articles.*
As, 24, *ashes.*
Ascence, 95, *ascent.*
Ascendis, 167, *ascends.*
Ascendit, 56, *ascended.*
Ascryue, 177, *ascribe.*
Asking, 63, *petition.*
Asse, 18, *ashes.*
Asse, 66, *ass.*
Assence, 107, *ascent.*
Assentioun, 39, *ascension.*
Assis, 180, *asks.*
Assis, 44, *asses.*
Asweill, 176, *as well.*
At the horne, 67, *outlawed.*
Athort, 95, *hither and thither.*
Atouir, 121, *above.*
Attour, 53, *above, over.*
Auance, 170, *advance.*
Auarice, 70, *avarice.*
Aucht, 40, *ought.*
Aueis, 152, *Aves.*
Augustinis, 179, *Augustines, or friars of the order of St Augustine.*

Glossary. 263

Auise, 201, *advise.*
Auld, 81, *old.*
Auoyde, 102, *put away.*
Austeir, 84, *austere.*
Authoure, 88, *author.*
Auysit, 201, *advised.*
Aw, 159, *awe.*
Awalk, 128, 195, *awake.*
Awalkis, 89, *awakes.*
Awin, 84, *own.*
Ay, 28, *aye.*
Ay, 169, *always.*

B.

Babling, 179, *babbling.*
Bad, 10, *bade.*
Bailfull, 147, *cruel.*
Bailfull, 142, *pitiless.*
Baill, 188, *sorrow.*
Baill, 84, *burning, hatred.*
Baine, 152, 169, *bone.*
Bair, 199, *bare.*
Bairne, 43, *child.*
Baith, 28, *both.*
Bak, 97, *back.*
Bak and syde, 97, *altogether.*
Balaamis, 156, *Balaam's.*
Bald, 88, *bold.*
Baldly, 150, *boldly.*
Baliallis, 142, *Belial's.*
Ballat, 25, 81, *ballad.*
Ballatis, 74, *ballads.*
Balulalow, 43, *lullaby.*
Ban, 161, *curse.*
Band, 68, *bond.*
Bandis, 69, *bonds.*
Bane, 158, *bone.*

Baneis, 129, *banish.*
Baneist, 159, *banished.*
Banis, 170, *bones.*
Banischit, 189, *banished.*
Bapteist, 13, *baptised.*
Baptisit, 5, *baptised.*
Baptisme, 12, *baptism.*
Bardit, 82, *equipped.*
Barne, 183, *child.*
Barnis, 49, *children.*
Barrane, 95, *barren.*
Barrounis, 196, *barons.*
Batell, 22, *battle.*
Battell, 122, *battle.*
Baudrie, 1, *lasciviousness.*
Bauld, 182, *bold.*
Be, 36, *by.*
Be war, 43, *beware.*
Beame, 151, *beam.*
Becaus, 6, *because.*
Becum, 156, *become.*
Becummin, 44, *become;* 53, *becoming.*
Befoir, 32, *before.*
Beforne, 23, *before.*
Beggand, 85, *begging.*
Begger, 35, *beggar.*
Beggaris, 165, *beggars.*
Begilit, 161, *beguiled.*
Beginnis, 74, *begins.*
Begouth, 31, *began.*
Begylde, 159, *beguiled.*
Begylit, 169, *beguiled.*
Behald, *behold.*
Behauiour, 125, *behaviour.*
Behauld, 129, *behold.*
Behuffit, 180, *behoved.*
Behuiffit, 180, *behoved.*
Beidis, 152, *beads.*

Beild, 93, *shelter, refuge.*
Beir, 193, *bear, carry.*
Beir, 163, *bier.*
Beiris, 26, *bears.*
Beist, 89, *beast.*
Beistis, 101, *beasts.*
Bek, 91, *bow.*
Belangis, 59, *belongs.*
Belangit, 86, *belonged.*
Beleif, 36, *believe.*
Beleif, 161, *belief.*
Beleuand, 102, *believing.*
Beleue, 3, *believe.*
Beleue, 98, *belief.*
Beleuing, 185, *believing.*
Beleuis, 5, *believes.*
Beleuit, 151, *believed.*
Bellie, 185, *belly.*
Bellis, 156, *Bel's, the great national idol of Babylon.*
Bellis, 47, *bells.*
Belleis, 168, *bellies.*
Bellyis, 164, *bellies.*
Belouit, 41, *beloved.*
Belyue, 186, *quickly, ere long.*
Bemis, 127, *beams.*
Bend, 95, *bound, leap.*
Bene, 48, *been.*
Benefites, 111, *benefits.*
Beneth, 2, *beneath.*
Benignitie, 81, *benignity.*
Bening, 43, *benign.*
Bequyeth, 136, *bequeath.*
Beseik, 115, *beseech.*
Beseiking, 114, *beseeching.*
Besettis, 109, *besets.*
Besyde, 80, *beside.*
Betakinnis, 107, *betokens, denotes.*

Betin, 133, *beaten.*
Betuix, 31, *betwixt.*
Bewtie, 188, *beauty.*
Bezond, 127, *beyond.*
Biddene, 33, *bidding, command.*
Biddis, 195, *bids.*
Big, 49, *build.*
Bill, 54, *record, writ.*
Birnand, 196, *burning.*
Birnist, 84, *burnished.*
Bis, 163, *hiss.*
Bischop, 158, *bishop.*
Bischoppis, 185, *bishops.*
Bissie, 124, *busy.*
Bitternes, 188, *bitterness.*
Bittis, 184, *bits, pieces.*
Blaid, 83, *blade.*
Blait, 163, *bleat.*
Blasphemis, 168, *blasphemes.*
Blasphemit, 103, *blasphemed.*
Blating, 161, *bleating.*
Blaw, 81, *blow.*
Blawis, 166, *blows.*
Blaw, 78, *blow, stroke.*
Blawin, 166, *blown.*
Bleid, 126, *bleed.*
Bleir, *dim.*
Blenk, 198, *look.*
Blerit, 179, *dulled, dimmed.*
Blinde, 59, *blind.*
Blindit, 159, *blinded.*
Blindlingis, 50, *blindfold.*
Blis, 186, *bliss.*
Blis, 65, *bless.*
Blissing, 65, *blessing.*
Blissit, 177, *blessed.*

Glossary. 265

Blys, *bliss.*
Blyssing, 38, *blessing.*
Blyssit, 61, *blessed.*
Blyith, 60, *blithe, merry, joyous.*
Blyithnes, 109, *gladness.*
Blude, 34, *blood.*
Bludie, 50, *bloody.*
Bocht, 20, *bought.*
Bodie, 82, *body.*
Bodyis, 102, *bodies.*
Boist, 78, *threatening.*
Boist, 91, *fraternity.*
Boist, 172, *vaunt.*
Boist, 53, *boasting.*
Bonet, 171, *bonnet.*
Bony, 180, *beautiful.*
Borne, 71, *born.*
Bosome, 36, *bosom.*
Bot, 14, *but.*
Bot, 84, *without.*
Bourd, 70, *jest.*
Bowne, 55, *destined.*
Bowne, 124, *ready.*
Bowne, 198, *prepared.*
Bra, 95, *steep hillside.*
Braid, 9, *broad.*
Braith, 190, *breath.*
Brak, 5, *break.*
Brak, 158, *broke.*
Brank, 181, *restrain, halter.*
Braull, 168, *brawl.*
Brawling, 171, *dancing.*
Breid, 75, *bread.*
Breidis, 188, *breeds.*
Breist, 144, *breast.*
Brek, 147, *break.*
Brekand, 111, *breaking.*
Breking, 88, *breaking.*

Brekis, 3, *breaks.*
Brether, 36, *brethren.*
Bricht, 74, *bright.*
Bringand, 127, *bringing.*
Bringis, 188, *brings.*
Brint, 113, 160, *burned.*
Brocht, 144, *brought.*
Brokin, 127, *broken.*
Browis, 185, *brows.*
Bruik, 10, 178, *enjoy.*
Bruke, 83, *possess.*
Brukkill, 174, *brittle, frail.*
Brukilnes, 131, *brittleness, frailty.*
Brunt, 190, *burned.*
Brym, 97, *raging.*
Buik, *book.*
Buird, 35, *board.*
Buke, 37, *book.*
Buklar, 93, *buckler.*
Bulrand, 97, *rushing, gurgling.*
Bullis, 154, *bulls.*
Bunnis, 180, (for the rhyme), *bums.*
Burbone, *Bourbon.*
Burding, 25, *burden.*
Bure, 122, *bore.*
Burges, 179, *burgess.*
Burgh and land, 62, *town and country.*
Burne, 30, *burn.*
Burnis, 97, *small streams.*
Burris, 91, *burrs.*
Buryit, 3, *buried.*
Busie, 166, *busy.*
But, 168, *without.*
But peir, 26, *unequalled.*
But weir, 130, *without doubt.*

Buyldit, *builded.*
By, 167, *buy.*
Bybill, 191, *bible.*
Bydand, 98, *waiting.*
Byde, 53, *remain, abide.*
Byke, 92, *hive.*
Byrd, 121, *bird.*
Byrne, 89, *burn.*
Byrth, 122, *birth.*
Byte, 91, *bite.*

C.

Cace, 106, *case.*
Caffe, 92, *chaff.*
Cankert, 163, *peevish.*
Caip, 152, *cap.*
Caip, 176, *cloak.*
Cair, 41, *care.*
Cairfull, 168, *sorrowful, woful.*
Caist, 180, *cast.*
Calfis, 113, *calves.*
Callis, 107, *calls.*
Callit, 32, *called.*
Calues, *calves.*
Campion, 99, *champion.*
Capitanis, 168, *captains.*
Captiuitie, 68, *captivity.*
Cardinallis, 179, *cardinals.*
Cariounis, 163, *carions.*
Carnall, 69, *carnal.*
Carue, 63, *carve.*
Caryit, 35, *carried.*
Casius, *Sinai.*
Castell, 190, *castle.*
Castis, 75, *casts.*
Catechisme, 2, *catechism.*

Catholick, 10, *catholic.*
Catiue, 65, *caitiff.*
Catyue, 35, *wretched.*
Caucht, 191, *caught.*
Cauld, 166, *cold.*
Caus, 74, *cause.*
Cause, 158, *because.*
Causis, 121, *causes.*
Causit, *caused.*
Ceis, 47, *cease.*
Ceiss, 90, *cease.*
Ceist, 153, *ceased.*
Celcitude, 45, *highness.*
Celsitude, 104, *highness.*
Ceremonyis, 195, *ceremonies.*
Certaine, 35, *certain.*
Citizenar, 31, *citizen.*
Chaftis, 99, *jaws.*
Chaist, 189, *chaste.*
Chaistitie, 8, *chastity.*
Chancit, 35, *chanced.*
Changeit, *changed.*
Changit, 51, *changed.*
Channoun, 195, *canon.*
Chanslar, 156, *chancellor.*
Chantour, 156, *chanter.*
Chaplane, 156, *chaplain.*
Chargis, 155, *charges.*
Chargit, 38, *charged.*
Cheif, 69, *chief.*
Cheikis, 109, *cheeks.*
Cheir, 32, *cheer.*
Cheis, 189, *choose.*
Cheritie, 60, *charity.*
Cheritabill, 174, *charitable.*
Childeris, 114, *children's.*
Chirurgiane, 149, *surgeon.*
Chirnesyde, *Chirnside.*

Chore, 156, *Korah.*
Chosin, 64, *chosen.*
Christen, 157, *Christian.*
Christianely, 14, *Christian like.*
Christin, 10, *Christian.*
Christinmes, 63, *Christmas.*
Christis, 20, *Christ's.*
Chylde, 74, *child.*
Clais, 44, *clothes.*
Claith, 171, *cloth.*
Claspit, 99, *clasped.*
Clatter, 170, 176, *resound, pour out.*
Cled, 55, *clothed.*
Cleif, 91, *cleave.*
Cleir, 20, *clear.*
Cleirar, 77, *clearer.*
Cleirly, 178, *clearly.*
Cleith, 178, *clothe.*
Cleithe, 32, *clothe.*
Cleirlie, 88, *clearly.*
Cleithing, 32, *clothing.*
Clek, 91, *hatch.*
Clene, 17, *clean.*
Clenar, 107, *cleaner.*
Clengeit, 67, *cleansed.*
Clensen, 107, *purification.*
Clerkis, 166, *clerks.*
Cleue, 90, *cleave.*
Cleuis, 181, *cleaves.*
Clink, 176, *tinkle.*
Clokit, 87, *cloaked.*
Cloikit, 90, *cloaked, disguised;* 161, *feigned.*
Closit, 154, *closed.*
Cloude, 151, *cloud.*
Clude, 151, *cloud.*
Clymmis, 145, *climbs.*

Coft, 172, *bought.*
Coist, 41, 193, *cost.*
Coist, 61, *exchanged*
Coistly, 35, *costly.*
Coistlie, 164, *costly.*
Coitis, 171, *coats.*
Coller, 158, *collar.*
Collectit, *collected.*
Come, 68, *came.*
Comforting, 124, *comfort.*
Commandis, 198, *orders.*
Committit, 54, *committed.*
Commouit, 74, *moved.*
Commoun, 102, *common:*
Commounis, 196, *commons.*
Commounweill, 160, *common good.*
Companie, 17, *company.*
Companzeoun, 30, *companion.*
Compassit, 58, *compassed.*
Compast, 102, *compassed.*
Compleit, 70, *complete.*
Compt, 202, *count.*
Conclude, 172, *concluded.*
Condampne, 86, *condemn.*
Condampnit, 21, *condemned.*
Condempne, 141, *condemn.*
Condempnit, 17, *condemned.*
Conding, 14, *fitting, becoming.*
Conding, 110, *condign.*
Confes, 16, *confess.*
Conforme, 37, *conform.*
Conforme, 68, *conformable.*
Confort, 47, *comfort.*
Conforter, 40, *comforter.*
Confoundis, 101, *confounds.*
Confoundit, 141, *confounded.*

Glossary.

Confyde, 141, *confide.*
Consait, 24, *conceit.*
Consaue, 1, *conceive.*
Consauit, 3, *conceived.*
Consecratit, *consecrated.*
Considerat, 90, *considered.*
Conspyre, 90, *conspire.*
Constantlie, 20, *constantly.*
Consumit, 92, *consumed.*
Contempne, 141, *contemn.*
Contemptioun, 77, *contempt.*
Contenand, 40, *containing.*
Contening, 2, *containing.*
Contenit, *contained.*
Continew, 163, *continue.*
Continewis, 3, *continues.*
Continewit, *continued.*
Contract, 14, *contracted.*
Contractit, 106, *contracted.*
Contrair, 32, *against.*
Contrair, 52, *contrary.*
Contrarious, 105, *perverse.*
Conuart, 110, *turn.*
Conuenientlie, 60, *conveniently.*
Conuersation, 78, *conversation.*
Conuert, 30, *turn.*
Conuertit, 50, *converted.*
Conuoy, 20, *convoy.*
Conuoyis, 80, *convoys.*
Conversioun, *conversion.*
Correctit, 37, *corrected.*
Corruptand, 158, *corrupting.*
Corps, 163, *corpse.*
Cot, 131, *coat.*
Couet, 8, *covet.*
Couetice, 163, *covetousness.*

Couetise, 175, *covetousness.*
Counsellis, 82, *counsels.*
Countis, 79, *accounts.*
Countis, 159, *reckons.*
Countrie, 63, *country.*
Coupe, 81, *cup.*
Courtes, 100, *courteous.*
Cousing, 74, *cousin.*
Cowper, *Cupar.*
Crakit, 152, *talked, chattered.*
Craif, 199, *desire, ask.*
Craif, 66, *importune.*
Craig, 94, *neck.*
Craig, 94, *rock.*
Creat, 18, *created.*
Crib, 66, *manger.*
Cribe, 43, *crib.*
Creddill, 45, *cradle.*
Creidis, 152, *creeds.*
Creid, 180, *creed.*
Creip, 153, *creep.*
Cressed, 187, *Cressida.*
Croce, 39, *cross.*
Croce, 29, *suffering.*
Croune, 91, *crown.*
Crop, 53, *produce, store.*
Crop, 91, *product.*
Crop and rute, 91, *growth and root.*
Croun, 198, *crown.*
Crownes, *crowns.*
Crownit, 39, *crowned.*
Crucifyit, 3, *crucified.*
Cruell, 147, *cruel.*
Cruellie, 39, *cruelly.*
Cruelnes, 86, *cruelty.*
Cruelteis, 99, *cruelties.*
Crummis, 35, *crumbs.*

Crune, 179, *sing.*
Cryand, 104, *crying.*
Cryis, 171, *cries.*
Cryit, 160, *cried.*
Cryme, *crime.*
Cuill, 36, *cool.*
Culd, 31, *could.*
Cullour, 160, *colour.*
Cum, cvm, 25, *come.*
Cumis, 131, *comes.*
Cummand, 33, *coming.*
Cummin, 144, *coming.*
Cumming, 64, *coming.*
Cummis, 189, *comes.*
Cummer, 93, *cumber.*
Cumpanie, 180, *company.*
Cunnand, 14, *covenant.*
Cunning, 14, *skilful.*
Cuntrie, 165, *country.*
Cunze, 171, *coin.*
Curage, 184, *courage.*
Curat, 180, *curate.*
Cure, 85, *care.*
Curious, 70, *anxious.*
Curis, 112, *carest.*
Curs, 88, *curse.*
Cursand, 160, *cursing.*
Cursingis, 176, *curses.*
Cursit, 153, *cursed.*

D.

Daill, 22, *deal.*
Daintelie, 164, *daintily.*
Daintie, 191, *dainty.*
Dallis, 168, *dawns.*
Dammis, 153, *dams.*
Dampnabill, 155, *damnable.*

Dampnatioun, 43, *damnation.*
Dampnatioun, 139, *condemnation.*
Dampnit, 89, *condemned.*
Dangeir, 197, *danger.*
Dansing, 33, *dancing.*
Dansit, 95, *danced.*
Dant, 202, *subdue.*
Dantis, 53, *subdues.*
Dar, 91, *dare.*
Dar, 116, *darest.*
Dartis, 87, *darts.*
Dathane, 156, *Dathan*
Dauid, 19, *David*
Dayis, 83, *days.*
Daylie, 41, *daily.*
Deale, *deal.*
Deand, 143, *dying.*
Deceis, 35, *die.*
Deceissit, 35, *died.*
Deceist, 26, *died.*
Declair, 13, *declare.*
Declaris, 15, *declares.*
Declynde, 177, *declined.*
Decoir, 52, *adornment.*
Decreit, 71, *sentence.*
Decretis, 82, *decrees.*
Dedicat, 101, *dedicated.*
Defectioun, *defection.*
Defendar, 141, *defender.*
Defendis, 86, *defends.*
Defendit, 197, *defended.*
Defyle, 190, *defile.*
Defylde, 191, *defiled.*
Defyling, 190, *defiling.*
Defylit, 101, *defiled.*
Degest, 93, *staid, sedate.*
Degre, 32, *degree.*

Glossary.

Deid, 54, *dead.*
Deid, 38, *death.*
Deid, 7, *deed.*
Deidis, 81, *deeds.*
Deidlie, 73, *deadly.*
Deidly, 126, *deadly.*
Deif, 63, *deaf.*
Deip, 186, *deep.*
Deip, 98, *depth.*
Deipest, 41, *deepest.*
Deir, 168, *dear.*
Deir, 144, *hurt, harm.*
Deirly, *dearly.*
Deit, 59, *died.*
Deith, 69, *death.*
Delatioun, 171, *accusation.*
Delf, 70, *dig.*
Delite, 63, *delight.*
Deliuer, 12, *deliver.*
Deliuerit, 5, *delivered.*
Deludit, 161, *deluded.*
Delyte, 81, *delight.*
Delyuer, 58, *deliver.*
Delyuerit, 58, *delivered.*
Delyuerance, 30, *deliverance.*
Delyverit, *delivered.*
Dence, 159, *Danish.*
Departit, 95, *departed.*
Dependis, 86, *depends.*
Depesche, 149, *send away.*
Derth, 82, *famine.*
Desaitful, 167, *deceitful.*
Desart, 139, *deserving.*
Deseruit, 197, *deserved.*
Destitude, 158, *destitute.*
Destroyit, 83, *destroyed.*
Desyre, 65, *desire.*
Desyris, 162, *desires.*

Determit, 177, *determined.*
Detestit, 63, *detested.*
Detfull, 55, *dutiful.*
Dettis, 17, *debts.*
Detteris, 17, *debtors.*
Deuice, 87, *device.*
Deuil, 21, *devil.*
Deuill, 11, *devil.*
Deuillis, 12, *devil's.*
Deuillis, 24, *devils.*
Deuise, 53, *devise.*
Deuoir, 153, *devour.*
Deuouring, 153, *devouring.*
Deuotioun, 170, *devotion.*
Deuyde, 31, *divide.*
Deuydit, 184, *divided.*
Deuyne, 17, *divine.*
Deuyse, 153, *devise.*
Deuyse, 82, *device.*
Deuysit, 87, *devised.*
Devorit, 97, *devoured.*
Dew, 70, *due.*
Dicht, 103, *adjudged, prepared.*
Differis, 181, *differs.*
Digne, 100, *worthy.*
Discend, 36, *descend.*
Discendit, 69, *descended.*
Disesit, 88, *diseased.*
Discipulis, 38, *disciples.*
Disches, 81, *dishes.*
Discripance, 146, *contradiction.*
Discriue, 68, *describe.*
Discryue, 100, *describe.*
Disherisit, 158, *disinherited.*
Dispise, 187, *despise.*
Dispair, 11, *despair.*
Dispens, 154, *dispense.*

Glossary. 271

Displesit, 162, *displeased.*
Dispone, 128, *give, dispose of.*
Dispyse, 133, *despise.*
Dispyte, 80, *despite.*
Dissaif, 82, *deceive.*
Dissait, 77, *deceit.*
Dissaue, 19, *deceive.*
Dissauit, 49, *deceived.*
Disseuerance, 53, *separation.*
Disswation, 186, *dissuasion.*
Distres, 36, *distress.*
Distroyit, 157, *destroyed.*
Diuers, 159, *diverse.*
Dochter, 192, *daughter.*
Dochteris, 96, *daughters.*
Doctouris, 91, *doctors.*
Doggis, 35, *dogs.*
Dois, 70, *does.*
Doing, 42, *action.*
Dolour, 177, *sadness.*
Dome, 198, *doom.*
Domeit, 26, *doomed.*
Dominiks, 179, *friars of the order of St Dominick.*
Domisday, 143, *doomsday.*
Dotit, 12, *endowed.*
Dotit, 94, *dowered.*
Doun, *down.*
Doun thring, 124, *thrust down.*
Doutles, 184, *doubtless.*
Dour, 110, *severe.*
Dout, 50, *doubt.*
Doutles, 145, *doubtless.*
Dow, 13, *dove.*
Do way, 152, *desist.*
Dowbill, 121, *double.*
Do weill, 181, *do well.*

Downe, 2, *down.*
Draif, 41, *drove.*
Draucht, 25, *last drawn breath.*
Drawis, 195, *draws.*
Dreid, 55, *dread, fear.*
Dreidis, 79, *fear.*
Dreidis, 101, *dread.*
Dreidis, 96, *dreads, fears.*
Dredour, 87, *dread, terror.*
Dremis, 168, *dreams.*
Drerie, 36, *dreary.*
Dres, 31, *address.*
Dres, 171, *redress.*
Dres, 184, *show.*
Dressit, 81, *dressed.*
Drest, 134, *procured.*
Dreuin, 185, *driven.*
Driue, 24, *drive.*
Driuis, 151, *drives.*
Drinke, 5, *drink.*
Drinkis, 6, *drinks.*
Drowne, 12, *drown.*
Drownit, *drowned.*
Drunkinnes, 17, *drunkenness.*
Dryue, 177, *drive.*
Dryuis, 80, *drives.*
Duche, 159, *Dutch.*
Dule, 27, *grief.*
Dulefull, 41, *doleful.*
Dulefully, 26, *wofully.*
Dullie, 89, *sorrowful.*
Dum, 63, *dumb.*
Dunbartane, *Dumbarton.*
Dundie, *Dundee.*
Dunfermling, *Dunfermline.*
Dure, 117, *door.*
Duris, 125, *endures.*

Dyne, 35, *dine*.
Dyntis, 110, *strokes*.
Dyte, 14, *indite*.
Dyte, 100, *writing*.
Dyter, 25, *inditer*.
Dytis, 92, *indites*, *states*.
Dwellaris, 82, *dwellers*.

E.

E, 86, *eye*.
Eare, *ear*.
Easit, 162, *eased*.
Edderis, 94, *adders*.
Edgeit, 87, *edged*.
Editioun, *edition*.
Edometis, 99, *Edomites*.
Edomeitis, 91, *Edomites*.
Ee, 179, *eye*.
Effairis, 195, *affairs*.
Effray, 202, *terror*.
Efter, 25, *after*.
Efter, 47, *according to*.
Efterwart, 29, *afterward*.
Eg, 158, *egg*.
Eik, 96, *also*.
Eik, 106, *add to*.
Eikit, 41, *added*.
Eild, 23, *old age*.
Eine, 69, *eyes*.
Eir, 195, *ear*.
Eir, 176, *auricular*.
Eird, 3, 6, 70, *earth*.
Eirdlie, 167, *earthly*.
Eirdly, 29, *earthly*.
Eiris, 98, *ears*.
Eirth, 2, *earth*.
Eis, 44, *ease*.

Eist, 62, *east*.
Eit, 101, *eat*.
Eitin, 38, *eaten*.
Eitis, 38, *eats*.
Ellis, 91, *else*.
Empreour, 148, *emperor*.
Enchiridion, 74, *handbook*.
Endis, 74, *ends*.
Endit, 188, *ended*.
Endles, 19, *endless*.
Ene, 35, *eyes*.
Enemie, 66, *enemy*.
Enemeis, 78, *enemies*.
Ennemeis, 158, *enemies*.
Enteris, 54, *enters*.
Enterit, *entered*.
Entised, 188, *enticed*.
Epecuriens, 185, *Epicures*.
Epistil, 5, *epistle*.
Epistill, 63, *epistle*.
Equall, 67, *equal*.
Equitie, 85, *equity*.
Erand, 201, *errand*.
Erle, 157, *earl*.
Erlis, 196, *earls*.
Ernestlie, 58, *earnestly*.
Erre, 160, *err*.
Errour, 157, *error*.
Esay, 42, *Isaiah*.
Eschaip, 25, *escape*.
Eschew, 70, *escape*.
Esperance, 53, *hope*.
Espye, 87, *espy*.
Estait, 24, *estate*.
Estaitis, 195, *estates*.
Esteme, 29, *esteem*.
Eternalie, *eternally*.
Euangelistis, 175, *evangelists*.

Euangell, 62, *gospel*.
Eue, 46, *Eve*.
Euermore, 22, *evermore*.
Euer, 82, *ever*.
Euer mair, 127, *evermore*.
Euer moir, 69, *evermore*.
Euerie, 35, *every*.
Euerie quhair, 155, *everywhere*.
Euerilk, 82, *every*.
Euerlastand, 127, *everlasting*.
Euerlasting, 140, *everlasting*.
Euil, euill, 35, *evil*.
Euill, 133, *wickedly*.
Euillis, 12, *evils*.
Euin, 158, *even*.
Euin, 63, *even, evening*.
Exaltit, 88, *exalted*.
Exampill, 192, *example*.
Exces, 17, *excess*.
Exectit, *exacted*.
Exempill, 152, *example*.
Exempillis, 159, *examples*.
Exemptioun, 77, *exemption*.
Exerce, 101, *exercise*.
Exercis, 85, *exercises*.
Exercisit, *exercised*.
Exersit, 101, *exercised*.
Exilit, 118, *exiled*.
Expellis, *expels*.
Expone, 138, *expound*.
Expres, 46, *express*.
Expres, 158, *expressly*.
Exyle, 42, *exile*.
Eyis, 82, *eyes*.
Ezechias, *Hezekiah*.

F.

Fa, 37, *foe*.
Factis, 190, *deeds*.
Faggat, 92, *faggot*.
Faggottis, 123, *faggots*.
Faid, 83, *fade*.
Faill, 40, *fail*.
Failzeit, 88, *failed*.
Faine, 57, *fain*.
Fainest, 35, *most willingly*.
Faining, 188, *feigning*.
Fair, 113, *fare*.
Fair, 42, *fare, go*.
Fais, 69, *foes*.
Fals, 47, *false*.
Falset, 178, *falsehood*.
Falt, 31, *want*.
Fand, 70, *found*.
Fang, *catch, seize, grasp*.
Fant, 31, *faint*.
Fantasie, 201, *fancy*.
Fastand, 6, *fasting*.
Fastit, 180, *fasting*.
Fatell, 162, *fatal*.
Fatheris, *father's, fathers*.
Faultie, 54, *typ. mistake for*
Faultit, *faulted*.
Faultis, *faults*.
Fauour, 178, *favour*.
Fauoris, 160, *favours*.
Faute, 78, *fault*.
Fautes, 80, *faults*.
Fay, 202, *faith*.
Fayne, 187, *feign*.
Febill, 166, *feeble*.
Febilnes, 109, *feebleness*.
Fecht, 177, *fight*.
Feid, 17, *feed*.

S

Feid, 53, *enmity, quarrel.*
Feidis, 164, *feeds.*
Feild, 92, *field.*
Feildis, 80, *fields.*
Feill, 15, *know;* 96, *feel.*
Feind, 169, *fiend, devil.*
Feindis, 27, *devil's;* 45, *fiends.*
Feinzetnes, 77, *feignedness.*
Feir, 41, *fair, strong.*
Feir, 195, *fear.*
Feird, 113, *afraid.*
Feirfull, 198, *fearful.*
Feist, *feast.*
Feit, 32, *feet.*
Feit, 179, *gave fees.*
Fell, 15, *keen.*
Fell, 45, *cruel.*
Fenzeit, 47, *feigned.*
Fenzeitnes, 58, *feignedness.*
Ferleis, 97, *wonders.*
Feruent, 70, *fervent.*
Feruentlie, *fervently.*
Feruentnes, 58, *fervour.*
Fill furth, 123, *fulfil.*
Fillit, 70, *filled.*
Fing, 72, *bundle of thread.*
Firme, 42, *firm.*
Firmelie, 146, *firmly.*
Fit, 182, *measure, tune.*
Fixit, 129, *fixed.*
Flatterie, 79, *flattery.*
Fleand, 93, *flying.*
Fle, 22, *fly from.*
Flee, 26, *fly.*
Fleiche, 180, *flatter.*
Fleis, 90, *flies.*
Flemit, 160, *banished.*
Flesche, 18, *flesh.*

Fleschely, 29, *fleshly.*
Fleschlie, 65, *fleshly.*
Fleshe, 58, *flesh.*
Fleshlie, 76, *fleshly.*
Flie, 181, *fly.*
Fling, 123, *throw.*
Flit, 89, *remove.*
Flockis, 172, *flocks.*
Flour, 26, *flower.*
Floure, 146, *flower.*
Flow, 88, *waver.*
Flude, 92, *flood.*
Flureis, 86, *flourish.*
Flycht, 152, *flight.*
Fo, 41, *fore.*
Foirbearis, 149, *ancestors.*
Foirbearis, 196, *forefathers.*
Foirfather, 174, *forefather.*
Folke, 120, *folk.*
Folkis, 170, *folk.*
Folie, 139, *folly.*
Follit, 102, *pursued, chased.*
Followis, 6, *follows.*
Followit, 47, *followed.*
Fontaine, 68, *fountain.*
Fontane, 5, *fountain.*
Forbiddin, 160, *forbidden.*
For caus, 38, *because.*
Forfair, 167, *perish.*
Forgeue, 115, *forgive.*
Forgeuin, 37, *forgiven.*
Forgeuis, 101, *forgives.*
Forgiue, 4, *forgive.*
Forleit, 99, *forsake.*
Forloir, 193, *lost.*
Forlorne, 30, *lost.*
Forme, 46, *form.*
Formit, 120, *formed.*
Forsaik, 123, *forsake.*

Glossary. 275

Forsuith, 62, *forsooth*.
Forsuke, 133, *forsook*.
Forthinkis, 155, *repents*.
Fortoun, 187, *fortune*.
Fortounis, 189, *fortunes*.
Forzet, 58, *forget*.
Forzet, 26, *forgot*.
Forzettin, 99, *forgotten*.
Foster, 179, *progeny*.
Fosterit, 34, *fostered*.
Foule, 172, *foul*.
Foulis, 101, *fowls*.
Foullar, 97, *fowler*.
Foundatouris, 163, *founders*.
Founding, 72, *found, foundation*.
Fourt, 2, *fourth*.
Fourtie, 6, *forty*.
Fra, 86, *from*.
Fra hand, 31, *immediately*.
Fragilitie, 55, *frailty*.
Fragill, 11, *fragile*.
Fragill, 106, *frail*.
Fragylitie, 14, *frailty*.
Frances, 179, *Francis*.
Fraternitie, 176, *fraternity*.
Fray, 24, *from*.
Fre, 66, *free*.
Fre, *noble*.
Fred, 200, *freed*.
Fredome, 98, *freedom*.
Freind, 37, *friend*.
Freindis, 182, *friends*.
Freir, 179, *friar*.
Freiris, 152, *friars*.

Freith, 41, *release, liberate*.
Frelage, 200, *right of heritage*.
Frelie, 85, *freely*.
Frely, 22, *freely*.
Frensie, 187, *frenzy*.
Fresche, 23, *fresh*.
Frute, 35, *fruit*.
Fry, 165, *spawn*.
Fridayis, 180, *Fridays*.
Foxe, 153, *fox*.
Fude, 65, *food*.
Fuffe, 164, 170, *puff*.
Ful, 101, *full*.
Fule, 87, *fool*.
Fulfill, 31, *fill*.
Fulfillit, 17, *fulfilled*.
Fulis, 152, *fools*.
Fulische, 89, *foolish*.
Fund, 195, *found, fond*.
Fundatioun, 186, *foundation*.
Fundyit, 69, *stiff, frozen*.
Fure, 179, *fared*.
Furth, 71, *forth*.
Furthe, *forth*.
Furthschaw, '79, *declare, show forth*.
Furthwith, 152, *forthwith*.
Fute, 94, *foot*.
Fyfe, *Fife*.
Fylde, 161, *defiled*.
Fylth, 92, *filth*.
Fyne, 28, *end*.
Fyre, 25, *fire*.
Fyue, 36, *five*.

G.

Ga, 50, *go*.
Gadderit, 164, *gathered*.
Gagioun, 156, *slander*.
Gaif, 20, *gave*.
Gaine, 187, *gain*.
Gaine, 156, *gone*.
Gaip, 152, *gape*.
Gais, 20, *goes*.
Gaist, 39, *ghost, spirit*.
Gait, 75, *way*.
Galles, *Gauls*.
Gallous, 152, *gallows*.
Gane, 153, *gone*.
Ganestand, 43, *withstand*.
Gang, 108, *go*.
Gar, 14, *make, compel*.
Garding, 120, *garden*.
Garris, 167, *causes, compels*.
Gart, 34, *compelled*.
Gat, 190, *begot*.
Gat, 157, *got*.
Gaue, 37, *gave*.
Ga will, 80, *go astray*.
Gedde, 163, *Ged*.
Geif, 88, *give*.
Geir, 26, *riches, wealth*.
Gentill, 121, *gentle*.
Gentilnes, 18, *gentleness*.
Geuand, 54, *giving*.
Geue, 150, *if*.
Geue, 76, *give*.
Geuin, 65, *given*.
Geuis, 26, *gives*.
Geuis, 87, *givest*.
Gevin, *given*.
Gif, 85, *give*.
Gif, 34, *if*.

Giftes, *gifts*.
Giftis, 65, *gifts*.
Gilt, 95, *gilded*.
Gilt, 135, *guilt*.
Giltles, 2, *giltless*.
Giue, 29, *give*.
Giue, 167, *if*.
Giuen, 114, *given*.
Ghaist, 3, *ghost*.
Glaid, 194, *glad*.
Glaidlie, 120, *gladly*.
Glaidly, 124, *gladly*.
Glaidnes, 33, *gladness*.
Glaidness, 99, *gladness*.
Glaik, 156, *trifle, spend time*.
Glas, 189, *mirror*.
Glie, 181, *glee*.
Gloir, 64, *glory*.
Gloird, 71, *gloried*.
Gloiris, *glories*.
Glorie, 62, *glory*.
Gloris, 44, *gloriest*.
Gluttoun, 34, *glutton*.
Gluttounis, 35, *glutton's*.
Gnashe, *gnash*.
Goddis, 52, *God's*.
Goddis, 152, *Gods*.
Godheid, 66, *Godhead*.
Godis, 2, *gods*.
Godles, 26, *godless*.
Godlie, 65, *godly*.
Goldin, *golden*.
Gospell, 73, *gospel*.
Gothis, *Goths*.
Gottin, 149, *begot*.
Gottin, 181, *got, won*.
Gouernance, 75, *government*.
Gouerne, 107, *govern*.

Gouerning, 72, *government.*
Gouernour, 50, *governor.*
Gouernouris, 92, *governors.*
Gowne, 91, *gown.*
Graip, 202, *feel, grope.*
Graith, 184, *clothing.*
Graith, 69, *prepare.*
Graithit, 16, *prepared, made ready.*
Grantis, 101, *grants.*
Grantit, 6, *granted.*
Gras, 187, *grass.*
Grasse, 83, *grass.*
Grat, 71, *wept.*
Gratious, 45, *gracious.*
Graue, 39, *grave.*
Grauin, 2, *graven.*
Grauit, 13, *buried.*
Gre, 90, *agree.*
Gredie, 65, *greedy.*
Gredynes, 185, *greediness.*
Greif, 102, *grief.*
Greif, 83, *grieve.*
Greit, 35, *great.*
Greitar, 113, *greater.*
Greitest, 44, *greatest.*
Greitlie, 155, *greatly.*
Greitnes, 100, *greatness.*
Grene, 179, *green.*
Gress, 202, *grass.*
Greting, 103, *weeping.*
Gretumlie, 125, *greatly.*
Greuance, 75, *grievance.*
Greuand, 8, *grieving.*
Greue, 39, *grieve.*
Greuis, 172, *grieves.*
Greuis, 134, *griefs.*
Greuit, 19, *grieved.*
Greuous, 92, *grievous.*

Greuously, 26, *grievously.*
Grevovs, 132, *grievous.*
Grip, 126, *lay hold, seize.*
Grit, 59, *great.*
Ground, 87, *whetted.*
Groundit, 141, *grounded.*
Ground-stane, 176, *foundation stone.*
Gruncheand, 26, *groaning and grinding the teeth.*
Gude, 65, *good.*
Gude, 45, *possession.*
Gude, 85, *property.*
Gudis, 34, *goods.*
Gudlie, 110, *goodly.*
Gude-man, 174, *good man.*
Gudnes, 68, *goodness.*
Guk, guk, 163, *cry of a fowl.*
Gyand, 82, *giant.*
Gyde, 20, *guide.*
Gydis, 92, *guides.*
Gydit, 184, *guided.*
Gyis, 195, *fashion.*
Gylis, 182, *guile.*
Gylt, 116, *guilt.*
Gyltie, 5, *guilty.*
Gyrne, 175, *gin, snare.*
Gyrne, 84, *grin.*
Gyrth, 94, *sanctuary.*

H.

Habitakill, 78, *habitation.*
Habite, 131, *habit.*
Haboundantlie, 115, *abundantly.*
Hadington, *Haddington.*

Haif, 58, *have.*
Hail, 81, *whole.*
Haill, 53, *whole, wholly.*
Haill, 73, *hail.*
Haillelie, 56, *wholly.*
Haillely, 192, *wholly.*
Haillis, 149, *heals.*
Haillit, 59, *healed.*
Hairt, 146, *heart.*
Haist, 153, *haste.*
Haist, 90, *hasten.*
Haistely, 26, *hastily.*
Haistie, 87, *hasty.*
Haistelie, 32, *hastily.*
Haistines, 186, *haste.*
Hait, 70, *hate.*
Haitit, 158, *hated.*
Hald, 30, *hold.*
Haldin, *held, compelled.*
Haldis, 168, *holds.*
Halie, 139, *holy.*
Halines, 115, *holiness.*
Hallowit, 4, *hallowed.*
Haly, 13, *holily.*
Haly, 28, *holy.*
Haly croce, *holy cross.*
Haly Gaist, *Holy Ghost.*
Haly kirk, 162, *holy church.*
Halynes, 183, *holiness.*
Haly Spreit, 47, *Holy Spirit.*
Haly Wryte, 48, *Holy Scripture.*
Hame, 32, *home.*
Handis, 89, *hands.*
Hand-madin, 125, *handmaiden.*
Hand write, 71, *hand-writing.*
Hang, 71, *hung.*

Hangit, 162, *hanged.*
Hant, 81, *to frequent.*
Happin, 192, *happen.*
Hard, 50, *heard.*
Harkin, 202, *hearken.*
Harlatrie, 34, *harlotry.*
Harlatrie, *villany.*
Harlottis, 190, *harlots.*
Harnes, 91, *harness, armour.*
Harnest, 182, *armed.*
Harnis, 99, *brains.*
Harpe, 81, *harp.*
Harpis, 99, *harps.*
Hart, 65, *heart.*
Hartfullie, *heartily.*
Hartfully, 11, *cordially.*
Hartis, 169, *hearts.*
Hartis, 47, *heart's.*
Hartly, 41, *beloved.*
Hartly, 66, *hearty, cordial.*
Hauand, 102, *having.*
Haue, 74, *have.*
Hauing, 116, *having.*
Hauld, 32, *hold, keep.*
Hay! 61, 168, *a joyous exclamation.*
Hecht, 35, *called.*
Hecht, 53, *promise, engage.*
Hecht, 17, 107, *promised.*
Hed, 144, *had.*
Heich, 47, *high.*
Heid, 170, *head.*
Heill, 114, *health.*
Heill, 170, *heel.*
Heip, 101, *heap.*
Heipand, 54, *heaping.*
Heipis, 81, *heaps.*
Heir, *hear.*

Glossary. 279

Heir, 25, *here*.
Heir and thair, 182, *here and there*.
Heirfoir, 69, *for this*.
Heirfoir, 76, *therefore*.
Heiris, 101, *hears*.
Heisit, 180, *heaved*.
Heit, 60, *heat*.
Helenis, 186, *Helen's*.
Helis, 158, *Eli's*.
Hellis, 52, *hell's*.
Helpis, 26, *helps*.
Helpit, 106, *helped*.
Helth, 63, *health*.
Hely, 157, *Eli*.
Helias, 157, *Elijah*.
Heretyke, 166, *heretic*.
Heretykis, 160, *heretics*.
Herisie, 50, *heresy*.
Heryit, 115, *plundered*.
Hes, 30, *has*.
Hes, 18, *hast*.
Hethin, 51, *heathen*.
Heuie, 25, *heavy*.
Heuin, 37, *heaven*.
Heuines, 114, *heaviness*.
Heuinlie, 52, *heavenly*.
Heuinly, 35, *heavenly*.
Heuinnis, 69, *heavens*.
Heuinnis, 167, *heaven's*.
Heuy, 126, *heavy*.
Heuynes, 105, *heaviness*.
Hew, 70, *hue*.
Hicht, 92, *height*.
Hidder, 198, *hither*.
Hiddertill, 112, *hitherto*.
Hidder socht, 193, *brought hither*.
Hie, 17, *high*.

Hiest, 18, 145, *highest*.
Hillis, 95, *hills*.
Him sell, 61, *himself*.
Hing, 46, *hang*.
Hinmest, 163, *the last*.
Hippis, 180, *hips*.
Hir, 45, *her*.
Hirdis, 164, *shepherds*.
Historyis, 191, *histories*.
Hoipit, 108, *hoped*.
Honest, 32, *respectable*.
Honouris, 66, *honours*.
Hony, 184, *honey*.
Hopeand, 108, *hoping*.
Horne, 105, *outlawry*.
Hornis, 91, *horns*.
Horribill, 196, *horrible*.
Hors, 8, *horse*.
Hors, 172, *horses*.
Hounger, 69, *hunger*.
Houngrie, 31, *hungry*.
Hount, 161, *hunt*.
Hous, 2, *house*.
Housis, 196, *houses*.
Hude, 91, *hood*.
Hudis, 169, *hoods*.
Huke, 80, *hook*.
Humanitie, 66, *humanity*.
Humbill, 68, *humble*.
Humbilnes, 66, *humility*.
Humelie, 96, *humbly*.
Humill, 115, *humble*.
Hunder, 160, *hundred*.
Hundis, 153, *hounds*.
Hundreth, 161, *hundred*.
Huntis, 153, *hunts*.
Hure, 164, *whore*.
Huredome, 158, *whoredom*.
Hurklit, 91, *folded*.

Hurtis, 78, *hurts.*
Hyde, 169, *hide.*
Hymne, 99, *hymn.*
Hymnis, *hymns.*
Hyne, 199, *hence.*
Hypocresie, 181, *hypocrisy.*
Hypocrisie, 87, *hypocrisy.*
Hypocritis, 91, *hypocrites.*
Hyrdis, 44, *shepherds.*
Hyre, 197, *hire.*

I.

Identlie, 22, *diligently.*
Idilnes, 173, *idleness.*
Idolateris, 152, *idolaters.*
Idolatrie, 50, *idolatry.*
Idoles, 63, *idols.*
Idoll, 91, *idle.*
Ilk, 25, *every, each.*
Imagerie, 176, *idols.*
Imagerie, 172, *image worship.*
Imagis, 95, *images.*
Imploir, 69, *implore.*
Imprentit, *imprinted.*
Impyre, 92, *empire.*
Impunge, 157, *impugn.*
In, 41, *into.*
Inche, 202, *inch.*
Includit, 161, *included.*
Inclusit, 166, *enclosed.*
Inclyne, 114, *incline.*
In contrair, 87, *against.*
In contrarie, 97, *in opposition.*
Incres, 57, *increase.*
Incressis, *increases.*

In deid, 65, *indeed.*
Indure, 89, *endure.*
Indure, 50, *harden.*
Induris, 14, *endures.*
Indurit, 163, *hardened.*
Indurit, 155, *endured.*
Infect, 191, *infected.*
Inglis, 159, *English.*
Ingrait, 135, *ungrateful.*
Inherite, 84, *inherit.*
Innocens, 61, *innocence.*
Innocentis, 30, *innocents.*
Inquyre, 87, *inquire.*
Inspyre, 70, *inspire.*
Institute, 14, *instituted.*
Instructioun, *instruction.*
Instructit, 178, *instructed.*
Inteir, 146, *entire.*
Intelligens, 186, *knowledge, intelligence.*
In till, 47, *into.*
Intill, 66, *into.*
Intill, 79, *unto.*
Into, 63, *in.*
Inuaid, 41, *invade.*
Inuent, 176, *invent.*
Inuentioun, 186, *invention.*
Inuentit, 152, *invented.*
Inuerkething, *Inverkeithing.*
Inwart, 40, *inward.*
Inwart, 91, *inwardly.*
Inwartlie, 131, *inwardly.*
In weir, 197, *doubtful.*
Ioy, 20, *joy.*
Isaack, 107, *Isaac.*
Isack, 70, *Isaac.*
Isackis, 70, *Isaac's.*
Isay, 37, *Isaiah.*

Glossary.

Ismalitis, 91, *Ishmaelites*.
Isope, 107, *hyssop*.

J.

Jabene, 91, *Jabin*.
Jacobinis, 179, *Jacobins*.
Jacobis, 95, *Jacob's*.
Jakmen, 172, *men in armour*.
Jelous, 200, *jealous*.
Jesew, 69, *Jesus*.
Jet, 182, *gad about*.
Jewes, 71, *Jews*.
Jewis, 147, *Jews*.
Jewis, 137, *Jew's*.
Johne, 59, *John*.
Jordane, 95, *Jordan*.
Jornay, 32, *journey*.
Josaph, 73, *Joseph*.
Josephis, 192, *Joseph's*.
Josias, 157, *Josiah*.
Josue, *Joshua*.
Joye, *joy*.
Joyes, *joys*.
Joyis, 45, *joys*.
Joyne, 192, *join*.
Joynit, 12, *joined*.
Jouk, 91, *nod*.
Joukis, 169, *bowings*.
Juda, 71, *Judah*.
Judethis, 192, *Judith's*.
Judgeing, 106, *judgment*.
Judgeit, 106, *judged*.
Juge, 197, *judge*.
Jugement, 158, *judgment*.
Junii, *June*.
Jurie, 135, *Jewry*.

K.

Kaill, 180, *broth*.
Keild, 158, *killed*.
Keill, 161, *kill*.
Keine, 166, *keen*.
Keip, 131, *heed*.
Keip, 155, *keep*.
Keipar, 142, *keeper*.
Keiping, 48, *keeping*.
Keipis, 2, *keeps*.
Keipit, 127, *kept*.
Ken, 48, *know*.
Kend, 25, *knew*.
Kend, 148, *know*.
Kend, 198, *known*.
Kend, 30, *made known*.
Kendlit, 97, *kindled*.
Kest, 41, *cast*.
Keyis, 6, *keys*.
Killis, 194, *kills*.
Killit, 137, *killed*.
Kin, 7, *kind*.
Kin, 64, *kind, sort*.
Kin, 70, *kindred*.
Kincarne of Neill, *Kincardine O'Neill*.
Kingdome, 4, *kingdom*.
Kingis, 154, *kings*.
Kinrik, 11, *kingdom*.
Kinroscheir, *Kinross-shire*.
Kirk, 43, *church*.
Kis, 138, *kiss*.
Kissit, 32, *kissed*.
Kittill, 179, *tickle*.
Knaw, 36, *know*.
Knaw, 79, *known*.
Knawand, 56, *knowing*.

Knawers, 16, *people who know.*
Knawin, 118, *known.*
Knawis, 154, *knowest.*
Knawis, 184, *knows.*
Knawledge, 27, *knowledge.*
Knelland, 195, *knelling.*
Kneill, 170, *kneel.*
Kneis, 45, *knees.*
Knicht, 24, *knight.*
Knittis, 130, *knits.*
Knot, 131, *pithy saying.*
Ky, 44, *cows.*
Kyd, 33, *kid.*
Kyis, 171, *cows.*
Kyithit, 40, *shewn.*
Kynde, 36, *kind.*
Kynde, 56, *sort, manner.*
Kyndely, 32, *kindly.*
Kyndnes, 46, *kindness.*
Kyson, 92, *Kishon.*

L.

Labouris, 130, *labours.*
Ladin, 25, *laden.*
Laif, 53, *the rest.*
Laik, *lack, need.*
Laip, 153, *lap.*
Lair, 11, *lore, learning.*
Lait, 180, *late.*
Lait and air, 142, *late and early.*
Laithly, 35, *loathsome.*
Laithsum, 191, *loathsome.*
Lambe, 37, *lamb.*
Lambes, *Lammas.*
Lambis, 95, *lambs.*

Lamit, 59, *lame.*
Lammis, 153, *lambs.*
Landis, 178, *lands.*
Lane, 79, *alone.*
Lang, 48, *long.*
Langest, *longest.*
Langing, 192, *longing.*
Lap, 95, *leaped.*
Lardounis, 179, *lumps.*
Laser, 23, *leisure.*
Lassis, 180, *lasses, girls.*
Lat, 118, *let.*
Latine, *Latin.*
Laubour, 89, *labour.*
Lauch, 84, *laugh.*
Laude, 71, *blessing.*
Laude, 100, *praise.*
Laudes, 137, *praises.*
Lave, 96, *the remainder, the rest.*
Law, 66, *low.*
Lawder, *Lauder.*
Lawis, 166, *laws.*
Lawit, 170, *lay.*
Lawly, 66, *lowly.*
Lawlynes, 38, *lowliness.*
Lawrel, 86, *laurel.*
Lay, 124, *pledge.*
Layit, 195, *laymen.*
Leand, 64, *lying.*
Lection, 196, *lesson.*
Legall, 71, *legal.*
Leiche, 159, *loiter, tarry.*
Leid, 27, *lead.*
Leid, 14, *watchword.*
Leidand, 151, *leading.*
Leif, 123, *leave.*
Leif, 84, *life.*
Leif, 64, *live.*

Glossary.

Leifis, 193, *leaves.*
Leigis, *lieges.*
Leill, 142, *constant.*
Leing, 77, *lying.*
Leip, *leap.*
Leir, 76, *learn.*
Leirne, 170, *learn.*
Leirning, 42, *learning.*
Leirnit, 160, *learned.*
Leis, 168, *lies.*
Leist, 30, *least.*
Leist, 36, *lest.*
Lely, 146, *lily.*
Leit, 169, *lied.*
Len, 79, *lend.*
Lenth, 49, *length.*
Les, 12, *less.*
Les and moir, 64, *small and great.*
Lesingis, 168, *lies.*
Lest, 82, *last, endure.*
Lestand, 144, *lasting.*
Lestis, 29, *lasts.*
Lestit, 180, *lasted.*
Lettis, 125, *lets.*
Leuand, 14, *living.*
Leuch, 102, *laughed.*
Leue, 64, *leave.*
Leue, 24, *live.*
Leuing, 114, *living, life.*
Leuis, 181, *leaves.*
Leuis, 83, *lives.*
Leuit, 187, *lived.*
Leuittis, 158, *Levites.*
Leyn, 199, *lean.*
Libertie, 67, *liberty.*
Licharie, 185, *lechery.*
Licharus, 190, *lecherous.*
Licherie, 65, *lechery.*

Licht, 78, *enlighten.*
Licht, 29, *light.*
Lichtin, 127, *enlighten.*
Lichtleis, 70, *slights.*
Lichtly, 95, *lightly.*
Lickand, 35, *licking.*
Lier, 154, *liar.*
Liftit, 39, *lifted.*
Lin, 102, *rock, precipice.*
Lippis, 77, *lips.*
List, 15, *chooses.*
Listis, 95, *lists.*
Litill, 195, *little.*
Liue, 51, *live.*
Lois, 174, *lose.*
Loissit, 23, *lost.*
Loist, 34, *lost.*
Lollaris, 11, *heretics, Lollard's.*
Lordis, 2, *Lords.*
Lordis, 30, *Lord's.*
Lose, 70, *loss.*
Loste, 189, *lost.*
Lot, 131, *possession.*
Loudlie, 168, *loudly.*
Loue, 100, *love.*
Louing, 48, *blessing.*
Louing, 111, *praise.*
Loup, 95, *jump.*
Loupe, 96, *leap.*
Louse, 168, *loose.*
Lownis, 185, *idlers, villains.*
Lowreis, 183, *foxes.*
Lowse, 193, *loose.*
Lowsit, 139, *loosed.*
Lowsing, 6, *loosing.*
Lowsis, 18, *looses.*
Lufaris, 34, *lovers, friends.*
Lufe, 62, *love.*

Glossary.

Luffis, 126, *loves*
Lufis, 81, *loves.*
Lufit, 201, *loved.*
Luifaris, 122, *lovers.*
Luifis, 161, *loves.*
Luiffing, 119, *loving.*
Luiffis, 85, *loves.*
Luk, 30, *Luke.*
Luke, 29, *look.*
Luking, 65, *looking.*
Lukis, 82, *looks.*
Lustie, 81, *pleasant.*
Lusting, 191, *lustful.*
Lustis, 27, *lusts.*
Lustit, 192, *lusted.*
Lusum, 100, *lovely.*
Ly, 66, *lie.*
Lychorie, 70, *lechery.*
Lychorus, 190, *lecherous.*
Lyfe, 20, *life.*
Lyfis, 179, *lives.*
Lyftit, 35, *lifted.*
Lyis, 43, *lies.*
Lyke, 37, *like.*
Lykenes, 138, *likeness.*
Lykis, 153, *likes.*
Lykit, 133, *liked.*
Lymmaris, 180, *worthless fellows.*
Lymmerie, 180, *villany.*
Lyonnis, 94, *lion's.*
Lyoun, 71, *lion.*
Lyre, 163, *flesh, skin.*
Lytill, 65, *little.*
Lytill quhile, 83, *a short time.*
Lytill stound, 33, *short time, a short space.*
Lyue, 143, *life.*
Lyues, 96, *lives.*

M.

Ma, 156, *more.*
Madionitis, 91, *Midianites.*
Magnifie, 43, *magnify.*
Mahomete, *Mahomet.*
Maid, 61, *made.*
Maidenheid, 127, *maidenhood.*
Maiestie, 67, *majesty.*
Maij, 120, *May.*
Mair, 12, *more.*
Mair, 38, *greater.*
Mair and min, 38, *greater and less.*
Maist, 82, *most, greatest.*
Maister, 153, *master.*
Majestie, 68, *majesty.*
Mak, 32, *make.*
Makand, 55, *making.*
Makis, 152, *makes.*
Makis, 19, *makest.*
Maledie, 94, *malady.*
Maling, 49, *malign.*
Malitious, 185, *malicious.*
Mammontrie, 63, *idolatry.*
Man, 42, *must.*
Maner, 152, *manner.*
Maneir, 30, *manner.*
Manesweir, 65, *perjure.*
Manis, 8, *man's.*
Mannis, 85, *man's.*
Mankynd, 76, *mankind.*
Mankynde, 73, *mankind.*
Mankynde, 59, *human nature.*
Mantene, 91, *maintain.*
Marche, *March.*
Mariage, 165, *marriage.*

Glossary. 285

Marie, *The Virgin Mary.*
Marie, 154, *marry.*
Marrit, 162, *marred.*
Mark, 93, *dark.*
Mark nor licht, 93, *dark nor light.*
Martine, *Martin.*
Maryit, 165, *married.*
Materis, 191, *matters.*
Matussalem, 146, *Methuselah.*
Mayd, 123, *maid.*
Meane, 186, *means.*
Mediatour, 67, *mediator.*
Meik, 142, *meek.*
Meiklie, 120, *meekly.*
Meine, 166, *mean.*
Meir, 139, *mere.*
Meit, 18, *meat.*
Meit, 32, *meet, fit.*
Mekill, 165, *much.*
Mekle, 33, *much.*
Mell, 62, *become acquainted with.*
Melodie, *melody.*
Memberis, 70, *members.*
Mend, 46, *amend.*
Mendis, 52, *amends.*
Menis, 33, *means.*
Menis, 83, *men's.*
Mennis, 30, *men's.*
Menstraly, 33, *minstrelsy.*
Mercat, 165, *market.*
Mercie, 2, *mercy.*
Mercyfull, 48, *merciful.*
Mercyfullie, 10, *mercifully.*
Mercyles, 103, *without mercy.*
Mercyles, 155, *merciless.*

Mers, *Merse.*
Meruellis, 37, *wonders.*
Meruellous, 111, *marvellous.*
Meruellouslie, 97, *marvellously.*
Merynes, 33, *merryness.*
Mes, 183, *the Mass.*
Messis, 181, *Masses.*
Mesure, 41, *measure.*
Meter, 6, *metre.*
Micht, 32, *might, power.*
Michtie, 73, *mighty.*
Michtis, 66, *powers.*
Michtis, 93, *strength, power.*
Michtiest, 92, *mightiest.*
Michtfullie, 94, *with power.*
Middis, *middle.*
Midnicht, 79, *midnight.*
Min, 38, *less.*
Minde, *mind.*
Minsing, 188, *mincing.*
Mirk, 179, *dark.*
Mirkness, 126, *darkness.*
Mirrie, 182, *merry.*
Mirrour, 196, *mirror.*
Mirrylie, *merrily.*
Mirrynes, 67, *mirth.*
Mis, 109, *miss.*
Mis, 46, *amiss.*
Mis, 60, *misdeed, sin, fault.*
Misauenture, 94, *misadventure.*
Mischeuouslie, 159, *mischievously.*
Misdeid, 55, *wrongdoing.*
Misericord, 49, *merciful.*
Miserie, 69, *misery.*

Misfair, 196, *fare ill.*
Misfortoun, 94, *misfortune.*
Misknaw, 64; Misknawis, 166, *ignorant of.*
Misken, 110, *be ignorant of.*
Misken, 84, *misunderstand.*
Miskennit, 113, *was ignorant of.*
Misknew, 71, *knew not.*
Misreule, 172, *misrule.*
Misthryue, 164, *thrive amiss.*
Mo, 58, *more.*
Moabitis, 91, *Moabites.*
Mockit, 102, *mocked.*
Moir, 57, *more.*
Moitis, 96, *motes.*
Molde, 82, 163, *earth.*
Mon, 198, *must.*
Mone, 193, *moan.*
Monence, *Monance.*
Monethis, 74, *months.*
Monkis, 169, *monks.*
Monstouris, 152, *monsters.*
Mont, 75, *mount.*
Montanis, 95, *mountains.*
Mony, 71, *many.*
Monyfald, 106, *manifold.*
Mony fauld, 167, *manifold.*
Morne, 198, *morrow.*
Mortifie, 37, *mortify.*
Mot, 68, *may.*
Mot, 103, *might.*
Moue, 27, *move.*
Mouit, 132, *moved.*
Mountit, 185, *mounted.*
Mouswobs, 96, *spider webs.*
Moyses, 36, *Moses.*
Mucke, 92, *dung.*

Mufe, 83, *move.*
Mufe thé not, 83, *be not disturbed.*
Muifit, 95, *moved.*
Mulis, 172, *mules.*
Mumleit, 152, *mumbled.*
Mumling, 183, *mumbling.*
Mummillit, 176, *mumbled.*
Murne, 24, *mourn.*
Murning, 77, *mourning.*
Murnis, 122, *mourns.*
Murther, 3, *murder.*
Mvsing, 145, 155, *musing.*
Mylde, 73, *mild.*
Myle, 160, *mile.*
Mynde, 36, 159, *mind.*
Myndes, *mines, remembrance.*
Myndis, 28, *minds.*
Myne, 42, *mine.*
Myne, 65, *my, mine.*
Myrrie, 46, *merry.*
Myrthis, 146, *gladness.*
Myster, 96, *need.*
Mysteris, 66, *needs.*
Myster maist, 96, *greatest need.*
Mysticall, 71, *mystical.*
Myte, 154, *mite.*

N.

Na, 6, *no, not.*
Naillit, 122, *nailed.*
Nalit, 134, *nailed.*
Na kin wise, 64, *nowise.*
Na kin wyse, 7, *no manner of way.*

Glossary. 287

Nane, 74, *no, none.*
Nathing, 56, *nothing.*
Natiounis, 74, *nations.*
Natiue, 14, *native.*
Natiuitie, 67, *nativity.*
Necessarie, 4, *necessary.*
Neid, 10, *need.*
Neidis, 16, *needest.*
Neir, 101, *near.*
Neir, 168, *nearly.*
Neist, 144, *next.*
Nek, 157, *neck.*
Nettis, 87, *nets.*
Neuer, 38, *never.*
Nicht, 5, *night.*
Nichtbour, 72, *neighbour.*
Nichtbouris, 3, *neighbours.*
Nixt, 72, *next.*
Nobilest, 38, *noblest.*
Nobill, *noble.*
Nobles, 202, *nobleness.*
Nocht, 172, *not.*
Nocht, 49, *nothing.*
Noddis, 169, *nods.*
Noe, *Noah.*
Noisthirlis, 96, *nostrils.*
None, 173, *noon.*
Notis, 195, *notes.*
Nouembris, *November.*
Nouther, 145, *neither.*
Nowellis, 43, *news.*
Nowther, 159, *neither.*
Noy, 24, *annoyance.*
Noyis, 78, *annoys.*
Noyis, 88, *noise.*
Nukit, 171, *nooked.*
Numerat, 176, *numbered.*
Nunne, 165, *nun.*
Nunnis, 180, *nuns.*

Nureist, 91, *nourished.*
Nurisching, 79, *nourishing.*
Nycht, 151, *night.*
Nymbill, 182, *nimble.*
Nyse, 132, *gross.*

O.

Obeyis, 82, *obeys.*
Obeyit, 33, *obeyed.*
Oblatiounis, 195, *oblations.*
Obserue, 85, *observe:*
Obseruance, 55, *observance.*
Obseruis, 79, *observes.*
Obsoluit, 154, *absolved.*
Obteine, 117, *obtain.*
Obtene, 12, *obtain.*
Occour, 79, *usury.*
Och, 138, *Oh!*
Ocht, 86, *ought.*
Ocht, 90, *ought, anything.*
Od, 176, *odd.*
Od or euin, 176, *odd or even.*
Of, 171, *off.*
Offendand, 11, *offending.*
Offendit, 195, *offended.*
Offeringis, 195, *offerings.*
Offerit, 151, *offered.*
Oist, *host.*
Oliue, 114, *olive.*
One, 20, *on.*
Onles, 153, *unless.*
Onlie, 56, *only.*
On liue, 96, *alive.*
On lyfe, 33, *alive.*
Ony, 91, *any.*
Ony wayis, 36, *anywise.*

Glossary.

Ophni, 157, *Hophni.*
Oppin, 127, *open.*
Oppinnis, 18, *opens.*
Oppres, 12, *oppress.*
Ordand, 13, *ordained.*
Ordour, 179, *order.*
Ordouris, 120, *orders.*
Organis, 81, *organs.*
Ornamentis, 81, *ornaments.*
Osan, 174, *Hosanna.*
Ouer, 120, *over.*
Ouercum, 126, *overcome.*
Ouerest, 38, *overest, greatest.*
Ouergane, 96, *overrun.*
Ouer gang, 94, *go over.*
Ouergang, 124, *oppress.*
Ouerlaid, 155, *overlaid, oppressed.*
Ouerquhelmit, 97, *overwhelmed.*
Ouerthrawin, 155, *overthrown.*
Ouerthrew, 91, *overthrew.*
Ouid, 187, *Ovid.*
Ouir, 202, *over, too.*
Ouirdriue, 23, *overdrive, spend, pass.*
Ouirquhelme, 99, *overwhelm.*
Ouirset, 23, *overset.*
Ouirspred, 151, *overspread.*
Ouirthraw, 102, *overthrow.*
Ouklie, 184, *weekly.*
Outher, 124, *either.*
Out tak, 128, *except.*
Out throw, 124, *throughout.*
Outwart, 91, *outwardly.*
Overthrowen, *overthrown.*
Ovr, 15, *our.*

Oxe, 66, *ox.*
Oxin, 44, *oxen.*

P.

Pacience, 29, *patience.*
Pacientlie, 29, *patiently.*
Pagane, 178, *pagan.*
Paine, 69, *pain.*
Paine, 17, *suffering.*
Paintit, 173, *painted.*
Paip, 169, *pope.*
Paipis, 195, *popes.*
Paith, 117, *path.*
Paithis, 85, *paths.*
Paithway, 117, *pathway.*
Pane, 167, *pain.*
Panis, 68, *pains.*
Pantounis, 171, *slippers.*
Papis, 172, *popes.*
Papistrie, 186, *papistry.*
Parabill, 30, *parable.*
Paramouris, 163, *paramours.*
Pareis, 180, *Paris, parish.*
Pardonis, 153, *pardons.*
Pardounis, 14, *pardons.*
Partis, *parts.*
Partit, 184, *parted.*
Pas, 67, *pass.*
Pascall, 38, *paschal.*
Pasche, *Easter.*
Passioun, 37, *passion.*
Passioun, 55, *suffering.*
Passis, 59, *surpasses.*
Passit, 38, *passed.*
Pater-nosteris, 176, *pater-nosters.*

Glossary. 289

Patter, 170, *chatter*.
Paunce, 182, *amble*.
Payit, 154, *paid*.
Peax, 90, *peace*.
Peblis, *Peebles*.
Peciabillie, 83, *peaceably*.
Pecis, 97, *pieces*.
Peice, 61, *peace*.
Peir, 26, *equal*.
Peirles, 35, *unequalled*.
Peirs, 139, *pierce*.
Peirsit, 147, *pierced*.
Peltrie, 154, *pedler's ware*.
Penneis, 154, *pence*.
Pennes, 93, *feathers*.
Penurie, 188, *penury*.
Pepellis, 82, *peoples*.
Pepil, pepill, *people*.
Perellis, 94, *perils*.
Perfit, perfite, *perfect*.
Performit, 70, *performed*.
Perfyte, 57, *perfect*.
Perische, 155, *perish*.
Perischit, 92, *perished*.
Perishe, 79, *perish*.
Perishit, 97, *destroyed*.
Perpetuall, 82, *perpetually*.
Perrell, 84, *peril*.
Perrellis, 94, *perils*.
Persaue, 137, *perceive*.
Persauis, 82, *perceives*.
Perseueir, 51, *persevere*.
Perseuerance, 20, *perseverance*.
Perseuir, 29, *persevere*.
Perseveir, 20, *persevere*.
Persew, 70, *pursue*.
Persewaris, 80, *pursuers*.
Persones, 195, *parsons*.

Persoun, 180, *parson*.
Perswaid, 72, *perceived*.
Perturbe, 92, *vex*.
Perturbis, 82, *disturbs*.
Peruerst, 186, *perverse*.
Perysit, 76, *perished*.
Petitiounis, 4, *petitions*.
Pittenweme, *Pittenweem*.
Pharesians, 168; Pharisians, 47, *Pharisees*.
Phenis, 157, *Phinehas*.
Picht, 190, *placed*.
Pietifull, 36, *pitiful*.
Pilgramage, 143, *pilgrimage*.
Pitie, 30, *pity*.
Pitious, 31, *piteous*.
Plaguit, 87, *plagued*.
Plaig, 99, *plague*.
Plaige, 20, *pledge*.
Plainlie, 166, *plainly*.
Plaintis, 196, *complaints*.
Plak, 179, *plack*.
Plane, 76, *to shew*.
Planelie, 195, *plainly*.
Plantit, 138, *planted*.
Pleasand, 74, *pleasant*.
Pleid, 130, *liability*.
Pleid, 61, *plead*.
Pleis, 77, *please*.
Plentie, 59, *plenty*.
Plenteouslie, *plenteously*.
Plenze, 59, *complain*.
Plesand, 81, *pleasant*.
Plesandlie, 88, *pleasantly*.
Plesit, 139, *pleased*.
Plesour, 88, *pleasure*.
Plesouris, 129, *pleasures*.
Plesure, 76, *pleasure*.

T

Plet, 24, *placed.*
Plicht, 14, *plea.*
Pluk, 170, *pluck, steal.*
Pluke, 144, *pluck.*
Plyabill, 30, *compliant.*
Poetis, 188, *poets*
Pointis, 37, *points.*
Polit, 180, *tickled.*
Pompe, 92, *pomp.*
Ponce, 3, *Pontius.*
Popische, 179, *popish.*
Port, *gate.*
Postle, *apostle.*
Posseid, 82, *possess.*
Posses, 58, *possess.*
Pot, 130, *pit.*
Pouertie, 184, *poverty.*
Powair, 100, *power.*
Poysonit, 185, *poisoned.*
Poysound, 46, *poisoned.*
Prais, 109, *praise.*
Pray, 27, *prey.*
Prayand, 67, *praying.*
Preceptis, 49, *precepts.*
Preclair, 80, *clear.*
Prefar, 76, *prefer.*
Preferrit, 162, *preferred.*
Preiche, 7, *preach.*
Preicheouris, 140, *preachers.*
Preicheris, 6, *preachers.*
Preichit, 48, *preached.*
Preichouris, 160, *preachers.*
Preif, 29, *proof;* 76, *prove.*
Preis, 25, *strive.*
Preist, 176, *priest.*
Preistis, 170, *priests.*
Prelatis, 195, *prelates.*
Prent, 12, *imprint.*

Prepair, 74, *prepare.*
Preparit, 200, *prepared.*
Presence, 163, *presents.*
Preseruis, 80, *preserves.*
Preseruit, 86, *preserved.*
Presoun, 198, *prison.*
Preuaill, 187, *prevail.*
Preuaricatioun, 158, *prevarication.*
Preue, 170, *prove.*
Preuene, 144, *prevent.*
Preuis, 185, *proves.*
Princelie, 195, *princely.*
Prisoun, 103, *prison.*
Priuelie, 87, *privily.*
Proceid, 71, *proceed.*
Proceiding, 149, *proceeding.*
Proceidis, 87, *proceeds.*
Prologve, *prologue.*
Promeis, 57, *promise.*
Promeist, 28, *promised.*
Promit, 77, *promise.*
Promittis, 98, *promises.*
Promittit, 98, *promised.*
Promysit, 126, *promised.*
Pronunce, 96, *pronounce.*
Propertie, 184, *property.*
Prophaine, 200, *profane.*
Prophesie, 73, *prophesy.*
Prophetis, 156, *prophets.*
Propyne, 28, *present.*
Proude, 125, *proud.*
Prouisioun, 120, *provision.*
Prouyde, 80, *provide.*
Pryce, 167, *price.*
Pryde, 80, *pride.*
Prydefull, 65, *prideful.*
Pryse, 76, *praise, esteem.*
Pryse, 22, *prize.*

Glossary. 291

Psalme, 99, *psalm.*
Psalmes, *psalms.*
Ptolomie, *Ptolemy.*
Pulis, 162, *pools.*
Pundis, 170, *pounds.*
Puneis, 167, *punish.*
Puneist, 103, *punished.*
Punische, 196, *punish.*
Punischement, 190, *punishment.*
Purches, 56, *purchase.*
Purchest, 75, *purchased.*
Pure, 103, *poor.*
Pureteth, 64, *poverty.*
Purgatorie, 63, *purgatory.*
Purgit, *purged.*
Purifyit, 77, *purified.*
Purpois, 37, *purpose.*
Purpour, 35, *purple.*
Purs, 171, *purse.*
Pursis, 176, *purses.*
Purteth, 92, *poverty.*
Puttand, 151, *putting.*
Puttis, 125, *puts.*
Pyke, 176, *pick.*
Pylate, 3, *Pilate.*
Pynde, 103, *pained, wasted.*
Pynde, 22, 120, *tortured.*
Pyne, 27, *pain.*
Pype, 182, *play, pipe.*

Q.

Quaik, 182, *quake.*
Queir, 176, *choir.*
Quha, 25, *who.*
Quhair, 58, *where.*
Quhairby, 118, *whereby.*

Quhair euer, 58, *wherever.*
Quhairfoir, 68, *wherefor.*
Quhair fra, 174, *where from.*
Quhairin, 44, *wherein.*
Quhair of, 80, *whereof.*
Quhairof, 11, *whereof.*
Quhair throw, 56, *wherethrough.*
Quhairwith, 30, *wherewith.*
Quhais, 55, *whose.*
Quhasaeuer, 5, *whosoever.*
Quhat, 34, *what.*
Quhat euer, 89, *whatever.*
Quhatsaeuer, 6, *whatsoever.*
Quhen, 30, *when.*
Quheill, 92, *wheel.*
Quhile, 83, *while.*
Quhilk, 34, *who, which.*
Quhilkis, 200, *which.*
Quhill, 149, *till.*
Quhill, *while, until.*
Quhisperit, 176, *whispered.*
Quhit, 178, *whit.*
Quhite, 63, *to cut with a knife.*
Quho, 116, *who.*
Quhome, 59, *whom.*
Quhy, 157, *why.*
Quhyle, 188, *short time.*
Quhylis, *times, sometimes.*
Quhyte, 154, *white.*
Quick, 10, *living.*
Quicke, 4, *living.*
Quicklie, 181, *quickly.*

Quiklie, 195, *quickly.*
Quod, 202, *quoth.*
Quyet, 190, *quiet.*
Quyte, 98, 202, *quit.*
Quyte, *quite, entirely.*
Quyte, 65, *free from.*
Quyte claime, 171, *quit claim.*
Qvhat, 74, *what.*

R.

Raif, 52, *tore.*
Ramis, 95, *rams.*
Rander, 142, *render.*
Ransoun, 68, *ransom.*
Rais, 195, *raise;* 96, *rose.*
Raisit, 71, *raised.*
Rasche, 99, *dash.*
Realme, 4, *realm.*
Rebelland, 104, *rebelling.*
Rebellis, 90, *rebels.*
Red, 93, *afraid.*
Red, 160, *read.*
Reddie, 100, *ready.*
Reddy, 117, *ready.*
Redeme, 37, *redeem.*
Redemed, *redeemed.*
Redemit, 69, *redeemed.*
Redres, 114, *redress.*
Reformit, 75, *reformed.*
Refraine, 37, *abstain from.*
Refresche, 18, *refresh.*
Refreschit, 66, *refreshed.*
Reft, 158, *snatched.*
Refusit, 152, *refused.*
Regnand, 101, *reigning.*
Regnis, 168, *reigns.*

Reheirs, 73, *rehearse.*
Reheirsis, 62, *rehearses.*
Reif, 8, *outrage.*
Reif, 65, *rob, steal.*
Reigne, 190, *reign.*
Reigne, 99, *kingdom.*
Reignes, 125, *reigns.*
Reid, 69, *read.*
Reid, *red.*
Reioyce, 34, *rejoice.*
Reioycit, 51, *rejoiced.*
Rejoyis, 88, *rejoice.*
Reik, 163, *smoke, incense.*
Reird, 84, *clamour;* 95, *noise.*
Rekning, 197, *reckoning.*
Releif, 36, *relieve.*
Releue, 93, *relief;* 12, *relieve.*
Relykis, 169, *relics.*
Remaine, 189, *remain.*
Remeid, 53, *remedy.*
Remedie, 56, *remedy.*
Remediles, 129, *without remedy.*
Remissioun, 4, *remission.*
Remittit, 102, *remitted.*
Remord, 158, *repent.*
Remord, 104, *make remorseful.*
Remoue, 65, *remove.*
Remufe, 75, *remove.*
Renoun, 18, *renown.*
Renowne, 160, *renown.*
Renownes, *renowns.*
Renunce, 131, *renounce.*
Repentand, 15, *repenting.*
Repleit, 113, *replete, filled.*
Repois, 146, *repose.*

Glossary. 293

Repreuing, 133, *reproving.*
Reprufe, 75, *reproof.*
Reprufe, 9, *reprove.*
Repute, 38, *reputed.*
Requyre, 7, *require.*
Requyris, 174, *requires.*
Requyrit, 99, *required.*
Resistand, 20, *resisting.*
Resistis, 75, *resists.*
Resistit, 104, *resisted.*
Ressaif, 65, *receive.*
Ressaue, 30, *receive.*
Ressauis, 29, *receives.*
Ressauit, 52, *received.*
Ressoun, 118, *reason.*
Restoir, 184, *restore.*
Restoird, 57, *restored.*
Restord, 115, *restored.*
Restorit, 70, *restored.*
Resurrectioun, 4, *resurrection.*
Retene, 6, *retain.*
Retenit, 6, *retained.*
Reuart, 67, *revert, turn back.*
Reuenge, 87, *revenge.*
Reule, 75, *rule.*
Reuth, 148, *pity.*
Reuthfull, 141, *pitying.*
Rew, 110, *regret.*
Rewaird, 130, *reward.*
Rewardit, 35, *rewarded.*
Rewlaris, 76, *rulers.*
Rewle, 190, *rule.*
Rewling, 127, *ruling.*
Rewlis, 38, *rules.*
Riche, 45, *enrich.*
Riche, 30, *rich.*
Richt, 66, *right.*

Richteous, 5, *righteous.*
Richteousnes, 10, *righteousness.*
Rin, 97, *run.*
Ring, 57, *reign.*
Ringand, 144, *reigning.*
Ringis, 48, *reigns.*
Rinnand, 152, *running.*
Rinnis, 102, *runs.*
Rissen, 69, *risen.*
Riuer, 147, *river.*
Riueris, 102, *rivers.*
Roboam, *Rehoboam.*
Rocke, 45, *rock, cherish.*
Rockit, 133, *shaken.*
Rod, 200, *road.*
Roddis, 183, *rods.*
Romanes, *Romans.*
Rottin, 162, *rotten.*
Rox, 153, *rocks.*
Rubbis, 153, *rubs.*
Rude, 168, *rood, the Cross.*
Ruddis, 169, *roods, crosses.*
Ruglane, *Rutherglen.*
Rute, 83, *root.*
Rutit, ruttit, *rooted.*
Ryall, 196, *royally.*
Ryatous, 35, *riotous.*
Ryatouslie, 31, *riotously.*
Ryches, 163, *riches.*
Rycht, 68, *right.*
Rychtcousnes, 76, *righteousness.*
Ryde, 190, *ride.*
Ryfe, *many, plentiful.*
Ryis, 198, *rise.*
Rype, 93, *matured.*
Ryse, 36, *rise.*
Ryue, 164, *tear, burst.*

S.

Sa, 32, *so*.
Sabboth, 2, *Sabbath*.
Sacrifying, *sacrifising*.
Said, 29, *long-continued*.
Saif, 46, *safe*; 30, *save*.
Saif, 53, *save, but*.
Saif, 82, *saved*.
Saift, 60, *saved*.
Saik, 64, *sake*.
Saikis, 159, *sakes*.
Saikleslie, 201, *without guilt*.
Saine, 26, *blessèd*.
Saintes, *saints*.
Sair, 29, 75, *sore*.
Sairis, 35, *sores*.
Sait, 82, *seat*.
Sal, 86, *shall*.
Salbe, 74, *shall be*.
Sald, 106, *sold*.
Sall, 59, *shall*.
Salomone, 157, *Solomon*.
Saluation, 177, *salvation*.
Saluatioun, 43, *salvation*.
Sanct, 34, *saint*.
Sanctandrois, *St Andrews*.
S. Andro, *St Andrew*.
S. Barnabie, *St Barnabas*.
S. Cudbert, *St Cuthbert*.
S. Dinneis, *St Denis*.
S. Jhone, *St John*.
S. John Euangell, *St John Evangelist*.
S. Johnis, *St John's*.
S. Johnstoun, *town of Perth*.
S. Katherene, *St Catherine*.
S. Steuin, *St Stephen*.
Sanctifyit, 101, *sanctified*.
Sanctis, *saints, saint's*.
Sandell, 44, *rich embroidered cloth*.
Sandellis, 171, *sandals*.
Sang, 67, *sung*.
Sang, 71, *song*.
Sangis, 61, *songs*.
Samin, 102, *same*.
Sathan, 52, *Satan*.
Sathanis, 9, *Satan's*.
Satisfie, 21, *satisfy*.
Satisfyis, 101, *satisfies*.
Sauch, 99, *willow*.
Saue, 77, *save*.
Sauer, 96, *savour*.
Saues, 193, *saves*.
Sauing, 137, *saving*.
Sauiour, 45, *saviour*.
Sauis, 86, *saves*.
Sauit, 52, *saved*.
Sauld, 37, *sold*.
Saule, 125, *sold*.
Saulis, 59, *souls*.
Saull, 175, *soul*.
Saullis, *souls, soul's*.
Sauour, 128, *savour*.
Sawin, 178, *sown*.
Sayand, 13, *saying*.
Sayis, 62, *says*.
Say weill, 181, *say well*.
Scarlat, 91, *scarlet*.
Scatteris, 125, *scatters*.
Schaip, 153, *scare away*.
Schaipis, 124, *aim*.
Schairp, 71, *sharp*.
Schairply, 105, *sharply*.
Schame, 24, *shame*.
Scharp, 87, *sharp*.
Scharplie, 97, *sharply*.

Glossary. 295

Schauelingis, 179, *shavelings*.
Schauin, 155, *shaven*.
Schauin sort, 155, *monks*.
Schaw, 75, *shew*.
Schawand, 169, *shewing*.
Schawin, 115, *shewn*.
Schawis, 29, *shews*.
Sched, 168, *shed*.
Schedding, 110, *shedding*.
Scheild, 158, *shield*.
Schent, 201, *destroyed*.
Schent, 39, *utterly lost*.
Scheip, 80, *sheep*.
Schew, *show, showed*.
Scho, 73, *she*.
Schoir, 172, *threaten*.
Schoir, 53, *threatening*.
Schoir, 167, *transgression*.
Schone, 32, *shoes*.
Schord, 78, *threatened*.
Schorit, 97, *threatened*.
Schort, 30, *short*.
Schortest, *shortest*.
Schot, 131, *penalty*.
Schyne, 83, *shine*.
Schynis, 126, *shines*.
Sclander, 58, *slander*.
Scoir, 182, *score*.
Scornis, 82, *scorns*.
Scornit, 188, *scorned*.
Sculptill, 200, *graven*.
Scurge, 29, *scourge*.
Scurgis, 133, *scourges*.
Scurgit, 39, *scourged*.
Se, 48, *see*.
Seasit, 163, *held*.
Seb, 92, *Zeeb*.
Secreit, 89, *secret*.

Secreitlie, 114, *secretly*.
Sectouris, 26, *executors*.
Seid, 85, *seed*.
Seik, 35, *sick*.
Seik, 69, *seek*.
Seiking, 140, *seeking*.
Seikly, 35, *sickly, feeble*.
Seine, 69, *seen*.
Seirche, 87, *search*.
Seis, 58, *sees*.
Selfis, 152, *selves*.
Sell, 14, *self*.
Sellis, 176, *sells*.
Sembling, 199, *seeming, show*.
Seme, 185, *seem*.
Semely, 182, *seemly*.
Semis, 168, *seems*.
Sempill, 63, *simple*.
Sen, 61, *since*.
Send, 74, *sent*.
Sendis, 86, *sends*.
Sene, 29, *seen*.
Sensualitie, 37, *sensuality*.
Sepulture, 102, *burial*.
Sepulture, 149, *grave*.
Seruand, 68, *servant*.
Seruandis, 101, *servants*.
Serue, 110, *deserve*.
Serue, 56, *serve*.
Seruice, 140, *service*.
Seruis, 72, *served*.
Seruit, 197, *served*.
Seruitour, 142, *servant*.
Seruitude, 68, *servitude*.
Seruiture, 150, *servant*.
Sesoun, 87, *season*.
Settis, 140, *sets*.
Seuin, 77, *seven*.

Seuinfald, 103, *sevenfold.*
Sew, *sue.*
Sex, 74, *six.*
Sex and seuin, 23, *six and seven (a game).*
Sext, *sixth.*
Sey, 95, *sea.*
Shawis, 155, *shews.*
Shortlie, 37, *shortly.*
Sic, 26, *so.*
Sic, 89, *such.*
Sic a kinde, 89, *such a fashion.*
Sicera, 91, *Sisera.*
Sich, 133, *sigh.*
Sicht, 29, *sight.*
Sicker, 94, *sure.*
Siclike, 92, *suchlike, like as.*
Siclyke, 71, *suchlike.*
Signe, 14, *sign.*
Sillie, 25, *feeble;* 179, *foolish.*
Siluer, 77, *silver.*
Sinay, 6, *Sinai.*
Sindrie, *sundry.*
Sing, *for* sign, 72, *aspect.*
Singand, 113, *singing.*
Sinnand, 106, *sinning.*
Sinnaris, 93, *sinners.*
Sinnes, 110, *sins.*
Sinnis, 92, *sins.*
Sinnit, 32, *sinned.*
Sisteris, 62, *sisters.*
Sittis, 3, *sits;* 114, *sittest.*
Skaith, 49, *harm.*
Skaldit, 163, *scalded.*
Skant, 31, *scarce, scant.*
Skarlat, 172, *scarlet.*
Skinnis, 153, *skins.*

Skyis, 81, *skies.*
Sla, 184, *slay.*
Slaik, 195, *slack.*
Slake, *slack.*
Slane, 21, *slain.*
Slaw, 100, *slow.*
Sleip, 101, *sleep.*
Sleipis, 144, *sleeps.*
Sleipit, 102, *slept.*
Sleuth, 89, *sloth.*
Slicht, 152, *cunning, fraud.*
Slie, 131, *sly.*
Slipper, 182, *slippery.*
Slokkin, 70, *quench.*
Slycht, 90, *cunning.*
Slychtis, 160, *tricks.*
Slyde, 100, *slide.*
Slyding, 72, *slipping.*
Slydrie, 89, *slippery.*
Slyme, 144, *clay.*
Smart, 118, *pain.*
Smellit, 151, *smelt.*
Smoir, 161, *smother.*
Smorit, 181, *smothered.*
Snair, 189, *snare.*
Snaird, 189, *ensnared.*
Snakis, 163, *snakes.*
Snaw, 107, *snow.*
Snib, 66, *hinder.*
Sober, 37, *small, mean.*
Sober, 137, *soir, suffering.*
Soberlie, 13, *soberly.*
Socht, 39, *sought.*
Sondayis, *Sundays.*
Sone and air, 34, *son and heir.*
Sone, 33, *son.*
Sone, 39, *soon.*
Sone, 144, *sun.*
Sones, 22, *son's.*

Glossary. 297

Sonnes, 30, *sons*.
Sonnis, 55, *son's*.
Soir, 58, *sore*.
Soirly, 54, *sorely, anxiously*.
Solempnitie, *solemnity*.
Solistatioun, 11, *anxiety, solicitude*.
Sorie, 78, *sad*.
Soueraine, 69, *sovereign*.
Spak, 74, *spoke*.
Spait, 97, *flood*.
Spectakill, 78, *spectacle*.
Speid, 153, *speed*.
Speik, 125, *speak*.
Speikand, 85, *speaking*.
Speikes, 85, *speaks*.
Speikis, 77, *speaks*.
Speir, 152, *ask*.
Speir, 108, *spear*.
Spendit, 84, *spent*.
Spill, 149, *destroy*.
Spill, 118, *mar*.
Spilt, 135, *destroyed*.
Spirituall, *spiritual*.
Spittit, 148, *spat*.
Splene, 146, *spleen*.
Spokin, 118, *spoken*.
Sponk, 163, *spark*.
Spousit, 73, *espoused*.
Spoylzeit, 52, *spoiled*.
Spred, 120, *spread*.
Spreit, 109, *spirit*.
Springis, 174, *springs*.
Sprinkill, 107, *sprinkle*.
Spyit, *espied, seen*.
Staffe, 80, *staff*.
Staine, 63, *stone*.
Stait, 82, *state*.
Stakerand, 88, *stumbling*.

Stakis, 163, *stakes*.
Stand, 97, *stood*.
Standand, 185, *standing*.
Standis, 183, *stand*.
Stane, 54, *stone*.
Stang, 71, *sting*.
Stangand, 163, *stinging*.
Stanis, 44, *stones*.
Stark, 23, *strong, powerful*.
Steid, 195, *stead*.
Steidfast, 62, *steadfast*.
Steidfastlie, 42, *steadfastly*.
Steik, 202, *shut*.
Steill, 65, *steal*.
Steir, 196, *government*.
Steir, 10, *stir*.
Stend, 95, *spring*.
Stepillis, 185, *steeples*.
Steppis, 202, *steps*.
Sternis, 127, *stars*.
Stert, 95, *start*.
Stife, 91, *stiff*.
Stinkand, 172, *stinking*.
Stok, 54, *stock*.
Stoir, 57, *store*.
Stomak, 31, *stomach*.
Stomokis, 65, *stomachs*.
Stoppit, 71, *stopped*.
Stormis, 186, *storms*.
Storie, 92, *story*.
Stound, 87, *aching, pain*.
Straif, 38, *strove*.
Straik, 191, *struck*.
Strang, 58, *strong*.
Strangair, 116, *stranger*.
Strampe, 94, *tread*.
Stray, 44, *straw*.
Streit, 102, *street*.
Stremis, 97, *streams*.

Strenth, 49, *strength.*
Strenth, 48, *strengthen.*
Stres, 105, *distraining.*
Stres, 113, *distress.*
Strickin, 168, *struck.*
Stringit, 81, *stringed.*
Striue, 24, *strife.*
Striuiling, *Stirling.*
Stroy, 124, *destroy.*
Stryfe, 27, *strife.*
Stryfe, 146, *striving, fighting.*
Stryke, 87, *strike.*
Stryuand, 91, *striving.*
Stryue, 75, *strive.*
Stude, 122, *stood.*
Stule, 44, *stool.*
Stummer, 100, *stumble.*
Sturdie, 186, *vexing.*
Subdew, 69, *subdue.*
Subdewit, 26, *subdued.*
Subtell, 131, *subtle.*
Subteltie, 160, *subtlety.*
Subtill, 190, *subtle.*
Suddand, 78, *sudden.*
Suddanely, 198, *suddenly.*
Suddanly, 28, *suddenly.*
Sufferit, 59, *suffered.*
Suith, 202, *true.*
Suith, 166, *truth.*
Suld, 29, *should.*
Sum, 60, *some.*
Sum deale, 181, *somewhat.*
Summe, 37, *sum.*
Sune, 89, *soon.*
Sunne, 2, *sun.*
Supplie, 72, *supply,*
Suppois, 183, *suppose.*
Sure, 94, *assure.*

Suretie, 59, *surety, certainty.*
Surfet, 65, *surfeit.*
Surmisse, 133, *surmise.*
Suspitioun, 87, *suspicion.*
Susseit, 149, *hesitated.*
Susteinit, 188, *sustained.*
Sustene, 30, *sustain.*
Swa, 150, *so.*
Sweilling, 44, *swaddling.*
Sweir, 198, *loth.*
Sweir, 79, *swear.*
Sweit, 88, *sweet.*
Sweiter, 146, *sweeter.*
Sweitest, *sweetest.*
Sweitly, 61, *sweetly.*
Swelland, 95, *swelling.*
Swyith, 44, *quick.*
Swyne, 165, *swine.*
Syde, 61, *side.*
Sylk, 35, *silk.*
Syle, 156, *betray.*
Syllie, *simple, harmless.*
Symeon, 57, *Simeon.*
Syne, 162, *after.*
Syne, 35, *afterwards.*
Synk, 162, *cesspool.*
Syse, 7, *assize.*
Syse, 115, *times.*
Syith, 91, *compensation.*

T.

Tabernakil, 78, *tabernacle.*
Tabernackles, *tabernacles.*
Tabill, 202, *table.*
Tabillis, 7, *tables.*
Tak, 109, *take.*
Takin, *taken.*

Glossary. 299

Takin, 12, *token*.
Takis, 22, *takes*.
Tak tent, 22, *be attentive*.
Tailit, 177, *tailed*.
Taine, tane, *taken*.
Tantonie, 153, *St Anthony*.
Targe, 82, *shield*.
Tarie, 154, *tarry*.
Taucht, 25, *taught*.
Tauld, 176, *told*.
Teiche, 63, *teach*.
Teichement, 77, *teaching*.
Teiching, 1, *teaching*.
Teichit, 25, *taught*.
Teind, 158, *tenth*.
Teindit, 164, *teinded*.
Teine, 78, *injury, loss*.
Teiris, 109, *tears*.
Teith, 14, 97, *teeth*.
Tempill, 101, *temple*.
Temptit, 30, *tempted*.
Tenderlie, 66, *tenderly*.
Termis, 195, *terms*.
Terribill, 35, *terrible*.
Testifyis, 200, *testifies*.
Thae, 102, *they*.
Thai, 36, *they*.
Thair, 1, *their*.
Thair, 58, *there*.
Thairby, 38, *thereby*.
Thairfoir, 29, *therefore*.
Thairin, 153, *therein*.
Thairof, 117, *thereof*.
Thairtill, 31, *thereto*.
Thairto, 57, *thereto*.
Thame, 167, *them*.
Thame self, 164, *themselves*.
Thame selfis, 87, *themselves*.
Thankis, 5, *thanks*.

Thay, 125, *they, those*.
Thé, 29, *thee*.
Theifis, 134, *theives*.
Thift, 8, *theft*.
Thine furth, 111, *thenceforth*.
Thingis, 69, *things*.
Thinkand, 180, *thinking*.
Thinkis, 195, *thinks*.
Thir, 78, *these*.
Thirlage, 85, *bondage*.
Thirldome, 99, *thraldom*.
Thirlit, 52, *bound to*.
Thirlit, 30, *enthralled*.
Thirlit, 118, *pierced*.
Thocht, 89, *thought*.
Thocht, 29, *although*.
Thochtis, 48, *thoughts*.
Thoill, 30, *suffer, endure*.
Thole, 89, *endure*.
Tholit, 67, *endured*.
Thousandis, 2, *thousands*.
Thow, 6, *thou*.
Thrall, 53, *servant*.
Thrall, 145, *stubborn, hard*.
Thrawardnes, 65, *perverseness*.
Thre, 60, *three*.
Threid, 72, *thread*.
Threitning, 3, *threatening*.
Thrid, 39, *third*.
Thrinfalde, 179, *threefold*.
Thring, 124, *thrust*.
Thrist, 131, *thirst*.
Throuchlie, 181, *thoroughly*.
Throtis, 96, *throats*.
Throw, 39, *through*.
Thyne, 54, *thence*.
Thyne, *thy, thine*.
Til, 101, *to*.

Till, 58, *to*.
Tint, 158, *lost*.
Tippet, 171, *short cloak*.
To, 166, *too*.
Togidder, 19, *together*.
Torment, 36, *tormented*.
Tormenting, 36, *torment*.
Tormentit, 162, *tormented*.
Tot quot, 154, *so much*.
Totcheit, 133, *tossed about*.
Toung, 36, *tongue*.
Toungis, 77, *tongues*.
Tour, 142, *tower*.
Traine, 188, *enticement, snare*.
Traist, 34, *trust*.
Traistand, 116, *trusting*.
Traistis, 76, *trusts*.
Transitoir, 72, *transitory*.
Translatit, 74, *translated*.
Trappit, 175, *trapped*.
Tratour, 37, *traitor*.
Trauel, 16, *labour*.
Trauell, 89, *trouble, pains*.
Tre, 44, *wood*; 167, *the Cross*.
Treasour, 34, *treasure*.
Tred, 94, *tread*.
Treis, 114, *trees*.
Trespas, 61, *trespass*.
Trespassis, 4, *trespasses*.
Treuth, 77, *truth*.
Trew, 160, *true*.
Trewar, 77, *truer*.
Trewlie, 60, *truly*.
Trewly, 36, *truly*.
Trick, 182, *artful, clever*.
Triffillis, 195, *trifles*.
Trimbill, 182, *tremble*.

Tripairtit, 184, *parted in three*.
Trothe, 54, *truth*.
Troubill, 58, *trouble*.
Troublis, 29, *troubles*.
Troublit, 15, *troubled*.
Trow, 63, *believe, trust*.
Trowis, 155, *believes*.
Trublit, 88, *troubled*.
Trumpettis, *trumpets*.
Trybes, *tribes*.
Tryflis, 177, *trifles*.
Trym, 32, *trim*.
Tryne, 91, *multitude*.
Tryne, 12, *retinue*.
Tryumphe, 52, *triumph*.
Tuik, 44, *took*.
Tuke, 184, *took*.
Tuke trauell, 89, *took pains*.
Tumbe, 137, *tomb*.
Tung, 173, *tongue*.
Tungis, tungs, *tongues*.
Turnand, 151, *turning*.
Turne, 37, *turn*.
Turnis, 55, *turns*.
Turnit, 144, *turned*.
Turs, 171, *truss*.
Twa, 30, *two*.
Twa edgeit, 87, *two-edged*.
Tway, 171, *two*.
Twelf, 3, *twelve*.
Twentie, 2, *twentieth*.
Twentie, 60, *twenty*.
Twin, 53, *separate*.
Twyse, 7, *twice*.
Tyde, 37, *time*.
Tyde, 101, *season*.
Tykis, 162, *dogs*.
Tyme, 29, *time*.

Glossary.

Tymes, 77, *times*.
Tyne, 31, *lose, be lost*.
Tyrane, 86, *tyrant*.
Tyrannis, 40, *tyrants*.
Tyrle, 81, *trill*.
Tyrranis, 86, *tyrants'*.
Tythingis, 43, *tidings*.

U.

Uengeance, 171, *vengeance*.
Unburyit, 102, *unburied*.
Unknawin, 117, *unknown*.
Unkyndly, 58, *unkindly*.
Utheris, *others*.

V.

Vaill, 65, *value*.
Vaine, vane, *vain*.
Valure, 146, *valour*.
Vangel, 30, *gospel*.
Vanitie, 64, *vanity*.
Vaniteis, 201, *vanities*.
Variance, 17, *change*.
Veirs, 14, *verse*.
Veluote, 172, *velvet*.
Veneis, *Venice*.
Vennemous, 68, *venemous*.
Verifie, 67, *verify*.
Veritie, 40, *verity, truth*.
Verray, 117, *very*.
Verteousnes, 80, *virtue*.
Vertew, 181, *virtue*.
Vexacioun, 11, *vexation*.
Vexit, 77, *vexed*.
Victorie, 75, *victory*.

Victour, 20, *conqueror*.
Vincust, 24, *vanquished*.
Visibill, 71, *visible*.
Visitis, 2, *visits*.
Vitious, 23, *unregulated*.
Vittel, 31, *grain*.
Vmbeset, 53, *surrounded*.
Vmest, 171, *uppermost*.
Vnbeleuaris, *unbelievers*.
Vnbeleue, 11, *unbelief*.
Vnclene, 177, *unclean*.
Vncouth, 93, *strange*.
Vnder, 2, *under*.
Vnderstand, 10, *understand*.
Vnderstude, 46, *understood*.
Vnfenzeitlie, 42, *unfeignedly*.
Vnforlorne, 127, *not lost*.
Vniuersall, 4, *universal*.
Vnitie, 157, *unity*.
Vnkynde, 122, *unkind*.
Vnkyndelie, 137, *unkindly*.
Vnkyndenes, 132, 133, *unkindness*.
Vnperfite, 63, *imperfect*.
Vnricht, 44, *unrighteous*.
Vnricht, 151, *wrong*.
Vnrichteousnes, 10, *unrighteousness*.
Vnschamefastnes, 65, *shamelessness*.
Vnstabill, 92, *unstable*.
Vnsure, 107, *uncertain*.
Vnthankfull, 150, *unthankful*.
Vntill, 5, *until*.
Vnto, 196, *unto*.
Vntraistie, 188, *untrusty*.
Vntrew, 127, *untrue*.

Vnworthelie, 15, *unworthily.*
Vnworthely, 5, *unworthily.*
Vnworthie, 24, *unworthy.*
Voce, 86; Voyce, 13, *voice.*
Voide, 102, *devoid.*
Voyde, 29, *void.*
Vowis, 14, *vows.*
Vp, 81, *up.*
Vpbring, 142, *rear.*
Vpon, 2, *upon.*
Vpper, 181, *upper.*
Vproir, 177, *uproar.*
Vs, 32, *us.*
Vse, vsis, *use, uses.*
Vsit, 177, *used.*
Vsurpit, 153, *usurped.*
Vther, 57, *other.*
Vtheris, 168, *others.*
Vtter, 92, *utter.*
Vyce, 166, *vice.*
Vylanie, 135, *villany.*
Vylde, vyle, *vile.*

W.

Wacht, 23, *quaff.*
Waigis, 195, *wages.*
Waik, 126, *watch.*
Waik, 193, *weak.*
Waiknes, 57, *weakness.*
Wairis, 195, *wares, goods.*
Waistit, 31, *wasted.*
Wait, 129, *know, knew.*
Wait, 198, *knowest.*
Waitis, 98, *waits.*
Wald, 31, *would.*
Walkand, 120, *awake.*
Walkins, 123, *wakens.*
Walkis, 88, *walks.*
Wallis, 113, *walls.*
Wallis, 97, 168, *waves.*
Wallowis, 83, *fades.*
Wallowit, 202, *withered.*
Wan, 174, *won.*
Wan, 28, *stroke, sickness.*
Wantand, 103, *wanting.*
Wantit, 35, *wanted.*
Wantounlie, 179, *wantonly.*
War, 32, *aware.*
War, 161, *were.*
Wardly, 64, *worldly.*
Wark, 88, *work.*
Warkand, 157, *working.*
Warkis, 80, *works.*
Warld, 120, *world.*
Warldis, *worlds, world's.*
Warldly, 122, *worldly.*
Warldlie, 24, *worldly.*
Warrand, 97, *warrant.*
Wat, 166, *know;* 168, *knows.*
Wate, 91, *knew.*
Wateris, 81, *waters.*
Watter, 14, *water.*
Wauer, 80, *waver.*
Wawis, 97, *waves.*
Way, 163, *wo.*
Wayis, 83, *ways.*
Wayis, 36, *wise.*
Waxit, 134, *became.*
Weddit, 46, *wedded.*
Weid, 93, *dwelling-place.*
Weilbelouit, 13, *well-beloved.*
Weild, 145, *possess.*
Weill, 159, *weal.*

Glossary.   303

Weill, 65, *well.*
Weill or wo, 53, *prosperity or adversity.*
Weind, 171, *fancied.*
Weip, 19, *weep.*
Weipit, 99, *wept.*
Weir, 130, *doubt.*
Weir, 197, *law phrase, referring to a doubtful debt.*
Weir, 158, *strife;* 22, *war.*
Weird, 24, *fate, destiny.*
Weiris, 185, *wars.*
Weirlie, 93, *happy.*
Weit, 36, *wet.*
Welcom, 150, *welcome.*
Welterand, 97, *rolling.*
Welth, 88, *wealth.*
Welth, 168, *gladness.*
Welthie, 189, *wealthy.*
Wemen, 186, *women.*
Wemis, *Wemyss.*
Wenche, 190, *girl.*
Wend, 25, *go;* 77, *gone.*
Wene, 30, *imagine, think.*
Went, 98, *gone.*
Wer, 29, *were, wert.*
Wes, 33, *was.*
Wesche, 105, *wash.*
Weschin, 148, *washed.*
Whill, *while.*
Wicht, 23, 75, *active, agile.*
Wicht, 117, *man, person.*
Wicket, 82, *wicked.*
Wickit, 55, *wicked.*
Wickitnes, 64, *wickedness.*
Widderit, 83, *withered.*
Wil, 78, *wilt.*
Will, 80, *wilfully.*
Win, 52, *won, gained.*

Win, 16, *gain.*
Win away, 97, *escaped.*
Windo, 116, *window.*
Wingis, 93, *wings.*
Winnis, 199, *gains.*
Wirk, 26, *work.*
Wirkand, 57, *working.*
Wirkar, 68, *worker.*
Wirking, 12, *working.*
Wirkis, 121, *works.*
Wirschip, 81, *worship.*
Wirship, 76, *worship.*
Wis, 8, *desire.*
Wis, 117, *know.*
Wisdome, *wisdom.*
Wist, 135, *knew.*
Withouttin, 28, *without.*
Witnessis, 37, *witnesses.*
Wittis, 75, *wits.*
Wo, 159, *sad.*
Wod, 200, *wood.*
Wolfis, 131, *wolves.*
Woll, 164, *wool.*
Worde, 12, *word.*
Wordis, 48, *words.*
Workis, 95, *works.*
Wormes, 24, *worms.*
Worschip, 57, *worship.*
Worschiping, 176, *worshipping.*
Worthely, 38, *worthily.*
Worthie, 32, *worthy.*
Wot, 154, *knows.*
Wount, 161, *wont.*
Wounder, 40, *wonder.*
Wounder, 32, *wondrous.*
Wounder, 131, *wonderfully.*
Wounder, 163, *wondrously.*

Woundis, 50, *wounds.*
Wrack, 162, *wreck.*
Wrait, 7, *wrote.*
Wraith, 19, *wrath.*
Wraithfulnes, 92, *wrath.*
Wrakkit, 99, *overthrown.*
Wrang, 167, *wrong.*
Wrangous, 152, *wrong.*
Wrangus, 86, *wrong-doing.*
Wray, 191, *betray.*
Wreist, 62, *wrest.*
Wretchit, 51, *wretched.*
Wretchitnes, 19, *wretchedness.*
Write, 68, *writing.*
Write, 98, *scripture.*
Writand, 1, *writing.*
Writtin, 30, *written.*
Wrocht, 193, *wrought.*
Wryt, 62, *writing.*
Wryte, 14, *write.*
Wryting, 39, *writing.*
Wrytis, 60, *writes.*
Wusche, 89, *washed.*
Wushe, 38, *washed.*
Wyde, 20, *wide.*
Wylde, 132, *vile, wicked.*
Wyfe, 114, *wife.*
Wyffis, *wife's, wives.*
Wyiffis, 184, *wives.*
Wying, 43, *pointing out.*
Wylde, 159, *wild.*
Wylis, 182, *enticements.*

Wyne, *vine, wine.*
Wynter, *winter.*
Wyse, 82, *wise.*
Wyte, 166, *blame.*

Z.

Ze, 29, *ye;* 7, *yea.*
Zeid, 36, *went.*
Zeild, 201, *yield.*
Zeill, 176, *zeal.*
Zeir, 49, *year.*
Zeiris, 71, *years.*
Zell, 96, *yell.*
Zet, 35, *gate.*
Zettis, 127, *gates.*
Zit, 57, *yet.*
Zing, 124, *young.*
Zock, 88, *yoke.*
Zockit, 161, *yoked.*
Zok, 25, *yoke.*
Zoue, 147, *you.*
Zoung, 153, *young.*
Zoungest, 31, *youngest.*
Zour, 62, *your.*
Zour sell, 62, *yourself.*
Zour selfis, 152, *yourselves.*
Zouth, 23, *youth.*
Zow, 24, *you.*
Zung, 85, *young.*
Zule, *Yule.*

PRINTED BY GEORGE ROBB, THISTLE STREET, EDINBURGH.

www.ingramcontent.com/pod-product-compliance
Lightning Source LLC
Chambersburg PA
CBHW030400230426
43664CB00007BB/685